P9-EDB-976

GARY YOUNGE

NO PLACE LIKE HOME

A BLACK BRITON'S JOURNEY THROUGH THE AMERICAN SOUTH

Gary Younge was born in 1969. He is a columnist and feature writer for the *Guardian*. Since joining the paper in 1994 he has written extensively from the United States, South Africa and throughout Europe. In 1996 he was seconded to the *Washington Post* after being awarded the Lawrence Stern fellowship.

Born and raised in Stevenage, Hertfordshire, he studied French and Russian at Heriot-Watt University and taught English to refugees in Sudan. He lives in London.

GARY YOUNGE

NO PLACE LIKE HOME

A BLACK BRITON'S JOURNEY THROUGH THE AMERICAN SOUTH

Cousin Whitney & Dean,

Great to meet you,
Wishing you all the best
in Egypt.

Gary Younge

PICADOR

3/2/01

First published 1999 by Picador

This edition published 2000 by Picador
an imprint of Macmillan Publishers Ltd
25 Eccleston Place, London SW1W 9NF
Basingstoke and Oxford
Associated companies throughout the world
www.macmillan.com

ISBN 0 330 36981 4

Copyright © Gary Younge 1999

The right of Gary Younge to be identified as the
author of this work has been asserted by him in accordance
with the Copyright, Designs and Patents Act 1988.

All rights reserved. No part of this publication may be
reproduced, stored in or introduced into a retrieval system, or
transmitted, in any form, or by any means (electronic, mechanical,
photocopying, recording or otherwise) without the prior written
permission of the publisher. Any person who does any unauthorized
act in relation to this publication may be liable to criminal
prosecution and civil claims for damages.

1 3 5 7 9 8 6 4 2

A CIP catalogue record for this book is available from
the British Library.

Typeset by SetSystems Ltd, Saffron Walden, Essex
Printed and bound in Great Britain by
Mackays of Chatham plc, Chatham, Kent

This book is sold subject to the condition that it shall not,
by way of trade or otherwise, be lent, re-sold, hired out,
or otherwise circulated without the publisher's prior consent
in any form of binding or cover other than that in which
it is published and without a similar condition including this
condition being imposed on the subsequent purchaser.

Contents

To Reba and Tara

Acknowledgements

First of all I would like to thank those who helped this book evolve with gentle criticism and warm praise in the right places and always at the right time. Donald Harding, Randeep Ramesh, Anna-Zohra Tikly, Sarah Davey and Mary Gilmartin – your advice and support were invaluable and went beyond the call of friendship. Special thank yous to my editor, Ursula Doyle, for keeping the art of thorough and disciplined editing alive, while maintaining a sense of humour, and to my agent, Jane Bradish Ellames, who from the beginning has been fighting corners I never even knew I had.

I am grateful to the editor of the *Guardian*, Alan Rusbridger, for welcoming me back to the paper after I had finished my travels and Carol Keefer for keeping things together while I was gone. I am also indebted to Michael Fletcher of the *Washington Post*, Charles Payne of Duke University and Penny Weaver from the Southern Poverty Law Centre for lending me their contacts books and passing on their reading lists. Thanks to Pat and Wayne for their protection, indulgence and support and for showing me the meaning of brotherhood – some of this is their story too.

And, leaving the largest debt of gratitude until the end, I thank Tara Mack, without whose encouragement, love, patience and honest appraisals this entire project would have remained in my imagination.

CHAPTER ONE

The Unlikely Lads

I was born and raised in the South – well, Stevenage in Hertfordshire, anyway.

The best thing to be said about Stevenage is that it was a good idea at the time. The time was the 1940s. Having secured victory against the Nazis abroad, people were now eager to win a caring peace through a Labour government at home. The idea, though it is funny to think of Stevenage in this way now, was to create a suburban Utopia thirty miles up the A1 from the capital – a concrete dream for London's poor who had been bombed out of their slums and were multiplying with gusto following the soldiers' return. It was to be a fresh start with gardens, parks and all the municipal amenities which had so far eluded working-class Londoners. So the planners set to work with a blank piece of paper and the post-war equivalent of magic markers, stencils and drawing boards and started to carve out a brave new world in the greenery of the Home Counties.

Years later friends in town planning would show a flicker of recognition when I told them I came from Stevenage because they had studied its conception and birth. They knew all about its odd and impressive quirks. With a population of around eighty thousand there was, to my knowledge, only one traffic light. But it was not uncommon to see three or four roundabouts in a stretch of road not more than a mile long, which made it a hell of a place to take a driving test. It also claimed the title of best cycling town in Europe. There were cycle paths that shadowed the major roadways and snaked through the underpasses beneath the roundabouts so you could, in theory, ride all the way around the town without ever having to cross a road, a fact that my mother used to boast about even before any of us had bikes.

Unless you ventured into pub land on a Friday or Saturday night, Stevenage was relatively quiet and safe. The whole time I was there I remember it making the national news only twice: once when a Chinese woman and her daughter were hacked to death in their room above a Chinese takeaway; and again when Shirley Williams, the Labour MP and Minister for Education, lost her seat to an unknown Tory in the general election of 1979.

But most of the time, Stevenage pretty much took care of itself. Each little area had its own community centre and a small concrete pedestrian shopping area with a greengrocer, butcher, newsagent, chip shop, a pub, a minimarket and maybe a launderette. And, just to make sure that you didn't get lost, each area also had its own colour. So you knew you were in the district of Shephall, say, because all the signs were red, or in Broadwater, where I lived, because they were brown. Not far from most people's houses there was a fair-sized clump of grass to play out on and at least one old person who lived nearby who didn't want you to play there. There was a bowling alley, swimming pool, cinema and leisure centre. There was a museum too and, though I visited it several times on school trips and took children there when I ran a holiday playscheme, I have absolutely no recollection of what they ever put in it. The leisure centre also had a theatre and while it did descend to the depths of *Cheggers Plays Pop* and Keith Harris and Orville in panto, especially over Christmas and the summer holidays, at other times it hosted Stephane Grapelli and professional productions of Shakespeare. Stevenage had a chess club, youth orchestra, amateur dramatic societies and a reasonably active CND.

There is nothing wrong with Stevenage. It's not the sort of place that you would visit and on your return tell everybody it was horrible – it's not the sort of place you would go to at all unless for a specific reason, and it would leave a scant impression. Stevenage is *all right*. The main problem with it when I was growing up there was that it still bore the indelible stain of the planner's magic marker. In human terms, it was still so very new – it was younger than my mum. And while lots of my friends, like me, were born in or around the town, almost everybody's parents came from somewhere else. That somewhere else was usually London or Essex, Wales or Scotland. But with a handful of exceptions there was no such thing as indigenous. As the Irish would say, we were all blow-ins.

There was an old part of Stevenage, a relatively small stretch of land with Tudor-looking buildings and narrow alleyways which obviously predated the war. But that was the Old Town and that was for shopping, drinking and, on Friday and Saturday nights, for fighting; a place where young women, their make-up ruined with tears, would hurl profanities at their young men full of beer in a vain effort to stop them from beating each other up.

Stevenage, I can safely say, had no long-standing tradition of racial prejudice. Stevenage had no long-standing traditions at all. It was not so much redneck as redbrick, a working-class town in the purest sense since, for all the time that I grew up there, most people could actually find work. I didn't know anyone whose dad was unemployed. Most friends' dads worked either at the British Aerospace (BAe) factory in the industrial area, or at the post office. Their mums either worked at home or in shops. It was a safe haven for your basic Steady Eddy. You could get a job that paid OK, a nice enough house with a garden, a holiday abroad every couple of years and a decent school for your children who were pretty much guaranteed a similar standard of living if that's what they wanted. Of course there were lots of ambitious people in Stevenage. But there were many more who fancied the sort of comfortable life that is now the object of scorn among metropolitan types, but which really was a dream come true for London's working class in the late 1940s.

In the eighties all that changed. By the middle of the decade, Stevenage had become something of a Thatcherite boom town, a working-class Tory town. House prices ballooned. Lots of my friends got little porches built on to their front doors. Manual, skilled and semi-skilled work was everywhere, and so were the living incarnations of Harry Enfield's Loadsamoney. Life, if many were to be believed, was just about the money in your pocket. There were about 150 kids who started in my school year in 1979. By 1985, when we were sixteen, all but around thirty of them, including many of my best friends, had left to get a job. Some went to work in insurance; others for BAe where their dads were; and a handful to the civil service. In an effort to clarify just how mistaken was my interest in higher education, one of my best friend's eldest brothers got out a pen, paper and calculator one night and worked out how much money I would 'lose' by going to university. He added up how much I could earn over my two years in sixth form and then my three years at university, calculated how much extra I could expect with promotions, and then compared it with how much a graduate earned where he worked. 'You're gonna be about thirty-five grand down, Gal, and that's without overtime. You want to think about it, mate,' he said. He was trying to be friendly.

When I finished school, I did what many seventeen-year-olds have done for several generations and went as far away as I could from the place where I had spent the previous seventeen years. I ended up teaching Eritrean refugees in Sudan for a year. When I came back I spurned the advice of my friend's brother and went to a redbrick university in Edinburgh called Heriot Watt where I studied French and Russian.

Whenever I returned to Stevenage after that I noticed that things were gradually changing. Boards went up over derelict shops in the town centre. A huge area of green in the middle of town was turned into a shopping centre with a drive-in Burger King, ice rink and DIY stores. A lot of the firms my friends had worked for had closed down, and by the age of twenty they had already faced their first redundancy. As the Cold War melted, BAe haemorrhaged staff. Steady Eddy could no longer promise his children anything any more, because there were no longer any certainties. His own job was under threat. By the beginning of the nineties, the town had become a metaphor for the eighties.

Quite how my mother, Reba, who was born in the parish of St Phillip in Barbados, ended up in Broadwater in Stevenage, is largely down to Mrs Stilling at number 16 Wychdell. Getting across the Atlantic was the easy bit. The government was so desperate for workers from the colonies to help it out with its labour shortage that it literally paid my mother's fare to get her there (and then asked her to pay it back later). All around the island, she told us, there were posters enticing people to come to England, the mother country, to work on the buses, tubes, the trains and in the hospitals. The British government gave orientation classes where they told people to wear flannelette pyjamas and bring woolly hats because it would be so cold. They never mentioned anything about racism.

My mother came in 1961 with a British passport. She told me that when she arrived at Victoria in London she was lined up with a lot of people from different islands. A man walked up and down the line calling out names and telling them what towns they would be going to and then handed each of them a train ticket. The handful of friends she had travelled with were scattered all over the country. She went to work in a hospital in Derby.

She said the thing that amazed her most was how little the English knew about their own country. Back in Barbados, thanks to the colonized education system, she had taken A levels in the British Constitution, European History and English Literature, and thought that English people would naturally know all about things like the Magna Carta and Shakespeare. She was fond of saying that she knew more about England than the English knew about themselves.

My father, Patrick, had arrived a few years before her and found work with a wine company. A few years after they married in London, the company moved to Stevenage. By that time, my brother Pat was almost two, and Wayne was a little baby.

It was 1966, two years before Enoch Powell invoked 'the River Tiber flowing with blood' if the government allowed any more non-white immigrants into the country, and the attitudes that launched him to prominence were hardening fast. The mantra went that if a black family moved next door they would have loud blues parties every night, try to fit twenty-five people into a two-bedroom house, kill goats and cows in the back garden, sleep with your job, steal your daughter and bring down the tone of the area and property prices with it. When my parents went looking for houses around Stevenage they were met with twitchy curtains and very cool responses – nothing overtly hostile, just the sharp glare of ignorant people who believed what they read in the papers.

But when they went to view 14 Wychdell, Mrs Stilling, an elderly lady even then, came out to greet them and asked my mother if she would like her to heat up Wayne's milk for him. She was the only person in their weeks of house hunting who had talked to my parents, and my mother decided that this was where we should live. Without Mrs Stilling, I dare say my parents would have found somewhere to settle anyway. They had to. But with her it seemed things would be a lot easier.

Not an awful lot of black people came to Stevenage. In fact the black community was small enough that almost everybody almost knew almost everybody else. We could not have numbered more than about three hundred, so you were never more than maybe two acquaintances removed from another black person in the town. There were three other black kids in my year, and no more than about ten of us in a school of eight hundred.

The black community's social life revolved around our cricket team, the Stevenage West Indians Sports and Social Club, or SWISSC. Both my father and my eldest brother used to play for SWISSC, and I used to score for them. About twice a year SWISSC would have a big party where each person would bring a dish (because there were no Caribbean caterers in the area), and a DJ who understood black music, generally from another town or someone's friend from London, would play calypso and reggae until the early morning. Our parents would dance until their glad rags were drenched with sweat, while we sat and looked on, familiar with the music because they played it at home, but not comfortable enough with it that we would want to go head to head on the dance floor with our parents in public. There were always two or three white people there, but rarely many more. They were second wives, girlfriends and occasionally workmates and usually, but not always, they were Irish.

Mrs Stilling embodied one of the three types of reactions a black family could expect in a place like Stevenage. There were those who, like her, welcomed us. There were those who tolerated us. And there were those who positively despised us.

You knew when you were in the company of the first group because when you met them it just felt right. They were not fazed by your race but they didn't try to ignore it either. They were just comfortable with you, which meant you could be comfortable with them. Occasionally the welcomers would say something dopey like, 'It'll be a while before I get a tan like yours,' or 'You'd better smile in the dark or I won't be able to see you,' but they never meant anything by it. They were good people who wanted to be friendly and were going about it in the best way they knew. There were more of them than you would imagine, but somehow there were never enough. The welcomers would cash my mum's cheques in the knowledge that they might just bounce; they would invite us around for fireworks nights or to birthday parties and would accept invitations from us on the rare occasions they were extended. They helped us when we needed help and accepted our help when it was offered.

Then there were the tolerators. They made out they were friendly. But really it was McFriendliness — a combo that came with a large order of patronizing behaviour and an unhealthy portion of stupidity. Their favourite lines would always come at bus stops in winter:

'Bloody hell, it's cold isn't it? Bet it's not like this where you come from.'

'I come from just down the road,' you would reply, but they weren't listening. They never listened.

'From Jamaica, are you?' they would ask and then not wait for the response, because Jamaica was the only country in the Caribbean that they had heard of. 'I had a friend once ... Winston his name was. Lovely bloke ... salt of the earth ... he had a beautiful wife ... gorgeous she was.'

It didn't have to be Winston from Jamaica. It could be Mandingo from Nigeria or Kunta Kinte from the Gambia. It didn't matter, because I'm sure most of the time they had made them up anyway. Whoever it was they were talking about and wherever he was supposed to be from, he always seemed to have a beautiful wife.

'I tell you he did like his rum, Winston ... great bloke...' And so it would go on. And on and on and on, while you just stood there and prayed for the bus to come soon.

Sometimes they would insist that you were as English as they were. Other times they would make out that you weren't. You were not allowed to mention your preference one way or another until they did. And it wouldn't matter even if you did, because they were only tolerating you anyway. They would quote you lines from their favourite Eddie Murphy and Richard Pryor videos and be offended if you didn't laugh. They would extend their hand in an attempt to do a black ghetto handshake – all fingers, thumbs and fancy flicks of the wrist – and be upset if you didn't have a clue what they were up to. They would insist on talking about cricketers you had never heard of and singers you didn't know, supposedly to make you feel at home. The trouble was, I *was* at home.

Then there were the despisers, like the Norrises, a scrawny white family at number 10 who used to stand at the top of the road and shout, 'Woggy, woggy' at us as we walked back from school.

Sometimes, when they got too much, Pat or Wayne would beat them up. But Mum didn't like us getting into fights because she knew that we would get the blame, regardless of whether we had been provoked or not. Once, when the Norrises had gone too far, she called the police. I was about five but I remember it well because it was the first time I heard the words 'ethnic minority'. The policeman said he wouldn't ask them to stop and explained his decision to my mother. 'I'm afraid that you are an ethnic minority in this area and you are going to have to put up with that kind of thing from time to time,' he said.

I asked my mum what an ethnic minority was, and she said it meant we were black and, according to the policeman, it also meant people could do what they wanted to us, and we couldn't complain. She called the station again saying she wanted 'a policeman, not an idiot' or she would take the law into her own hands. A younger man came who did talk to the Norrises. God only knows what he said. Whatever it was, it didn't stop them.

The despisers were the ones who called social services and told them that my mother could not look after us and that we should be taken into care for our own protection; the ones who refused to get off the party line so Mum could call the ambulance when Pat, who was nine, broke his finger in the back door; the ones who forced my mum to leave the school she was teaching at in Stevenage after the headmaster refused to punish children who carved racial insults into the desk she had to look at every day.

One of the skills I developed growing up was to spot the number of white people relating to me on an upgrade – the tolerators masquerading as welcomers, and the despisers trying to make out they are really tolerators: people who wanted your friendship but refused to challenge any of their prejudices in order to get it.

In general, Stevenage was a town of tolerators. And while the despisers outnumbered the welcomers, it was never so bad that you couldn't bear it. The despisers were despicable and the tolerators were tolerable. It was rarely dangerous but always irritating. It meant that you could never forget and were always on your guard.

Fortunately, my mother had prepared us for this. Under the reign of Reba, there was a tiny adhesive flag stuck to the front door of 14 Wychdell. From left to right it was blue, then gold and then blue again and had a black trident in the middle. It is the Barbadian flag, and the rule was that whenever we entered the house we were not English. We were in Barbados and we would behave accordingly. The English were these 'other' people with whom we mixed all day but who were different from us in the most basic ways. Of course, we liked many of them. But, as many of them would never let us forget, we were also unlike them.

'They' had 'their' own flag and 'their' own anthem. 'They' didn't rinse the dishes; 'they' ate bad food like fish fingers and pre-packed paella instead of stewed beef, peas and rice for tea; 'their' parents didn't slap 'them' enough; 'they' starved all week just so 'they' could have a big Sunday roast.

'We' on the other hand had our own flag on our own door and a map of the country tacked to the living-room wall. Mum photostated the Barbadian national anthem for us to learn as well as the date of Barbados's Independence Day. Before we had ever been there we would refer to Barbados as 'home'.

'You can do what you want out there but step into this house and you're in Barbados,' Mum used to say. If we did anything she didn't like or something she just didn't understand she would suck her teeth and say, 'Nah! You all are too damn English,' and that would be that. It was an insult.

Depending on who we were talking to, we were as likely to say we were Bajan as British. If we were at home, and Mum was chiding us for being too 'English', then we were Bajan. If we were at school, and someone was telling us to go back to where we came from, we would say we were British – somehow Englishness was never something any of us rushed to claim – and had as many rights as they did. But if someone at school or in the street tried to claim there was no difference between us and them and said, 'You're British, just like us,' we would immediately revert to being Bajan, since we knew there was a difference. We would pick'n'mix, and the answer we gave depended partly on what we thought the motivation for the question was, partly on the fact that nobody gave us the option of being both at the same time and partly on what we perceived our interests to be at any given moment. When it became apparent to me, several years later, that there was more to racial identity than nationality and that, in any case, I didn't have to cement myself in one identity and stay there for the duration of an entire conversation, let alone my whole life, it was a great relief.

Quite how this did not turn us into despisers of the English I am not sure. Numbers almost certainly had something to do with it. Almost everything in which we took part, be it the youth orchestra, rugby, football or chess, we were usually the only black people there. My mother's extensive voluntary work – adult literacy, local youth clubs, benefits for the disabled, play centres – took place in the predominantly white community. Despising the English was not really an option if we wanted to get on with our lives. But being wary of them was essential if they weren't going to stop us living it.

So our scorn was reserved for the symbols of Englishness. We kept our seat when the flag was raised, and our mouths closed when the anthem was played. We would not merely miss the Queen's speech on Christmas Day. We waited until it got to three o'clock so that we could turn the television off and deliberately not watch it. For football we supported the Brazilians; with cricket we went for the West Indies; in rugby it was usually the Welsh – God knows why, I think it was something to do with Shirley Bassey. Even when we watched *It's a Knockout* or *International Superstars*, we would cheer for the Dutch, the Germans, the Italians – even the Belgians. Anyone but the English.

But looking back on it the one group I am amazed we didn't encounter more often was the disbelievers: people who thought we confirmed all their racial prejudices only to be left in disbelief when they discovered that for every stereotype we conformed to there were at least another two that we defied.

The Younge household was a statistic waiting to happen: a black one-parent household in 1970 (my father left when I was fifteen months old), with three boys and one of the messiest houses on the street. Our house was on a par with the Norrises'. It didn't smell or anything. It was just a mess – the sort of mess which meant you could hardly ever have your friends around, and if you did you would have to tidy up for hours beforehand and then they would still come in and say it was a state. It was just a three-bedroom semi-detached house packed to the rafters with three boys and a working mother who hated housework and loved hoarding. There were three sets of PE kit, school uniforms, swimming gear, school books, comics and toys. Then there were all the cheap clothes, curtains, bits of cloth and pillowcases that mum had accumulated and intended to send back to family in Barbados – bundles of good intentions. She never did send them; she was too busy, too tired and after a while she couldn't afford to, because there was just too much of it. So she kept on collecting stuff until there was no more space in her own bedroom and she had to sleep downstairs.

We were all on free school dinners and got grants to help buy our clothes when we stayed on at school. Having one parent meant we were worse off than most others, including, I would guess, the Norrises.

But it was a special brand of penury – teacher poor. Mum had made a career move from nurse to teacher when I was about four so that she could be with us during the holidays and would no longer have to do shift work. Like most teachers, she was paid pitifully but, also like most, she took what felt at the time like an unhealthy interest in her children's academic welfare. She read our reports, scrutinized our exam results and never took our side if we got into trouble with teachers. She preferred to invest in a cultural trip abroad than a video recorder – we didn't get a VCR until I was seventeen, by which time I had been to France twice and to Germany once thanks to an IOU deal between my mum and the school. There was never any money for sweets and trendy clothes, but always cash for subs so that we could play football, cricket, rugby, chess, join the orchestra and do gymnastics because extra-curricular activities were considered important.

I never knew a time when it was not assumed that I would stay on at school and go to university. No future career was ever dictated. It was just made clear that whatever our 'English friends' were doing, our education wouldn't finish until we were twenty-one. And whatever we did we had to be good at it. 'If you go for a job and an Englishman goes for a job, and he's got eight O levels, you are going to have to have nine or you're not going to get the job. It's as easy as that,' my mum used to say. And so we all got stacks of qualifications (thirty-one O levels and twelve A levels between the three of us, and we know because we were counting), and then we all scattered to the outer reaches of the United Kingdom – Pat to Cardiff, Wayne to Belfast and me to Edinburgh.

In short we were almost everything a racist could expect from a black family. Except that we weren't.

On a warm day in May 1988, Mum came back from a shopping trip in the town centre and stopped off at Alan and Sue's at number 8 for a chat. She left soon afterwards saying she felt flushed, and walked three doors down to our home and died. She was forty-four; I was nineteen.

Because of all the community work she had done, her sudden death made it to the front page of the *Stevenage Gazette*. She had always insisted that she wanted to be buried in Barbados – 'not this cold place' – and we obliged, but also held a service in Stevenage. The church was packed. Right at the back, behind her friends, former students, colleagues and the SWISSC crowd, standing in the far right-hand corner with less hair than I remembered him having, was Bob Norris. The head of the Norris household, paying his respects.

With her anthems, flags, maps and dates of independence, Mum had tried her best to ensure that we had a secure footing in our racial identity. When she started commuting to London to run a supplementary school for the Caribbean Teachers' Association, she would bring back birthday and Christmas cards with black people on them. In a drawer in the kitchen there were stacks of plastic bags, emblazoned with a silhouette of the capital's skyline and the slogan

LONDON AGAINST RACISM, courtesy of the Greater London
Council. The family deck of playing cards had famous black
Americans on it. She would also take me (both Pat and
Wayne had grown up and moved on by this stage) on trips
to museums and seaside resorts with black youth groups run
by friends she knew in London.

Whenever possible her efforts extended beyond Barbados
to the black Diaspora at large. During my first year at junior
school I brought in my Anansi stories – children's tales from
Africa about a crafty spider who always gets his way. When
I was about eight she organized a school trip to see the
South African musical, *Ipi Tombi*. When I was a little older
we went marching against the South African President P. W.
Botha's official visit to England. A few years later we were
both regular Friday-night pickets outside the South African
Embassy calling through megaphones (mostly to baffled
tourists) for Nelson Mandela's release.

This wasn't always a smooth baton transfer of racial and
political awareness from one generation to the next. When I
was younger I used to find a lot of these museum excursions
and other 'black stuff' a real bore. The black greetings cards
Mum brought home made Wayne and me gag because they
were so badly produced. We used to moan when she made
us use the 'black' playing cards rather than the 'proper' ones.
At *Ipi Tombi*, my brothers and I spent most of the perform-
ance arguing over custody of the binoculars so that we could
have a close-up look at the bare-breasted dancers. And I
particularly loathed the trips with the black kids from
London, partly because I didn't know anybody and was so
obviously an outsider. Since they all came from the same area
of Peckham, they were all good friends and were generally a
lot tougher than I was. They were also fluent in the kind of
black-London street lingo that never made it to Stevenage.
They could say 'Wicked' and click their fingers and look

cool, but if I tried it with my flat Stevenage vowels, I just sounded stupid. Often, I used to spend the days wandering around on my own and would be back at the coach about an hour before we were supposed to leave. The other kids would mistake this enforced solitude for arrogant aloofness and accuse me of 'thinking I was white'.

Even so, I am glad my mum made the effort, because I have no idea how I would have made sense of my experiences otherwise. I never learnt one thing about black British history or culture at school. It was entirely possible to go through school in Stevenage and not know that black people existed at all (other than the few you saw on television or around town), let alone that they had been in Britain for centuries.

Nobody told me that there were at least two black women in the Scottish royal court in 1513; that Olaudah Equiano, an Igbo from eastern Nigeria, toured the country during the latter part of the eighteenth century putting the case for the abolition of the slave trade. No one mentioned that the country's first race riot took place in Butetown near Cardiff in 1919, or that the first black MP, Shapurji Saklat-vala, a Parsee, was elected to represent North Battersea in 1922. There was not one word that would have located me in the country in which I was born, not one scrap of information to challenge those among my peers who knew no better than to repeat their parents' claims that I had just come off the banana boat and was now (I never did get this) set both to steal their jobs and sponge off the welfare state. Nothing. Not one point on a compass that would have helped me navigate my way from my mother's past to my own present.

This chasm in my education was thanks largely to the collective and selective myopia that Britain has about its place in world history, but at the coal face that was my school the crime was negligence rather than anything sinister. It is not as though my teachers deliberately went out to deny me access to my own history. My guess would be that most of them didn't know any of this themselves.

When you are being forced into a vacuum you will take your oxygen from wherever you can. Without even really knowing I needed it, I found mine several thousand miles away, across the Atlantic Ocean and on what was the wrong side of the Mason–Dixon line.

Barbados may have been where my mother came from and where many of my family remain. The country's flag may well have been on my door and I may even have called it 'home', but Barbados never surrounded me in the way that America did. Bajan culture does not exist on that kind of scale. With the exception of music (and most of that was from Jamaica), Barbados just physically couldn't reach me in Stevenage unless my mother went out of her way to put it there. The United States did not have that problem. From Spiderman comics to *Pulp Fiction*, via Elvis and *Dallas*, America's icons have a habit of becoming Britain's – a truism for all races.

But America's dominance was especially strong among black Britons because our numbers were so few and our own reference points so well hidden. From the turntable to the fashion store, black America became our influence almost by default. When I was about eight, we got a rabbit which we called not Thumper or Flopsy but Mohammed after Muhammad Ali. At the age of four, I had a T-shirt that stretched over my toddler's pot belly proclaiming that I could 'float like a butterfly and sting like a bee'.

Quite where my fascination with the South started I don't know. It could have been with the televising of Alex Haley's *Roots*, which I was forced to stay up and watch. My brothers and I could recite the lineage all the way from Kunta Kinte down to Haley himself, and I can still remember it as far as Tom the Blacksmith. It could have begun when I was studying *To Kill a Mockingbird* for English O level, or watching Alice Walker's *The Color Purple*, or humming Shug Avery's 'Sister' for what seemed like years after. Or maybe it was B. B. King's blues and Billie Holiday's 'Strange Fruit'. Had I been born slightly later, or been slightly hipper, I could have gone for the East or West Coast, fired by hip hop and the bad-boy antics and lyrics of the rap world. But it was the South that spoke to me urgently about the things I instinctively felt I was lacking – a sense of place and history, a feeling that the collage of insignificant experiences that made up my everyday life was in some way linked to a broader 'whole' that existed before me and would continue long after I was gone.

By the time I had reached my early twenties I had devoured all five volumes of Maya Angelou's autobiography, Alice Walker's entire *œuvre* and everything from Ntozake Shange to Toni Morrison, whose books I somehow managed to enjoy without really understanding.

As a student, I monopolized the television in my flat and watched every edition of *Eyes on the Prize*, seeing the civil rights era unroll in black and white, yearning for a time when political morality appeared that simple, and political activity was executed with such style and dignity. Birmingham, Selma, Montgomery, Little Rock and Jackson – I could not have found them on a map, but each town was located in a very specific place in my imagination thanks to 1960s newsreels showing water cannons, vicious dogs and brutal cops turning on black men and women of around my own age. For the most part I was enjoying a well-constructed, historical documentary series that championed causes I strongly identified with. But there was one still photograph,

19

of a group of civil rights activists called the Freedom Riders, that reached a place in my subconscious I had not visited for many years.

On one of those trips with black youth groups that my mother was so keen on, I went to the seaside in Brighton. I was about twelve. I was sitting on my own by a window, reading a book, when the coach stopped at the traffic lights on the front not far from the pier. It was hot, the sort of unlikely heat that descends on English shores only two or three times a year. The beach, like the roads, was gridlocked with underdressed sunseekers, their skin red raw from overexposure.

On the other side of the road about six skinheads – shaved scalps, bleached jeans at half mast, thin Lonsdale T-shirts and eighteen-hole brown Doctor Marten boots – were walking in the other direction carrying cans of cheap beer, laughing and shouting at each other, when one of them spotted us, a bus full of black kids, aged roughly between eight and fourteen, dressed up for a day out (we always had to put on our best clothes for these trips) and stuck on a red light. Nobody else noticed them at first. They were too busy enjoying themselves. But since I didn't know anybody, and my mum was up at the front with her friends, I had nothing better to do than alternate reading with looking out of the window.

The first one to see us had difficulty containing his excitement and even greater difficulty in making his friends pay attention. I saw him grab their arms, first playfully and then with urgency, and point. It took a while. I shifted over to the aisle seat to look down the centre of the coach and see if the light was anywhere near turning, and if the grown-ups had noticed them. They hadn't. When I sat back by the window they were already on their way. By the time they reached the middle of the road they had started chanting. 'Nigger ... Nigger ... Nigger, Nigger, Nigger.'

Now the whole bus knew what was going on. Everybody had moved over to my side to see what was happening. The grown-ups at the front of the bus were striding to the back, telling everyone to return to their original seats. But rushing up the aisle, bringing their panicky voices with them, just made everything worse. Within seconds the crowd on the bus had gone from the boisterous kids about to get dropped off at the seaside to a bustling, yelling house of panic on four wheels. The smaller children were starting to scream.

Meanwhile, the skinheads were weaving through the stationary traffic, chanting as they strode. 'Nigger ... Nigger ... Nigger, Nigger, Nigger.' The light had just turned green, but we couldn't move because there were still cars in front of us. Still sitting by the window, I was immobilized, partly transfixed by the drama and partly fazed by the unreality. I saw the frozen glare of resentment in the eyes of the motorists around us who feared they were about to get caught up in something that they felt did not concern them.

The skinheads were upon us, bashing on the window, shouting, 'Nigger!' and trying to rock the coach. The look on their faces was not one of hate but sport. We were terrified, and they were enjoying themselves. Inside, it felt as though the coach was shrinking, leaving childish shrieks to reverberate around an increasingly small space.

The first sight of clear road emerged, and the driver pulled off. For a moment, the skinheads stopped thumping but kept up their chant. But the lights were against us. Red returned just as we made it to the crossing. As they ran forward to continue their torment, the driver jumped the light. A car coming in the other direction beeped, but he kept going. The chanting grew fainter, and the atmosphere

21

switched from fear to relief. The leaders, all women, cursed the 'damn fools' and once again told everyone to calm down. The children recounted the episode in hushed voices. My mother came up to see that I was all right – I was stunned and slightly tearful, but fine. That evening, as my mother and I made our way back to Stevenage from Peckham by bus and train, she jokingly said it was a good thing we had a black driver, because a white one would not have known to jump the lights. After that, it was never mentioned again. What was there to say, and whom would you say it to anyway?

The picture of the Freedom Riders did not force the dormant memories of that day in Brighton upon me like a thunderbolt, or drown me in a tidal wave of harrowing, emotional flashback. It drew them back slowly, as though through a filter that shut out my forty-five seconds of isolated helplessness and allowed a sense of dignity and perspective to seep through. Before, I had been watching history unravelling in a faraway place. Now, it felt closer and more immediate.

For me, the South was a small rural town carved in celluloid with a court house in the middle of a dusty square. Either Danny Glover or Samuel L. Jackson would play the part of the libidinous preacher with an angelic, dutiful wife (Vivica Fox) staring longingly at her man as he gives his sermon and looking the other way when he seduces the voluptuous vixen (Vanessa Williams), returned from the North with her fast, urban ways. There would be a matriarch (Irma Hall), with Bill Nunn cast as her hardworking eldest and devoted son who would always wear dungarees and short-sleeved shirts that left the depth of his brawn beyond all question. Hall, whose religious fervour precludes any form of emotional indulgence, lives in a clean but tumble-down house off a dirt road, and is capable of displaying affection only through the artery-clogging meals she cooks for her son.

There would be a part reserved for Anthony Hopkins as a racist judge for whom sending a black teenager down for three years for looking a white woman in the eye and then nipping off to the segregated country club for a shot of Jack Daniels is all in a day's work. His wife (Susan Sarandon) spends most of her time in bed suffering from the vapours and being waited on by a black maid.

Matthew McConaughey, of course, would be the liberal lawyer who will, against all odds, save Nunn from the electric chair by convincing an all-white jury that he is innocent of the crime that everybody knows he couldn't possibly have committed.

And there would be at least two poorly shaven rednecks (Kevin Bacon and Woody Harrelson) who double up as Klansmen. Drunk and jobless they ride around in a battered red Ford pick-up shouting crude insults at women and racial epithets at blacks and are always in trouble with the law. Before the film is over they will engage in an act of extreme racist depravity that will audibly disgust and physically revolt the audience. And while the judge will not approve of what they have done, he will not condemn them with his gavel either, for he does not want to set a precedent and does very much want to be re-elected.

Along with close-ups of Hall honey-roasting hams, frying chicken and dunking ribs in blood-red barbecue sauce, there would be pan shots of cotton fields and meadows full of violet. All of the main action would take place at either the church, the court room, the juke joint or on the porches where the men (black and white) chew tobacco and then spit it on the floor while their women carry them large glasses of sweet, iced lemon tea.

The music would be by Quincy Jones. The season would be summer. And despite McConaughey's courtroom victory, the theme underpinning the entire production would be tragedy.

I longed for the heartfelt affinity that both blacks and whites in the South seemed to have with their environment. They were Southerners and, whatever that meant to them, they were proud of it. Even those who were forced to leave would refer to it with a tender, bitter-sweet longing. I ached for that all-immersion sensuality that came with a rich diet, hot sun and a passionate faith, delivered in deep tremulous tones, either from the pulpit or the soap box – or both.

Clichés immortalized in film and fiction they may be. But to me, these Southern characters spoke of rural beauty and sumptuous food in a rich and lyrical language. They spoke of unbending resistance, uncompromising dignity and undeniable faith in a hostile world. They sang, danced, preached and polemicized. Across the ocean, up the A1 and along the SB5/15 route from the town-centre bus station they spoke to me – Gary Younge in Broadwater, Stevenage.

CHAPTER TWO

Five Points South

The Freedom Riders were a group of black and white civil rights workers who set off from Washington DC on 4 May 1961 to challenge the practice of racial segregation on interstate travel through the Southern states, which had only recently been outlawed.

The law in question stemmed from the judgement in the *Boynton vs. the Commonwealth of Virginia* case, handed down in December 1960. The Supreme Court had ruled it illegal to enforce racial segregation on facilities like wash rooms and lunch counters for passengers travelling from one state to another within the US. Before the judgement, each state could decide whether to segregate those facilities or not. So a black and white couple travelling together from New York State to Virginia would have been able to get off the bus and eat together in New York (where segregation was not enforced) but not in Virginia (where segregation was still practised).

The strategy of the Freedom Riders, according to James Farmer, who organized the Rides, was to force the government either to uphold the law or bow to the Southern racists. In his autobiography, he writes: 'What we had to do was to make it more dangerous politically for the federal government not to enforce federal law than it would be for them to enforce federal law. We decided the way to do it was to have an interracial group ride through the South. We felt we could count on the racists of the South to create a crisis so that the federal government would be compelled to enforce the law.' So the activists planned to travel by bus from Washington to New Orleans.

This was not the first time that Farmer's organization, the Congress of Racial Equality (CORE), had been involved in something like this. In 1947 it had co-sponsored the Journey of Reconciliation with a British-based pacifist organization, the Friendship for Reconciliation, to test another Supreme Court decision on the segregation of interstate travellers.

But a lot had changed between 1947 and 1961. In 1954 there had been the landmark ruling on segregation, *Brown vs. the Board of Education of Topeka, Kansas*, which had outlawed the principle of 'separate but equal' and therefore removed the Supreme Court's official stamp of approval for segregation.

Then came the Montgomery bus boycott when, under the leadership of the twenty-six-year-old Reverend Martin Luther King Jr., blacks had walked for over a year rather than travel at the back of the Montgomery buses. A few years later, the world witnessed the integration of Little Rock High School in Arkansas at federal gunpoint as black teenagers parted a sea of baying bigots. And the sixties had started with a wave of student-led sit-ins during which young people from the South had led the challenge to segregation in public places like restaurants and libraries.

Many of these changes were reflected in the types of people who were selected for the Freedom Ride in 1961. In 1947 all the travellers had been men. In 1961 there were three white women. In 1947 all of the blacks apart from one were from the North. In 1961 they were all from the South. In 1947 they would confront segregation only in the upper South (Virginia, North Carolina, Kentucky and Tennessee).

By 1961 they were bold enough to take on the Deep South – all the way through Georgia, Alabama and Mississippi.

On 1 May 1961 six whites and seven blacks assembled at Friendship House in Washington DC to take part in the Freedom Rides. Only one, James Peck, had been on the Journey of Reconciliation fourteen years earlier. Quite how Peck, who was white, came by his radical streak is a mystery. As the heir to the Peck & Peck clothing fortune, he was assured of a comfortable future among New England blue bloods if he wanted it. But he dropped out of Harvard and spent three years in a Connecticut prison during the Second World War as a conscientious objector before working full time for the civil rights movement.

James Farmer, the black son of a preacher and a teacher from rural Mississippi, had been a teenager of precocious intellect who was already in college by the age of fourteen. In June 1943 he founded CORE, and in between a series of union jobs, half-paid activist work, one failed marriage and one successful one (to a white woman – a fact that would prove an obstacle to his political advancement several times in the future), he dedicated himself to the organization.

The youngest member of the group was John Lewis, a twenty-one-year-old black man born to a sharecropping family in rural Alabama whose family could never understand the motivation for his political involvement. 'You were sent to school to get an education,' his mother told him when he became a student radical. 'You should get out of this move-ment, just get out of that mess.' The oldest member was Walter Bergman, a sixty-year-old white man who had been a professor at Wayne State University in Detroit and an activist in the teachers' union and the Socialist Party.

Following the Gandhian strategy of warning your opponent of what you plan to do before you do it, Farmer had written to the President, the Attorney General, the Director of the FBI, the Chairman of the Interstate Commerce Commission and the Presidents of both the national bus companies, Greyhound and Trailways, explaining CORE's intentions and including a copy of their itinerary. The plan was simple. They would split up into two groups; the first would travel by Greyhound, and the second on Trailways. Whites would travel at the back of the buses, and blacks at the front – the direct opposite of custom, practice and, in some places, local law in the South. At every stop, blacks would get off and use the whites-only facilities, and whites use the blacks-only facilities. They were scheduled to arrive in New Orleans on 17 May, where they would attend a rally to celebrate the sixth anniversary of the Brown decision. Peck would lead the group on Trailways, while Joe Perkins, the CORE Field Secretary, would head those on Greyhound.

The first few days went by without any major incidents. In some areas of Virginia, the authorities had recently painted over the WHITE and COLORED signs in anticipation of the Riders' arrival. In North Carolina the signs remained unchanged and became commonplace, but segregation was rarely implemented. It was not until Rock Hill, South Carolina, that Farmer's strategy of waiting for Southern racists to provoke a crisis started to bear bloody fruit.

As Lewis stepped off the bus and made his way to the white waiting room, he was punched repeatedly by young white thugs. Two other Freedom Riders were attacked, although neither seriously injured, before the police stepped in and broke it up.

The next few days' journey, through South Carolina and

Georgia, ran smoothly. In Atlanta, the Riders had dinner with Martin Luther King, who offered warm words of encouragement. That night, Farmer's father died, and he left the Rides to attend the funeral in Washington DC. The others went on to Alabama, one of the most racist states in the Union, without their leader. Within days they would be on front pages all over the world.

At the small town of Anniston, a reception committee of white men armed with iron bars, chains, knives, clubs and axes was waiting for those travelling on the Greyhound bus. The Riders made a collective decision that to test the facilities there would be suicide and told the driver to drive on. But before he could pull off, the mob slashed one of the bus's tyres.

After a brave but futile attempt to escape on three wheels, the driver abandoned the bus and left the activists to the mercy of the mob which had chased them up the highway in around fifty vehicles. Some of the gang tried to force the doors open, while others smashed the windows with bricks and axes. Then one of them threw a firebomb through the back window, and soon the bus was engulfed in flames. An Alabama plain-clothes policeman, who had been on the bus since Atlanta, pulled out his gun and forced the mob back as the Freedom Riders tumbled out, choking, to receive a vicious beating.

Meanwhile the group on the Trailways bus, which had left Atlanta slightly later, was arriving back at the station in Anniston to the sound of wailing ambulance sirens but with no idea of what had happened. Around eight white men got on the bus and physically moved the black Riders to the back and the white ones to the front. They sat in the middle seats to make sure their work was not undone.

With the South's racial order restored, the Trailways bus left for Birmingham, where the police had done a secret deal with the Ku Klux Klan. The police, an FBI informant later revealed, gave the Klan fifteen minutes to beat the Freedom Riders before they would appear.

The Klansmen used their fifteen minutes efficiently. Peck and a black Freedom Rider called Person were the first to leave the bus. Within minutes Peck had been knocked unconscious, and Person was being savagely attacked. When the others saw what happened, they tried to run, but the Klansmen caught them and beat them up too.

Tom Langston, a photographer for the *Birmingham Post & Herald*, just had time to finish a roll of film and hide it before the mob turned on him, hitting him with lead pipes before taking his camera and smashing it. Peck and Person were put in private cars and sent to the nearest white and black hospitals. The first one Peck was taken to refused to admit him because he was a civil rights protester. The second gave him fifty stitches in his head.

It was Sunday 14 May, Mother's Day, and when the Birmingham Commissioner for Public Safety, Eugene 'Bull' Connor, was asked where the Birmingham police were, he said they were probably spending the day with their mothers. The Governor of Alabama, John Patterson, held a news conference where he blamed the Freedom Riders for their own misfortune: 'When you go somewhere looking for trouble, you usually find it,' he said.

By the next day, the film that Langston had saved from the mob had gone all over the world. There was one shot of several whites stomping on Peck's head. There was one, taken later, of a bandaged and bruised Peck standing in front of a placard saying WELCOME TO BIRMINGHAM, and another, by an agency photographer in Anniston, of thick black smoke pouring from the bus. The Freedom Rides were international news.

The *Daily Mirror* in London said: 'President Kennedy is

now facing one of the supreme tests of his ability to lead America.' The *Diario de Buanda* in Angola lamented 'the tragedy of Negro life in America'. In Tokyo, the President of the Birmingham Chamber of Commerce, Sidney Smyer, was leading the city's business delegation at the International Rotary Convention. Smyer, a confirmed segregationist, found himself subject to hostile questioning about his home town from his Japanese hosts whose interest in doing business with the Birmingham traders waned considerably thereafter.

But the most swingeing criticism, and the one which would hurt the White House most, came from the Kremlin. *Izvestia*, the official paper of the Supreme Soviet, wrote that the incidents in Alabama revealed another 'example of wild bestial morals in a country pretending to teach others how to live'.

Back in Birmingham, Minister Fred Shuttlesworth, Alabama's most prominent spokesman on civil rights, was trying to rescue the Riders from further attacks. An armed cavalry of black churchmen went hurtling up Highway 78 to bring the Riders back from Anniston, where hospital workers were refusing to treat them. Those in Birmingham who did not need hospital treatment were taken back to his house.

The next day, the Riders pondered their next move. Clearly it was too dangerous to try and get out of Birmingham that night and head for their next stop in Montgomery. Realistically it looked as though it might be several days before they could leave the city. Either way, they would miss the rally in New Orleans.

They took a vote and decided to fly to New Orleans for the rally (only Peck voted to continue). The first Freedom Ride was over.

*

But another one was about to begin. In Nashville, Tennessee, Diane Nash, leader of the Student Non-Violent Co-Ordinating Committee (SNCC), had anticipated the first group's decision and already called Farmer at his parents' home to ask if he would have any objections to her organization taking up the Ride. The US Attorney General, Robert Kennedy, who had sent his aide, John Siegenthaler, to Birmingham to help the first group of Freedom Riders escape, called everyone he knew in Nashville and urged them to try and dissuade Nash. But Nash was not for turning.

The Nashville students set off for Birmingham the next day without Nash, who was considered too important an organizer to have in the field. Some had written their wills.

A few days later President John F. Kennedy sat in the White House in his pyjamas, hearing updates from his agitated younger brother, Robert, whose aides advised the President to try to avoid federal military intervention at all costs.

It took two days and Robert Kennedy's bullying to find a driver to take the Freedom Riders from Birmingham to the Alabama state capital, Montgomery. At 8.30 a.m. on Saturday 20 May, the St Petersburg express pulled out of the station, protected by state police.

'We got on the bus, and a great many Riders took a nap,' said John Lewis. 'I sat on the front seat, right behind the driver. About forty miles or less from the city of Montgomery, all signs of protection disappeared. There was no plane, no patrol car, and when we arrived at the bus station, it was eerie. Just a strange feeling. So quiet, so peaceful, nothing. And the moment we stepped down the steps of that bus there was an angry mob.'

Lewis had got off first and begun to deliver his statement to the press when a crowd of white men armed with lead pipes, bottles and baseball bats ran towards him. Within minutes, three Freedom Riders lay unconscious and bloody on the street, and a mob of around a thousand whites would disperse only after the head of the Alabama state police held a gun to the head of a rioter. By the time the local police got there, the violence was over, and the Attorney General's personal aide, who had been bludgeoned with a lead pipe, was on his way to hospital.

The next day both Farmer and Nash flew into Montgomery. So did Martin Luther King, who was going to address a public meeting in support of the Freedom Riders in the First Baptist church that night. Word of the meeting soon leaked, and by the time it was due to start a large group of angry whites had gathered outside and were burning cars, hurling bricks, firing shots into black homes and lobbing petrol bombs on to the church roof.

Inside the church, terrified, trapped worshippers sang hymns as their leaders tried to force Robert Kennedy to intervene and guarantee their safety. At the eleventh hour, just as US marshals were poised to take over, Governor Patterson declared a state of martial law, and Montgomery police were making their way towards the church in great numbers. But it was not until 4.30 a.m., after bitter and confused negotiations between King, the Kennedys and Patterson, that the weary and harassed congregation at the First Baptist church were allowed to return to their homes under the protection of the Alabama National Guard.

In Washington the Kennedys were losing their patience with both sides. It was a difficult time for President Kennedy. He had been in office only four months. Within the first few months he had been humiliated at the Bay of Pigs in Cuba and lost the first leg of the space race to the Soviet Union, who had sent Yuri Gagarin into orbit. Bolstered by Kennedy's weakness, the Soviet premier, Nikita Krushchev, had agreed to a summit with the President, which was now only weeks away. The last thing Kennedy needed, as he roamed the globe talking about the need to defend freedom and liberty from the red menace, were headlines suggesting that he could not uphold the same principles at home. And he knew that he had to come to a compromise with the racist Southern Democrats who had supported his election. Unbeknown to the protesters, they clinched a deal with the rabid segregationist senator James Eastland from Mississippi. If Eastland could keep the mobs at bay in Jackson, Mississippi – the Riders' next stop – then the federal government would not challenge the state's right to arrest and detain them.

Early on Wednesday morning, the Freedom Riders went to Montgomery's Trailways bus station. Only protesters and reporters were allowed on the bus. Then twelve National Guardsmen boarded, saying their job was to protect the Freedom Riders. Once on board, the Freedom Riders were told they would be skipping all stops between Montgomery and Jackson.

Farmer, who rejoined the trip in Montgomery, said the journey was conducted as though it were a military operation: 'There were police cars screaming up and down the highway with their sirens blaring. There were federal, state and county police. That did not ease our fear. If anything, it increased it. We didn't know which way the National Guardsmen would point their guns in the event of a showdown.'

At the Mississippi state line, the Alabama National Guardsmen handed over responsibility to their Mississippi peers.

In Jackson, the state Governor, Ross Barnett, had spent much of the morning on the radio asking people to stay at home and let him handle the Freedom Riders. When both the Trailways and the Greyhound group arrived, they went to use the whites-only facilities and were immediately arrested, ushered into paddy wagons and carted off to jail. The next day, they went to court where they all pleaded guilty to violating Mississippi's segregation laws. SNCC and CORE urged all those who could do so to remain in jail rather than post bail. In the spirit of Gandhi, they planned to fill up the jails until the injustice had been eradicated. By this time the Freedom Rides had become a cause célèbre for radicals. From prison, Farmer got word to his staff to keep activists coming into Jackson on almost every bus. SNCC was similarly mobilizing its supporters. By the time that Farmer had done his time, a total of 355 Freedom Riders had been arrested.

But as the activists geared up, public interest in the campaign petered out. Robert Kennedy questioned the Freedom Riders' patriotism – a serious accusation in the America of the early sixties. By June, a Gallup poll showed that sixty-three per cent of all Americans disapproved of the Freedom Rides.

With the scenes of brutal beatings off the television screens and front pages, and public opinion moving in his direction, Robert Kennedy twisted arms and concentrated minds at the Interstate Commerce Commission, which had jurisdiction over interstate transport, in order to bring the matter to a close. Within four months, the ICC had handed down a ruling that would enable the federal government to implement the Supreme Court decision of *Boynton vs. the Commonwealth of Virginia.*

The battle was over. The Freedom Riders had won. For several years after that, black Southerners called any campaigners who came to work in the South 'Freedom Riders'. The words became synonymous with those who came, stayed and fought. The campaign which had started with thirteen men and women at the Greyhound and Trailways bus stations

in Washington DC in the full of spring had defended the
right not just of ordinary Americans to ride wherever they
liked on the buses, but of civil rights activists to take the
fight against racism right on to the segregationists' home
turf. Violence would not stop them. The South would never
be the same again.

This was the journey I decided to retrace, from Washington
DC to New Orleans, through the Deep South, on a Greyhound bus: a personal journey on a historic route heading for
familiar places to which I had never been. I 'knew' it as a
land of lynching, blues and burning crosses. I had seen its
battles unfold in black and white and heard its speeches and
screams from over the Atlantic. Now I needed to see it in
colour and hear it up close. I had to feel the fear, taste the
food and ride at the front of the bus. I wanted to breathe life
into the legend of my formative years.

Shortly before I went to the US, I asked an American
journalist what kind of reaction I could expect as a black
Briton.

'Well, when they hear your accent, white Americans will
usually add twenty points to your IQ,' he said. 'But when
they see your face, they most definitely won't.'

Recalling that the authors of *The Bell Curve* had claimed
that black people have an IQ on average fifteen points lower
than whites, I was heartened to think that even in the eyes
of the most hardened racist I would still come out at least
five points ahead.

I was taking my five points and heading South.

CHAPTER THREE

Washington DC: My new best friend

For two days before their journey, the thirteen Freedom Riders underwent a course in orientation in Washington DC. An attorney detailed the federal and state laws regarding interstate transportation. A social scientist explained the racial customs in the areas they would be travelling through, and the lengths to which some of the local people might go to defend them. Farmer spelt out the principles of non-violence and peaceful resistance on which the Rides were based. And finally came role-playing sessions in which each participant took it in turns to heap verbal and physical abuse on the others in order to simulate the kind of situations they expected to meet on their way.

Over on Capitol Hill, Simeon Booker, a reporter for the black magazine Jet, *had dropped in on Attorney General Robert Kennedy to tell him that he was going to travel with the Freedom Riders and write a story. He also wanted to warn him that there would probably be trouble. 'OK, call me if there is,' Kennedy replied. 'I wish I could go with you.'*

On the night of Wednesday 3 May, on the eve of the Freedom Riders' departure, Farmer took them all out for a meal at a Chinese restaurant in downtown DC. Many referred to it, half jokingly, as the last supper.

'We were told that the racists would go to any extent to hold the line on segregation in interstate travel,' says Farmer. 'So when we began the Ride, I think all of us were prepared for as much violence as could be thrown at us. We were prepared for the possibility of death.'

*

The day I arrived in Washington DC from London, a half-million-strong battalion of 'muscular Christians' called the Promise Keepers were in town. They had come to 'display their spiritual poverty so that God might influence them' and demand a return to the patriarchy they felt was the natural order of things. The day before, one of their directors had knelt down before a crowd of thousands and called on other whites to join him as he prayed: 'Lord, I confess that we are an arrogant people, that we have deeply wounded African-Americans and Jewish and Native American and Hispanic friends in the story of this land,' he said. 'Even unconsciously, the way we stand, the way we talk, the way we think about ourselves projects an incredible sense of superiority about everything. We don't even see it.'

In the *Washington Post* came news that Supreme Court judge, Sandra Day O'Connor, would cast a deciding vote on a crucial ruling on affirmative action. At the University of Mississippi in Oxford there was a huge row over the Confederate flag. The school coach had asked supporters to stop waving it at football games because it was scaring away promising black athletes. Students responded by turning out en masse to wave their flags at the next game. And in the White House, Clinton's attempt to promote racial harmony through a high-powered working group was foundering because nobody knew what they were supposed to be talking about.

On the arts pages was the full text of a speech delivered by General Colin Powell, following the unveiling of the memorial to Robert Gould Shaw and the 54th Regiment of black soldiers who fought in the Civil War.

My girlfriend lived in Washington, and in her mailbox there were two letters: the quarterly bulletin from the National Association of Black Journalists, and a letter from her company informing her that a dispute concerning race and sex discrimination had been resolved with the union.

Race in America is everywhere. From the pulpit to the football field, from the newsstand to the mailman, you cannot get away from it. For a black Briton this is both a relief and a burden.

In Britain race ranks alongside sex, politics and religion as a subject best not discussed in polite company. One of my colleagues at the *Guardian* once described me to someone as a short, stocky guy with an earring, even though there were only three other black reporters in the building. To notice difference in Britain is tantamount to saying that difference is bad. One of the highest compliments people thought they could pay me when I was growing up was to say that they did not even think of me as black.

'What do you think of me as, then?' I would ask.

'Just Gary,' they would say.

'And what colour is Gary?' I would insist, and their eyes would roll as if to say: 'Here you go again, forcing it down my throat.'

Being black is not the most interesting thing about me. Nor is it usually the most important. But it is definitely the most obvious. When people proudly tell me that, when it comes to race, they are colour blind, I want to shake them and remind them that blindness is a disability. Nobody would choose to be blind. And in any case, blindness doesn't mean that the grass is not green or the sky blue or my skin brown. It just means that a blind person can't see it.

To point this out to most white English people is to provoke their ire. Mention racial slights you have encountered, and they will accuse you of being chippy; bring up a topic of conversation that has a racial dimension, and you will be rubbing their noses in it; write too many articles about race, and they will warn you about being ghettoized. The result is an awkward, stifling silence. At times, being black in Britain feels like my worst-kept secret.

The US could not be more different. Americans are as upfront about race as they are about their salaries or visits to their therapists. McDonald's puts advertisements in black magazines praising the contributions of their African-American staff; most major cities have a Black Chamber of Commerce and a Black Pages, a directory of black-owned businesses in the area.

While working for the *Washington Post* on a three-month fellowship in 1996, I called the Republican Party – a party of the right which is opposed to affirmative action – to discuss a story I was doing about black Republican candidates for the congressional elections. I had a long and interesting conversation with their press officer and was faxed a list of people to talk to.

A year later, back at the *Guardian*, I called the Labour Party – a party of the left which supposedly supports affirmative action – to ask what their strategy was for getting out the black vote for the general election. They said they had no such strategy and would not dream of targeting voters in terms of race. Nor, they insisted, did they have a list of black candidates. 'That's not the kind of thing we would keep a tally of,' claimed the press officer.

The US, in this respect, is extremely liberating. There is a level of honesty there about race that one simply wouldn't get in Britain. You do not have to walk around with a crucial part of your identity in hiding, only to take it out on special occasions, give it some air, let it breathe and then put it away again. But it is a double-edged sword. For in the US, issues of race do not just surround you. They define you. More often than not, race in America dictates where you live, where you worship and how you socialize. At times you wonder if people ever think about anything else. There are places where black people are supposed to be – culturally, philosophically and geographically – and others where they are not. The same is true for whites.

Television viewing figures provide a brilliant example. When it comes to watching TV, black and white Americans might as well live on different planets. According to the research group TN Media, fourteen of the twenty most popular shows among African-American viewers don't make it to the top 100 among whites. Turn the racial classifications around and the same is more or less true. The number one show among blacks, *Between Brothers*, is 117th for whites. The number four show among whites, *Friends*, is 118th with blacks. Not a single show that is in the top ten for whites is also in the top ten for blacks. If one thinks of how much time is spent not just watching television but talking about it, it becomes clear how much of a cultural rift this represents. There is no point in talking to your white colleague about a joke you saw on *Living Single* the previous night, because you know he wouldn't have seen it. And if a situation arises in the office that reminds your white colleague of a scene in *Seinfeld*, he might as well keep it to himself.

I am sure there are not too many black Brits who watch the *Antiques Roadshow* or too many whites who were ardent fans of *Desmond's*. But there is enough common ground on *EastEnders'* Albert Square or on Brookside Close, not to mention *Gladiators* and *Blind Date*, for a chat with a stranger of almost any hue at a bus stop.

In Britain you are encouraged to keep your racial identity under lock and key; in America you are prisoner to it.

There are few places where this is more true than Washington DC. The nation's capital – also known as Chocolate City – is around seventy per cent black and thoroughly segregated. This is a city where the former mayor,

Marion Barry, was filmed smoking crack, jailed for six months, went on television and said he was a nymphomaniac, ran for mayor again and won. How? Because he said he was framed by the white establishment, and such is the mistrust among blacks of the media, police and judiciary that most of them would rather believe him than his detractors.

According to some, DC is already in the South. Since there is no official definition of what the South is, there is no sure way of telling. The South is not a place so much as a construct – a distinctive but undefinable fabric into which history, economics, culture, race, prejudice and cuisine have been woven. The one thing it has very little to do with is geography, given that there are plenty of places (like Nevada or Arizona) which sit in the south of the United States and yet would never be mistaken for being in 'the South'.

'There are lots of ways to define the South,' said Susan Glisson, a Ph.D. student at the Center for Southern Culture at the University of Mississippi in Oxford. 'You can do it historically [by the eleven Confederate states], economically [adding the other seven states that had slavery] and then literally in terms of a sense of place and religiosity. It is grounded in a sense of place but also in a state of mind.'

Whichever way you slice it up, some places would be undeniably of and in the South: Virginia, the Carolinas, Georgia, Alabama, Mississippi, Louisiana, Tennessee and Arkansas. All of them were slave-owning states which fought for the Confederacy and hosted major showdowns during the civil rights era.

After that you can take your pick. The version most widely known is the one used by the Bureau of Census Statistics which includes all of the former slave-states (with the exception of Missouri) whether they fought in the Civil War or not, as well as Washington DC and Oklahoma (which was not a state at the time of the Civil War). This includes the nine above-mentioned states as well as Texas and Florida (which did fight in the Civil War) and Oklahoma, Maryland, Delaware, West Virginia and Kentucky (which didn't).

The Americans have the English to blame for this confusion. Charles Mason and Jeremiah Dixon surveyed the land south of the Pennsylvania–Maryland boundary in 1760, when the country was still a colony. By the nineteenth century, all the states north of the boundary had abolished slavery, and the rest hadn't. 'Below the Mason–Dixon line' became synonymous with 'in the South'.

Both the strength and the weakness of this definition is its inclusivity. 'The South' can be construed so broadly as to be meaningless. It is a moot point whether a state like West Virginia really has that much in common with Mississippi apart from a historical coincidence which ceased to exist more than a hundred years ago.

Others prefer to stick to the eleven states which fought for the Confederacy during the Civil War, when the South tried to split from the rest of America to preserve slavery and greater autonomy for individual states. On the face of it, this definition has the benefit of absolute clarity and cohesion. All of them opted to secede from the union, laid down the lives of their young men in a bloody struggle to fulfil that wish and lost with drastic consequences.

But a lot has changed since the 1860s. The largest minority in Texas is no longer black, but Hispanic. The same will soon be true of Florida. The presence of newly arrived immigrants (primarily from Mexico, Cuba and Puerto Rico) over the past twenty years has radically altered the political and social cultures there. Meanwhile, Kentucky and Missouri both had representatives in the Confederate capital of Richmond (as well as Washington), and wavered between both sides for a long time during the Civil War. And the status of

West Virginia, which seceded from Virginia because it did not want to fight, was never fully recognized by the Confederacy.

To come down definitively on one side or the other would leave you with some strange omissions. Take out Kentucky, and you are saying that Uncle Tom, the central character of Harriet Beecher Stowe's novel, did not have his cabin in the South. It would also exclude Muhammad Ali, who joined the Nation of Islam following his experiences of segregation in Louisville, Kentucky. Leave out Maryland, and the abolitionist Frederick Douglass was not born in the South. Take away Florida, and you exempt the state in which blacks suffered the greatest threat of lynchings in the fifty years after Reconstruction (from 1882 to 1930), and leave the celebrated Harlem Renaissance author, Zora Neale Hurston, who was born in the Florida panhandle, in cultural limbo. Omit Texas and you will have trouble explaining the lynching in Jasper in 1998 when a black man was brutally murdered by two Klansmen. 'Texas was the last state of the Confederacy to surrender,' says Glisson. 'If the South is defined by rebellion, then Texas is definitely in the South.'

'There is one South and many Souths,' chimes the mantra of students of Southern culture. 'There are small Southern diasporas all over the place,' says Glisson. 'If you go to parts of Brazil, where they maintained slavery after America abolished it, there are gravestones with many Southern names on them.'

At the end of the day the safest definition is that the South is where people say it is. I would say Washington is borderline, but the fact that segregation was legally enforced in DC until well into the sixties locates it in the South. You can get grits in DC (a gooey, porridgy dish that Southerners have with their breakfast and few Northerners can bear) but you will have to look for them. Having been the headquarters for the Union forces during the Civil War, and remaining the seat of government, it can hardly lay claim to the rebellious, anti-federalist rhetoric which infects so much of Southern culture. Yet the former Confederate capital is barely a hundred miles away, and as any Southern Confederate general would have told you, Virginia is no further away than a determined wade over the Potomac.

The Greyhound bus company has a seven-point set of core standards which it distributes to all of its staff, designed, it seems, to ensure customer care with split-second precision. It is a list of orders that assumes maximum obedience and minimum intelligence, so much so that its employees are not even trusted to work out for themselves what time of day it is or whether they are serving a man or a woman.

The notice, as seen on the wall of the customer service office in the Greyhound bus station in Charlotte, North Carolina, a few weeks later, reads:

1. Customer is acknowledged with eye contact and a smile upon arrival at all service areas.
2. Customer is verbally greeted with 'Good morning' (afternoon, evening), How may I help you?' with a smile and eye contact within ten seconds.
3. Customer is listened to without interruption while maintaining eye contact. All facts are repeated and confirmed.
4. Customer is given current, accurate information and options available.
5. Customer is asked 'Is there anything else I can help you with?'
6. Customer is thanked. 'Thanks for choosing Greyhound,' by surname or by 'Sir/Madam'.

7. All Greyhound staff in full uniform: no rips, stains or
tears and shoes shined.

The only thing I am really bothered about on Greyhound's seven-point plan is number 4. Point 2 would be
nice, point 3 is polite, and the other four points would not
be unpleasant. But to get points 1–3 and then 5–7 without
point 4 amounts to the kind of wanton provocation that
could result in serious injury.

This is not the traditional gripe about Americans grinning
inanely and saying, 'Have a nice day.' I actually like that. I
don't care if it's shallow. My point is that points 1–3 and
5–7 on the Greyhound customer service plan will work only
if point 4 is working. Without point 4, it is just a racket
devised to drive you insane. My point is that being chirpy is
not, in itself, customer service.

At the Washington DC Greyhound station, where I went
to buy my bus ticket, the staff clearly agreed. Their motto
seemed to be if you cannot get point 4 right you may as well
ignore the other six points as well.

Standing at the door to the customer service room, I
watched three people talking on the phone. None of them
acknowledged my presence. One woman was technically not
on the phone, but was talking into the microphone on her
phone. Actually picking it up looked like it would have been
much too much trouble. The man in the corner finished his
call. I directed my gaze towards him hopefully and smiled,
but he looked right through me. Then he got up. I smiled at
him again as he walked in my direction, but by that stage he
seemed intent on knocking me over. I moved out of his way.
He walked past as though I was invisible. After a couple of
minutes the woman who was on the speakerphone realized I
was not going to go away and asked if she could help. I told
her I wanted to travel around on Greyhound for a couple of

months and I understood there was a ticket I could buy for the entire trip. Could she tell me what it was called and how much it would cost? She pointed me in the direction of her other colleague, who was still on the phone, and said I would have to ask her.

When the woman in question got off the phone I asked the question again.

'Do you want to travel somewhere and stay for two months, or do you want to travel around for two months?' she asked.

'I want to travel around for two months,' I said.

'Then you need an Amayoreepass,' she said and turned to go back to her phone.

'A what?' I asked.

'An Amayoreepass,' she said a bit louder.

'Sorry,' I said, trying to sound as English, and therefore foreign and therefore in need of some slow and deliberate speech with all the consonants and vowels thrown in for free, as I possibly could. But she took my elaborate pronunciations as a signal that I was either hard of hearing or had learning difficulties, and turned up the volume.

'AMAYOREEPASS,' she yelled. 'It's like America and then pass but without the "ca",' she said. 'You can have them for fifteen, thirty or sixty days.'

'Oh right, an Ameripass,' I said. 'How much are they?'

She pointed me to her colleague, the one who pointed me to her in the first place, and who was, once again, talking to the air over her phone.

'She will help you,' she said.

I waited for her colleague to finish her call and then asked how much an Ameripass would cost.

'How long you travelling for?'

I planned to travel for two months but wanted to break the journey in the middle with a trip to Chicago for

Thanksgiving. 'Probably thirty days,' I said, figuring there was no point in paying for a week when I would not be using it.

She tapped around on her computer and came up with $399. I asked, just out of curiosity, if the sixty-day pass was simply double that. 'Yes, sir,' she said, unflinching in her certainty, and pointed me in the direction of the ticket desk. Then she called me back. She was having second thoughts. In a fit of industry, she reached for her keyboard again. 'Wait there, let me just check that, sir,' she said and tapped away. 'Oh no, a sixty-day pass is $600,' she said.

I thanked her. The only piece of extraneous activity that I had seen her make in the ten minutes I had been in the room had saved me $198.

The queue at the ticket counter was short, and the procedure simple. I asked for a sixty-day Ameripass and I got one. It is one small piece of paper, the size of two playing cards, wrapped in a thin Greyhound envelope. I had been hoping for something just a little bit more substantial for my $600 and I began to get jittery. This flimsy piece of paper had to last me sixty days.

Just as the saleswoman was writing down my details I anticipated my own failings and asked her what I should do if I lost the ticket.

'Sir, that ticket is your best friend. Whatever you do don't lose your Ameripass,' she said.

'Believe me, I'm not planning on losing it,' I said. 'But just say I did, then what would I do?'

The saleswoman started malfunctioning. She did not know what to say apart from what she had said already. So she said it again. 'Sir, that Ameripass is your best friend. You do not want to lose that. Believe me, sir, I have seen people when they have lost their Ameripass, and they are so upset, and there is nothing I can do for them.'

That was just the kind of reassurance I did not want.

'I really do not want to lose it. But in the same way that I might fall out with my best friend even though I might not mean to, I might just . . . you know . . . lose it.'

By this time she had finished with my details and was not at all interested in my getting cute. She just stapled the ticket to another, slightly larger piece of paper and handed it back to me with a smile and a warning. 'Look after it, sir.'

I left with my new best friend.

CHAPTER FOUR

Virginia: Looking local.
Sounding foreign

The Freedom Riders saw their first white and coloured signs on the wash-room doors in the Greyhound station in Fredericksburg, Virginia, only fifty miles outside Washington. This would be their first test. Charles Person, a black student from Atlanta, went into the white wash room. James Peck went into the black one. Nothing happened. Further down the state, in Farmville, the segregation signs had been deliberately freshly painted over. But even where segregation was not being enforced, Peck noticed blacks and whites remained separated by habit rather than law: 'It is disheartening to me that in a city such as Richmond, which is not far from the nation's capital and where the color signs had been removed, Negroes were sticking to the formerly separate and grossly unequal colored waiting rooms and restaurants,' he wrote.

Danville was the first place anyone was refused service. Ed Blankenheim, a white carpenter from Tucson, Arizona, sat for ten minutes at a coloured counter, until his bus was ready to leave, and was not served. Peck and some other Riders, who came through the town on a later bus, had the same problem, but were finally seen to after a brief discussion with the manager.

'The ride through Virginia was routine,' recalled Farmer. One Rider joked: 'They knew we were coming and they baked a cake.'

It was a cold, clear October morning when I boarded the nine forty-five from DC to Richmond. At the gate, a man took my ticket, which until then I hadn't believed anyone would accept as a document in lieu of payment, and asked me kindly and apologetically for some ID.

Struggling with my rucksack, my computer and a shoulder bag (a sorry sight that was to hold up a number of queues over the next two months), I reached for the first thing that was available, which happened to be from work.

He smiled. 'You're a newspaper man,' he said. 'I tell you what. I'll get you on the bus and you get me on the news.' He laughed, waved me on and then turned to the woman behind me who had no idea what he was talking about and said, 'That man there's gonna get me on the news.'

The bus was fairly empty at first, and in line with Greyhound-traveller's etiquette which dictates that so long as there are empty double seats only freaks and stalkers invade someone else's space, I picked a seat on my own. It was cold, and the air conditioning was on strong. Two guys at the back of the bus shouted down to the driver at the front, 'Hey man, turn down the ACs.'

The bus took off out of the Greyhound station, turning its back on the Congress, and headed south down I-95, passing some of the textbook urban desolation – empty lots of concrete land with grass growing through it, surrounded by abandoned houses and boarded-up shop fronts – that stands rotting in the shadow of Capitol Hill. Within minutes, we were on the motorway, where on either side Virginia's trees were performing their annual striptease for fall and decking the ground in moulting browns and yellows.

At Fredericksburg, with the bus gradually filling up, a man with thighs that would not have shamed an ox took the seat next to me and sat with legs akimbo, as though he had woken up with the sole intention of squashing an Englishman against a Greyhound bus window. A spate of undignified, low-level jostling ensued – the daily bump and grind of

GARY YOUNGE

crowded public transport involving elbows, knees and feigned politeness – as I tried to claw back the space to which I felt I was entitled. But the big guy from Fredericksburg was having none of it, and after five minutes, because he was bigger than me and because it was only a two-and-a-half-hour journey, I gave up. The terms of my surrender were punitive. Not only did I have to pay with my discomfort, but I was also prevented from reading my book because there was not enough room to move my elbows in order to turn the pages. To avoid further humiliation, I closed my eyes and soon fell asleep. When I woke up, my persecutor had gone, and so had everyone else. I was in Richmond, and the bus driver was waiting impatiently for me to leave. As I got off I saw my cousin Natalie waiting, with a car, a smile and a spare bed in her room for three nights.

One of the great things about having parents who come from a tiny island with a labour force that has been ravaged by the demands of post-war economic migration is that whichever side of the Atlantic you are on you are never short of a place to stay. Of my mother's five siblings, only one came to England, while the rest stayed in Barbados. But my father is one of ten children, and all but two left to make a life elsewhere. I have an aunt in Savannah, Georgia; one in Houston, Texas; and one in London; a couple of uncles in Toronto; one in Florida (I think); and another who has now retired to Barbados after several years in the States.

Natalie, the twenty-two-year-old daughter of my father's sister Velma, grew up in Barbados but left to study in America when she was eighteen. She wears her national identity on her car number plates, BAJAN WI, and is one of those people with whom you spend five minutes and then wonder what the hell you've been doing with your life. She

is the kind of person who makes you want to throw away
your television, pour all of your beer down the sink and
join an evening class, go jogging or read a hardback political biography – anything that would make you feel that
your every waking moment is being used constructively.
Natalie runs the university chapter of the National Association of Advancement for Colored People, the oldest civil
rights organization in the country; she is heavily involved
in the campus's black caucus; and is a senator on the student
government. She also has a part-time job as a manager at
the student union and is, judging by the certificates on her
wall, an excellent student.

Her friend and flatmate, Lenell, whose parents left Trini-
dad for Brooklyn and then Brooklyn for Virginia, is similarly
hyperactive. The sheer volume of confidence generated by
the two of them together should carry a government health
warning that anyone who feels in any way insecure should
keep well out of their way.

On the first night I took them out for a meal at an Italian
chain restaurant, the Olive Garden. Like movie stars in a
Beverly Hills eaterie, they nodded hellos to four or five
people in the room. One woman came over to ask if Natalie
was going on the Reclaim the Night torch-lit demonstration
on campus. She was. Another wanted to check with both of
them how plans were going for the trip to the million-
woman march. They were going fine. But in between courses
and hellos, our conversation dwelt not on the dry stuff of
politics but on the urgent matters of love and the single black
woman – a crucial conversation in America, given the alleged
dearth of eligible black men which is a perennial topic of
black women's magazines and talk shows. I brought up the
issue mostly because I felt it my birthright to do so. As the
youngest of three boys I spent my entire adolescence being
interrogated by my elder brothers about every female phone

call or furtive dalliance that did or didn't come my way. Since I have no younger brothers of my own to annoy, I now consider it my responsibility to pass the tradition on via my younger cousins. At first Natalie told me to grow up and wondered out loud whether my questions did not reveal some inadequacies in my own private life. A good point but, unfortunately for her, not good enough. After a little more prodding – I take this birthright thing seriously – it turned out that neither had a boyfriend at the moment.

Lenell said she might soon have to start dating white men. 'Some black guys you know, it's like chilling is all they're doing. I want a man with ambition who wants to do something with his life and has some goals,' she said. Natalie said so long as she could find a man who would treat her like a queen she didn't care what colour he was. Lenell said, 'Amen.'

I used to think that. I remember saying that race had no place in my love life. But then I noticed a pattern in many of my relationships, which, given the small number of black women in both Stevenage and Edinburgh, always involved white women until the age of twenty-three.

First came the discovery that their parents were racists, which was always a surprise for them but never for me. Then came their belief that if only their parents got to know me they would change their minds, and everything would be fine. Feeling myself being converted from a boyfriend to an educational aid for improving race relations, I would then insist that this was an issue between them and their parents and was not something I was prepared to get involved in, since I had no interest in 'getting to know' a racist. Then they would say I was ungrateful for the efforts they were making; I would tell them I was going out with them not their parents; they would say I didn't want to make the relationship work; I would ask them if they thought they were doing me a favour by going out with me, thinking, but never saying, scratch the surface and this racism thing appears to be hereditary. And then we would break up.

The last time I got involved in something like this was at university, where the parents of my girlfriend at the time had promised to cut off her financial support in the middle of her degree if she carried on seeing me. One Christmas, her elder brother had told her she could come to Christmas dinner only if she left me behind – 'I'm not spending Christmas Day with a coon,' he said. She spent Christmas Day with me but had taken it upon herself to persuade her parents to have a Boxing Day meal with both of us. She didn't tell me of the plan until Christmas Eve. I was not impressed. I told her that I didn't want to spend Boxing Day with her parents, but if she did that was fine. I had friends I would rather spend time with.

She hit the roof. She had spent all this time setting up dinner between me and a couple of racists and now I was letting her down. I told her if she had told me before I could have saved her the trouble, but that whoever the compromise was supposed to please it definitely wasn't me. By New Year we had broken up – needless to say there were other problems with that relationship – and by February I had decided that life was too short to go out with white women unless they had a basic level of racial awareness. Not that I would present a prospective mate with a questionnaire asking them to name the first five black MPs or trace and describe the events leading up to the 1981 uprisings in Brixton in an attempt to ascertain her suitability; but if there was no instinctive will to understand what going out with a black person entailed, I knew it just could not work. In other words, race mattered; it was in my love life whether I wanted it there or not.

I didn't bother telling Natalie and Lenell all of this, partly because it would have been horribly patronizing – 'I used to think that but then I grew up,' is hardly the way to endear yourself to a younger cousin – but also because I think they had given the issue every bit as much thought as I had and, in a completely different set of circumstances, had not surprisingly come up with a completely different conclusion. I did ask them if they felt it likely that they could meet a white person with sufficient racial sensitivity. Both of them thought it was possible. I hope they are right.

As we drove home from the Olive Garden Natalie warned me to be careful in Richmond after dark. One of her friends had been robbed at gunpoint; the friend of one of her friends was shot dead in another attack; and a woman from university had been raped by a burglar – all within a few blocks of her student dorm, all within the last few months.

In daylight, much of downtown Richmond looks as though everybody just upped and left after the Second World War and came back a week ago to open some shops. There are some pretty parts: well-tended parks, the impressive grounds of the state capitol and neat, shiny, office blocks. This, after all, was the capital of the Confederacy, the political focal point of Southern efforts to establish their own country, independent of the Yankees. Next door to what would have been the Confederate White House is a Confederate museum. If the South had won the Civil War, this would now be the capital city of a separate country. The main thoroughfare, Broad Street, is an uneasy mix of the grand and the derelict. Jackson ward, once the home of a vibrant African-American community which during the fifties attracted some of the biggest names in music and dance, is now a shell, victim of one of the main paradoxes of integration: the economic, social and cultural life was sucked out of the area as soon as official racial barriers started to fall, and blacks could live, shop, eat and party almost anywhere they wanted to in the city. For all that, Richmond, which is fifty-five per cent black, has the benefit of still being a city in the way the rest of the world understands the term – a place where you can walk for thirty minutes in almost any direction and still not run into a motorway.

Walking almost a straight path from Natalie's student residence past an expensive hotel and through the urban desolation of downtown, I came to a neat little building with a gold plate signalling the office of the attorneys Hill, Tucker and Marsh. In the reception area, many of the legal and political signposts mapping out the historical route of African-Americans' legal battle for equality were hanging on the walls: the Declaration of Independence, the Bill of Rights, the Gettysburg Address and the Emancipation Proclamation. In the top left-hand corner of the wall facing the entrance was another poster, showing a black hand with a pen against the backdrop of cotton fields, and the words HANDS THAT PICK COTTON CAN PICK OUR PUBLIC OFFICIALS – REGISTER AND VOTE.

I introduced myself to the receptionist, who directed me to a seat and then called through to announce my arrival. Still staring at the posters on the wall, I heard a voice, faint but firm, from the offices at the back. 'What line's he on?' it asked.

'He's not on the phone, Mr Hill, he's here,' said the receptionist and smiled at me. 'He's got confused. He thinks you're on the phone ... He's here,' she shouted. Within seconds a tall, stooping figure in a grey two-piece suit and an olive waistcoat guided his Zimmer frame out of his office and slowly up the corridor and offered me his hand.

This was Oliver Hill, graduate from the class of '33, a ninety-year-old attorney and civil rights veteran who waged war with the American judiciary to bring about the end of legal segregation through his work on the *Brown vs. Board of Education* case. Hill was one of an ambitious group of young black men who graduated from the historically black Howard University law school in Washington DC under the strict tutelage and guidance of Charles Houston, the school's Vice-Dean, whom Hill described as a tough disciplinarian. In the classroom he told students that they were not just learning for their own personal gain, but so that they could go into the court room and uplift the race. The first class to graduate since the school ran a full-time law course under Houston's reign were handed their degrees in 1933. First in the class was a tall, jovial and highly motivated man called Thurgood Marshall, who went on to become the first African-American on the US Supreme Court. The second, and one of Marshall's best friends, was the even taller Oliver Hill.

In the first decade or so after Hill's graduation, the strategy of these black lawyers was not to challenge segregation so much as to make sure it kept true to its word. American law at the time stated that separation of the races was legal so long as the facilities provided to both races were 'equal'. Hill and his peers argued, with varying success, that Southern authorities were legally bound to bring facilities in black institutions up to the standards provided for whites. According to the *Richmond Times Dispatch*, Hill's legal team filed more civil rights suits in Virginia than were filed in any other Southern state during segregation. The *Washington Post* once estimated that Hill's team was responsible for winning more than $50 million in higher pay, new buses and better schools for black teachers and students.

But by the late forties the strategy had changed. The NAACP (National Association for the Advancement of Colored People) now felt it was time to challenge the validity of the 'separate but equal' doctrine itself and started scouring the country looking for test cases.

Hill found his case – or rather it found him – in the small rural town of Farmville at the black school called Moton High. On Monday morning, 23 April 1951, the phone in principal Boyd Jones's office rang with news that two of his students were about to get in trouble with the police unless he came to the Greyhound bus terminal immediately.

As soon as Jones left, there was a mutiny in the school. Its leader, and the voice behind the hoax telephone call, was sixteen-year-old Barbara Johns. With the principal out of the way, Johns and four friends, who had been plotting for several weeks, went to each classroom with a message slip announcing that school assembly would be at eleven. When the students and teachers arrived in the main hall they were met by a strike committee, headed by Johns, who dismissed the teachers and told her peers it was time the students fought for a decent school. It was time to walk out and return only when the white community was prepared to give them a reasonable response. As some took up picket signs, others sought a meeting with the white Superintendent of Schools and the Chairman of the county school board.

On the third day of the strike, the students met Hill and his friend and colleague Spottswood Robinson. The lawyers had no desire to start their battle against segregation in a conservative backwater like Farmville. 'Only these kids turned out to be so well organized and their morale was so high, we just didn't have the heart to tell 'em to break it up,' said Hill in Richard Kluger's book *Simple Justice*. They told the children and their parents that the only way the NAACP would become involved was if they were prepared to sue for an end to segregation. The parents and students agreed to do it.

A month after the strike began, Hill filed suit. Two years later, the federal district court unanimously ruled against them, arguing that the separate schools were not the product of racism but Southern mores. Hill and Robinson appealed to the Supreme Court, which decided to hear the case along with *Brown vs. the Board of Education of Topeka* (often referred to just as *Brown*), which dealt with the same issue. Thus Oliver Hill began his involvement in the legal battle that would transform the racial landscape of America. 'There's no doubt about it. *Brown* was the greatest legal case this century. It gave Negroes their rights under the thirteenth, fourteenth and fifteenth amendments. We knew we could win it; we just had to educate the courts.'

The fruits of that victory were a long time coming. The courts decided that the South needed time to break down segregation and so ordered the authorities to enforce integration with 'due deliberate speed'.

'As white folks interpreted it, due deliberate speed meant as long as hell if any time at all. At that time we had separate everything: separate cemeteries, hospitals, every damn thing was separate. And uncomfortable, too. Our coaches were up by the engine. They were hot. When I was fighting all this I faced everything: bad telephone calls, vile letters, that kind of junk. Once they burned a cross on my lawn. But life is dangerous just driving an automobile down the street.'

He sounds casual about it now, but in those days Hill did not let his young son answer the telephone. We were in a little back room of his practice, with a large desk covered in folders with a vase full of plastic flowers on it. His memory is still sharp and his speech fluent, although, being ninety, he has so much to remember that any question about the past is followed by a few seconds' silence as he strains, with his eyes closed, to give you as accurate an answer as possible.

'I was born in Richmond but moved to Roanoke when I was in elementary school and then I went to high school in DC. My grandfather was a preacher and he wanted my father to be a preacher too, but my father wanted to be a seaman. My father deserted my mother when I was one. The divorce papers say he was an alcoholic.' His mother remarried. 'To be honest, I had very little contact with white folks. Economically, we were middle-class Negroes. As it was, I was an only child growing up in what would then have been called luxury. When I was nine, my grandmother tried to tell me something about her experiences of slavery, but I wasn't that much concerned at that age.'

Hill believes that despite his legal victories not much in the South has changed. 'Nowadays we are dealing with the same issues. The white man still don't want to accept Negroes as fully fledged citizens. All immigrant minorities strove to be white, and all of them were accepted as white unless their skin was a little bit too dark. Negroes couldn't get into restaurants, but foreigners could. We were the ones who put up a big fight, but everybody else moves faster than us. White women have benefited more than Negroes from the civil rights Acts of 1964 and '65.'

So were all the legal battles worth it?

'Of course they were. There are certain things you get from just mixing with other people. White kids and their parents control everything, and black kids aren't going to know who's controlling everything if they can't mix.

'We have to try to make progress through inclusion. It is evolutionary change. Everything changes. I don't think that we have to approach every issue and think, what did the founding fathers think? We have to say, what is the most important issue for the founding fathers today?

GARY YOUNGE

'You see, in England you have always had all the
privileges of being an Englishman. But we didn't have that
here. The difference is that we have a written constitution
and you all don't.'

My initial reaction when Mr Hill said this was to inform
him politely that he was dead wrong. I have never had all
the privileges of being an Englishman. Just about every time
I return to the country, I have to deal with an immigration
official who will put my passport under a special light and
ask me lots of dopey questions because he thinks I might
have stolen it. Even now, there are places – pubs and
restaurants mostly – right in the centre of London that don't
allow black people in unless they have to. Of course, they
don't say, 'Sorry, sir, we are operating a colour bar tonight.'
They say it's a private party, or members only. I tried to meet
some friends a few years back in Covent Garden. The man at
the door said it was a private party. I asked him if my friends,
who were all white and all inside, had been invited to the
party, and if so who was throwing it, because the chances
were I would know them as well. Without a blush, explanation or apology, he let me in. 'Go on, then,' he said with a
sigh, as though he were doing me a favour. None of that
feels much like a privilege.

But then I caught myself. For even though segregation
was not always against the law in England – the country's
first piece of anti-racism legislation did not appear until 1965
– there were never laws in England, like there were in the
United States, that actively enforced and codified it. You
can't legislate for the unfriendly stares my parents received
when they went house hunting.

Whatever I might have said to him, had I been stupid
enough and rude enough to interrupt him (which I nearly
was), would not have been quite right. But while I do know
there is a big difference between not being able to do

something because people won't let you and not being able to do it because it is forbidden by law, I also know that, as long as you are not allowed to do it, the difference doesn't feel that big.

I asked Hill if he considered himself patriotic.

'As far as I am concerned, the first thing I am in the US is a black man. But the only reason that Negroes are a homogenous group in the US is because the white man thinks so. Some Negroes are so white their pigmentation is almost indiscernible. I know I am the descendant of African, Indian, white and Semitic, so what the hell is homogenous about me?'

With the interview drawing to a close he told me he served in England as a sergeant during the Second World War. 'I never did get to London. We went to Herefordshire, Carmarthen and Southampton. We used to play bridge with quite an upper-class family in Hereford.' I tried to imagine this – a group of black soldiers from the American South playing bridge over Pimms with some Hereford toffs – and it made me laugh.

'The white soldiers did used to resent it that the white girls dated Negro soldiers, but there wasn't anything they could do about it. The local people used to think that the Americans were arrogant. You know the little engines you have on your cars, well the Americans used to laugh at those. They used to laugh at the money you made too, because they earned a lot more.' Hill laughed and then stopped and wiped some spittle from his mouth. 'I was thirty-six years old and I had better sense than to date white women then or run around getting drunk. It was the English that invented segregation, after all.'

By the time I had left Mr Hill's office and made my way back up the long road towards Natalie's dorm, it was late afternoon. Around the university, students lounged on the rickety front porches of what looked like fraternity houses, drinking beer from cans covered in brown paper, while loud rock music poured from the windows above them. This could have been Bohemia. But it looked more like sloth and privilege marinating in Budweiser. The campus police were on patrol, and several students were leaving their classes and jumping into large Jeeps for the short drive home.

With a few hours to kill before Natalie or Lenell returned from classes, I set about looking for Monument Avenue. After some poor directions from a police woman and some excellent ones from a young man with a can, I found it just in time to see dusk descend on the captains of the Confederacy.

Monument Avenue is one of the most bizarre pieces of urban landscape America has to offer, a mile-long stretch of historical confusion and political duplicity cast in bronze and elevated for all to see. Coming from the town centre it starts with a line of monuments to Confederate military supremos who spearheaded the battle to preserve, among other things, slavery. And it ends with a statue of Arthur Ashe, a black humanitarian sportsman who fought against racial inequality and was forced to leave Richmond, his home town, because the tennis courts were segregated.

Coming from the town centre, it is Robert E. Lee who really strikes you first. He sits upright and proud on his sculpted horse, whose muscular flanks are keenly chiselled. Shoulders back, chin out, perched on marble and standing about sixty feet tall, Lee, who led the Army of North Virginia and co-ordinated much of the military strategy for the Confederacy, is the very symbol of Southern heroism. 'A people carves its own image in the monuments of its great men,' said Richmond's mayor, Archer Anderson, at the ceremony to mark the unveiling of the monument in May 1890.

That the principal monument should have been dedicated to Lee should be of little surprise. For Lee is the embodiment of the way many Confederate sympathizers would like those who fought for their cause to be remembered, as a chivalrous tribe of gents who abhorred slavery – 'a moral and political evil' – and fought not to preserve human bondage, but for blood, honour, land and the 'freedom' of the individual states.

'I cannot raise my hand against my birthplace, my home, my children,' said Lee after he resigned from the Union Army to join the Confederates. 'Save in defense of my native state, I never desire to draw sword again.' But when the war was over and the South had lost, he rejoined the Union and worked for the common good.

With Lee leading the charge into Southern mythology, apologists for the Confederacy can reduce the Civil War to the following: 'The war was not about slavery but states' rights. Our ancestors fought for what they believed in. They fought courageously, and they lost, and we are glad and proud that they fought.'

Here lies the moral foundation for the notion, popular among many white Southerners, that the Civil War was nothing worse than a noble lost cause, a war that was worth both fighting and losing. '*Because* I love the South, I rejoice in the failure of the Confederacy,' said former President Woodrow Wilson. '[Nevertheless] I recognize and pay loving tribute to the virtues of the leaders of secession ... the righteousness of the cause which they thought they were promoting – and to the immortal courage of the soldiers of the Confederacy.'

By the time I left Lee's statue and made my way to see his lesser contemporaries, the crickets were out and house lights were coming on. The Avenue is flanked by turn-of-the-century houses and has a large grassy tranche in the middle which looks bigger than both of the roads to its sides put together. Soon joggers appeared, along with wealthy, healthy-looking thirty-somethings walking the sorts of dog that wealthy, healthy-looking people walk. I walked through the middle, kicking up the leaves, and since I had neither a dog nor tracksuit trousers I looked out of place.

Just before Lee comes to the statue of Jeb Stuart. After comes the statue of Jefferson Davis who, given the lateness of the hour, was now bathed in lights. Davis was the wartime president of the Confederacy who accepted his new position with the words, 'The time for compromise has now passed. The South is determined to make all who oppose her smell Southern powder and feel Southern steel.' Now he stands on Monument Avenue with his hand outstretched, and a quote saying: 'Not in hostility to others, not to injure any section of the country, not even for our own pecuniary benefit, but from the high solemn motive of defending and protecting the rights we inherited and which it is our duty to transmit unshorn to our children.' Fine words for a man who approved the summary execution of black soldiers during the Civil War as an 'example' to discourage the arming of slaves. After him come the Confederate leaders General Stonewall Jackson and finally Commodore Maury.

Then, just when you think the Avenue must either come to an end or go on into an eternity of self-delusion, there is Arthur Ashe. With his tennis racket in his left hand and a book in his right, he is surrounded by a multiracial group of children all clamouring to touch him. In his glasses and tracksuit trousers he cuts an avuncular figure. The inscription on the back is from the Bible: Hebrews 12:1 'Since we are surrounded by so great a cloud of witnesses let us lay aside every weight, and sin which so easily ensnares us, and let us run with endurance that which is set before us.' At the back it carries the date it was erected, 1996, and its purpose: 'to inspire children of all nationalities'.

I turned around to walk back up Monument Avenue, feeling angry and confused. The anger was not difficult to explain. I had spent about an hour walking along a road in which four men who fought to enslave me (in the midst of this rage, the slight geographical fact that I am from England and not the American South felt like an irrelevance – they stole my ancestors and just took them somewhere else) have been honoured and exalted. I resented the fact that on the way to work every day, black people have to look at that. Imagine how black children must feel when they learn that the people who have been raised and praised up the road are the same ones who tried to keep their great-great-grandparents in chains. And I was angry at what they have done to Arthur Ashe. It looks like an afterthought. Not only is Ashe severely outnumbered by racists, but whoever decides these things has established some sort of equivalence between them all – as though these are just famous people from the South, regardless of what each of them fought for.

Mr Hill had proposed a compromise on this point earlier in the day: 'I didn't have any problem with putting Arthur Ashe up there. The only thing I wanted to do was to make a clean break and have him further away from those old Confederate generals. Those old losers. I wanted to say, here is Arthur Ashe – a clean break, representing a new era. Here is Arthur Ashe starting the twenty-first century.'

And while all the others, with the exception of Davis, just sit on their plinths without any explanation, presumably because everyone knows why they should be there, Ashe needs the excuse of being someone for 'all nationalities'. This, I am sure, is in part due to the row that followed putting him there in the first place – some whites claimed his presence would bring down the historical tone of the area. It also marks another in a long line of great Virginia botches when it comes to making principled decisions about what the state's heritage means to its inhabitants.

For years, a fierce debate raged over what to do with the official state song. The first stanza reads:

> Carry me back to old Virginia
> There's where the cotton and corn and 'tatoes grow,
> There's where the birds warble sweet in the springtime,
> There's where this old darkey's heart am long'd to go.
> There's where I labor'd so hard for old massa
> Day after day in the field of yellow corn,
> No place on earth do I love more sincerely,
> Than old Virginia, the state where I was born.

Blacks protested for a long time, but only in January 1997 was it finally retired. Even then, it was not abolished but demoted to state song 'emeritus'.

On the first Monday after Martin Luther King's birthday, when the rest of the country is celebrating Martin Luther King Day and the great works of the civil rights leader, Virginia is marking Lee–Jackson–King Day, which honours Robert E. Lee and Stonewall Jackson as well. One day which honours two men who fought to preserve slavery and one who died trying to rid the country of its vestiges – who, one wonders, could possibly be happy with that?

But my anger surprised me. Sculptures and monuments are not generally the sort of thing that get me excited one way or another. Europe in general and England in particular are full of statues to people who did revolting things but who are fêted for their bravery and Christian rectitude. They are everywhere: Churchill, Queen Victoria, Wellington, on street names, tube stops, in parks and on pub hoardings. I barely notice them any more, and when I do, my expectations of what they might represent are so low that it would be almost impossible for me to be disappointed.

If I see a statue then I presume that behind the official story of derring-do and boundless courage there is inevitably some horrible denial of my history. The only one I have ever seen that I liked was of the Irish trade unionist Jim Larkin, on O'Connell Street in Dublin. Larkin stands with his arms held high and his palms to the sky, with the inscription: 'Arise, the great appear great because we are on our knees. Let us rise.' That could speak to everyone about almost anything.

But these Confederate generals fought for a cause that was commonly believed to be wrong at the time, and is almost universally believed to be wrong now. And they lost. I cannot think of any other culture in the world that would erect such massive memorials to a war that was fought for such an ignoble cause and which was lost. Depending on your politics, the Vietnam memorial in Washington might fit the bill. But its simple design bears no hint of triumphalism, just sorrow at the immense human waste. Monument Avenue felt like the cultural and political equivalent of putting a huge statue of Adolf Hitler and his sidekicks up on Kurfürstendamm Platz in Berlin – not as trite a comparison as it might appear, given the number of blacks who died in slavery.

I also felt a certain amount of confusion. The idea of ripping down monuments makes me nervous. I was in the Soviet Union when people started removing the busts of Lenin, and when the city of Leningrad was renamed St Petersburg. I sympathized, but it looked as though people were trying to deny that Communism ever happened. Somehow, for me, removing monuments is in the same ball game, although definitely not in the same division, as burning books – a very violent and insecure way of excising parts of the past because people do not like them. So while I hated to see the generals on Monument Avenue, I wasn't absolutely sure that I wanted to see them go.

I turned off Monument Avenue to find a bar and a toilet, and by then I was almost certainly seeing things; being black and surrounded by Confederate captains after dark will do that to you. The first bar I got to had only white people in it. I saw a skinhead playing pool with what looked like a red-faced Southern-type good ol' boy with a beard and cap. I would go there if I had to but I kept walking up the street to see if I could find somewhere else. As I turned away from the bar, I understood precisely what was wrong with the statues I had just seen. They had intimidated me, threatened me and left me deeply suspicious of the white people around me, and whatever else a monument is supposed to do, it is not supposed to do that.

In his book *Standing Soldiers, Kneeling Slaves*, the historian Kirk Savage writes of the thirty-year period after the Civil War when the first statue was put up: 'Public monuments were meant to yield resolution and consensus, not to prolong conflict ... Even now to commemorate is to seek historical closure, to draw together the various strands of meaning in an historical event or personage and condense its significance.'

To this definition of what makes a good monument I would add one more qualification, suggested to me a month later by Odessa Woolfolk, the President of the board of directors of the Civil Rights Institute in Birmingham, Alabama. When I asked Ms Woolfolk if memorials to the Confederacy offended her, she said: 'Not if they are honest, no.'

Judged on these criteria, Monument Avenue is the main street in the metaphorical capital city of bad monuments. Not only do the statues there not represent a consensus now, when most of the city's inhabitants are black (when I mentioned the statues to African-Americans, they called them 'crackers', 'racists' and 'losers'). They never did. It is not even as though the Civil War was uniformly supported by whites in the South. In 1863, in the middle of the war, Davis had to put down a massive riot at gunpoint in Richmond after white civilians protested at the hardships inflicted upon them by the war economy. 'We are going to the bakeries and each of us will take a loaf of bread. That is little enough for the government to give us after it has taken all our men,' said one woman at the time. The *Richmond Dispatch* of 6 September 1887 reported that the city council had refused to endorse subsidies for the first statue in what was then a suburban location because it would 'benefit only a certain class of people'.

Nor do they mark closure. America is still dealing in a very real way with the legacies of slavery. That, despite the denials of the hard right, is what the debate over affirmative action is all about.

Given that the vast majority of people on all sides of the political spectrum now believe that slavery was a bad thing which had to stop, and that America does need a cohesive, federal government, they can hardly be accused of passing the test of time.

And they are dishonest. Davis's statue describes him as an 'exponent of constitutional principles. Defender of the rights of states', and then come the words '*Crescit occulto velut arbor aero fama.*' I do not read Latin, but unless this inscription means 'Here stands a man who fought tooth and nail to defend the bankrupt ideology of human bondage', then it is an incredibly misleading appraisal of Davis's legacy.

So while I believe that to remove monuments is to pretend that an ugly period in history never happened, the history reflected in these statues really didn't ever happen. At least in England, most people think Winston Churchill was a great bloke. An awful lot of West Indians must have done as well, otherwise they wouldn't have named their children after him. Whatever I might think of Churchill and Queen Victoria, they do represent a popular consensus and reflect a (mistaken in my view) sense of resolution. If I have a problem with them being there, then it is not with the monuments, but with the society that is pleased to see them. On Monument Avenue, the monuments make me mad all by themselves.

The next day I went to get my hair cut. In London, this is a relatively simple and usually enjoyable exercise. At my hairdresser's in Hackney, there are two guys, one from Antigua, the other from St Lucia, who actually cut hair, and at least two or three others who are there just to make conversation. All are between forty and sixty and engage in raucous banter only half of which I understand because their accents are so broad and their vocabulary is still peppered with island colloquialisms that are truly beyond my ken. On the walls, there are pictures of great West Indian cricketers like Clive Lloyd and Brian Lara, footballers like Ian Wright and John Barnes, and topless models, like Linda Lusardi and Pamela Anderson; on the radio there is calypso; and on the bench there is the day's copy of the *Daily Mirror*, usually open at the racing page.

Whenever you go, there is rarely a queue. They beckon me over, and I ask them for a flat top – number two on the top and one at the sides – which suits me fine, although I don't know whether anything would suit me better because I have never asked for anything else. At least twice during the fifteen to twenty minutes it takes them to finish, they will stop when someone pokes their head around the door, and start to chat. And when it is over, I give them eight pounds, seven pounds for the cut and a pound tip, and I am on my way.

. Compared with the ordeal I had to go through in Stevenage, this is bliss. For even though nobody in the town could cut black hair professionally, it had become a popular myth in the Younge household that the Greek man at Marymead shopping centre knew what he was doing. He didn't. But every few months we would go there anyway and ask him for a flat top, or to cut some off round the sides and leave the top long, or for something else we had seen on *Top of the Pops* or in *Melody Maker*. Every time he would nod knowingly and then do the same thing – shear me like a sheep and leave my head looking like a chocolate treat with a small coating of fuzz on top.

When I reached fifteen I broke with tradition. I decided that, since Afros were out, and having short hair and a sense of dignity was not possible, I would pay my cousin Sophie, who had come to live with us from Barbados, to put my hair in plaits every few months. I was still the butt of many jokes in the playground, but at least I liked it and I kept it like that for eight years.

In the black barbers I went to in Richmond, I was spoilt for choice. On the wall, next to a poster with the African continent coloured in black, gold and green, calling for black customers to 'protect yourself, respect yourself' against HIV/AIDS, hung another poster headlined NEW YORK STYLES. Underneath were pictures of about twelve men, each with a different hairstyle, some relaxed, one with a curly perm, some with patterns, and one who was completely bald apart from a little bit of slick, wavy stuff right on top of his cranium. Asking for a flat top under these circumstances seemed a bit lame. The barber, Greg, was putting the finishing touches to a man whom he had made completely bald, and talking about American football. As he called me over, I was trying to think what else I could ask for that would sound more adventurous than a flat top.

'Flat top, please,' I said to Greg.

'Do you want a case?' asked Greg.

I know that the obvious thing to do in a situation like this is to own up and say that you don't know what a 'case' is. Greg did not yet know I was English, which could have provided the perfect excuse to request an explanation. But there was something so embarrassing about not being able to answer what seemed like a simple question about my own hair that the most sensible thing to do seemed to be to acquiesce. How bad, I thought, could a 'case' be?

'Yeh, go on then,' I said.

But Greg was not stopping there.

'Do you want it cut with the grain or against it?'

Another chance to confess my ignorance. Not only was I out of my depth; I was taking in water. But if Greg had said do you want some mayo and a side of potato salad on there I would probably have cheerfully agreed. Play safe, I thought.

'With, please,' I said.

Greg nodded reassuringly and started telling me why he supported the Dallas Cowboys even though he had lived in either North Carolina or Virginia all of his life. (I do not remember the reasons now.)

I wanted to talk to him about civil rights, but when he found out I was English he wanted to quiz me about Lady Di. He thought Di had been killed by the British establishment because she was having a relationship with a non-white Muslim.

'What was Charles doing with her anyway, man? She was much too young for Charles. He was never going to keep up with her. That's why he ended up running off with that old Camilla thing.'

Greg knew as much about the royal family as any Brit and had just as many opinions about them. By the time he had finished my hair and was looking for his mirror, we were on to women.

'You married?' he asked.

'I have a girlfriend,' I said.

As though that didn't count, Greg then proceeded to tell me that there were plenty of women in Richmond I could have (as though they were his to give), especially with my accent. 'Don't matter what color either although lot of them got children, so you got to like children.'

He turned me around and held the mirror to the back of my head and asked me what I thought. I was speechless. Whatever a 'case with the grain' might be, it didn't suit me. It made me look like Captain Scarlet.

'That's great,' I said and walked out to uproarious ridicule at the hands of Natalie and Lenell.

It was Lenell's turn to cook that night. The evening before it had been mine. I had made guacamole and spaghetti carbonara with chicken instead of bacon because Lenell won't eat bacon — 'Swine is a filthy animal,' she said. It had taken me about two hours to prepare. The guacamole had been tried precisely once each by Natalie and Lenell, and the carbonara had been eaten but not, I think, particularly enjoyed. In about half the time I had taken, and with a quarter of the fuss, Lenell turned out chicken in breadcrumbs, macaroni cheese, cornbread and potato salad. It was delicious.

My humiliation complete, I asked Natalie if she would take me to the station the next morning.

At 6.45 a.m. the Richmond Greyhound terminal was busy. In the coffee shop, a guard was trying to coax some of the tramps out into the cold sunshine. 'Go fuck with someone else,' shouted one of the vagrants, and the guard moved on to an old white man, dribbling in his beard in the corner, to ask him, out of politeness, if he had a ticket to ride. I got a coffee and then performed a curious dance as I struggled to balance the hot cup, a rucksack, a shoulder bag and a leather bag with a laptop without scalding myself.

There were confusing signals coming out of the tannoy about which bus I should get. I got in line for the one which had Danville, my next destination, on the sign above the door, but I was on my own. I moved over to the next door, advertising buses for Nashville, and asked a man in a Greyhound suit if that was the door for Danville. 'Yes it is,' he said. That should have been enough. But since I had no desire to ask the same question of someone in a similar suit in Nashville several hours later, I put the same question to the same man slightly differently.

'The seven fifteen for Danville?' I asked.

'Listen, sir, this is the bus for Danville. If you're going to get on, get on.' Then he shut the door so I couldn't get on.

By the time he had opened it again and put my rucksack in the back, there were only a few seats left. One was next to a punk woman who had clearly staked out her territory with her sleeping bag, so I moved to the back where there was a young black man wearing a green Gap sweater who grudgingly moved over a little so I could sit down.

Then I started my morning ritual. Nothing too gross, just a few sneezes to start the day. Not a big women-and-children-run-for-cover sneezing fit, just two firm but reasonably controlled explosions that visit me every morning.

The man sitting next to me was not impressed. By the time I got to the third sneeze, he had had enough. 'Do you mind covering your mouth if you're going to cough? I'm not planning on getting sick,' he said.

This, I thought, was a bit much. I had turned my back to him and put my hand over my mouth and nose when I did it. And as nobody else was talking on the bus, his claim that I was polluting the atmosphere filled a big silence. I had to say something, and since there was nothing sensible I could say, I said something utterly smart-arsed, English and stupid that makes me cringe just to write it down.

'You sneeze through your nose not your mouth. Sneezing through your mouth is called coughing and I didn't cough. And I don't plan to get you sick,' I said.

That showed him.

'I don't plan on having a discussion about it either,' he said, and that was that. To continue would have been foolish, possibly dangerous and, judging by my first retort, pathetic. I could see from his ticket that he had been travelling since eleven thirty the previous evening so I knew that he was tired and decided that was why he was crabby.

Still, I was not looking forward to the next three and a half hours sitting shoulder to shoulder with Mr Grouch. I lived in fear that I might sneeze again and in so doing unleash the unknown demons that were playing havoc with his mind. My nose did not let me down. But living in fear of sneezing, I discovered, is almost as bad as sneezing itself.

The driver introduced himself and read us our rights. 'There is no smoking or drinking of alcoholic beverages on the bus, and I will presume that anybody caught doing so will have reached their final destination. There is a rest room for your convenience in the back. Gentlemen, please remember that there are ladies on board so be careful and remember to lift the lid. And as always, may God bless you on your journey.' The microphone clicked off.

By the time we left Richmond, the sun was coming up, and there was about a foot of morning steam rising from the Appomattox River as though in a state of suspended animation. We stopped at a Hardees for a burger. Mr Grouch, it transpired, was with a couple of dreadlocked friends, at least one of whom was tucking into a can of Guinness before we had left Richmond city limits. I contemplated shopping him to the driver.

At Farmville, somebody got off, leaving a spare seat towards the front that I was quick to claim as my own. And there I stayed, until the bus crossed the River Dan and rolled into the tiny depot at Danville.

I got off and went to get my bag. The driver asked me for my luggage ticket. I told him nobody had given me a ticket. He told me they had. I told him they hadn't. And so it went on until he gave my rucksack to a woman with very bad teeth who dragged my bag to the counter and made me fill out a docket so that if I was stealing it I would be easily traced.

The bus station at Danville was little more than a room with a couple of electronic game machines and a man with a taxi called Julian who said he would take me to see Mr Louis Cobbs, a spokesman for the local branch of the NAACP. I called Mr Cobbs's home to get directions, and soon all meaningful communication broke down. His home help said he lived on Gay Street. I heard Day Street. Julian said he had never heard of Day Street. I called her back and asked her to spell it. She spelt it with a 'G'. I heard a 'D'. I turned to Julian triumphantly and said, 'She says Day Street.' Julian shrugged his shoulders. I handed him the phone. 'Gay Street. Why didn't you say so?' I apologized.

I asked Julian to tell me about Danville, and he told me about the murder of a young boy who had been shot in a drug-related crime just a couple of days ago.

'Ain't nothing good at all. Everything here's bad.'

Louis Cobbs was a small man in a checked shirt, trainers and bad health. He had an impressive repertoire in pithy one-liners. 'Two hands and a strong back ain't worth much nowadays'; 'The man who wins the war doesn't sit at the peace table'; 'White people will get out the ballot for you but they won't go out on a limb for you.' Kernels of eternal truths which I appreciated for their lyrical quality even when I didn't always understand what they meant.

Sitting in the smoky darkness of his front room and hearing him carefully outline struggles past and present while alternately puffing and wheezing, I got the impression that little had changed in Danville since the fifties. 'Does it bother you?' he asked as he took out a packet of cigarettes. 'Not morally, I mean, but physically. You see, I'm addicted, and I don't get on too well without it.' He didn't seem to be getting on too well with it either.

He told me the story of his return from the war when he got off a bus rather than sit at the back; of the man who had been run out of town because of his relationship with a white woman – 'he should have known better'; of how white flight to private education and the suburbs was resegregating the schools – 'we are losing a lot of what we gained'; and of the nurses at the hospital who were being forced to take a general test in order to keep their present jobs – 'They make the rules to suit themselves, and so people find themselves out of work on just the slightest pretext.'

Halfway through the interview, a woman named Roshelle Guynn, a friend of Mr Cobbs, arrived. She was a tallish, full-figured woman who, when she had something important to say, somehow managed to move her neck to the rhythm of her voice without moving her shoulders. Whatever Mr Cobbs said, she would embellish with some lurid detail or scandalous aside. I would scribble her comments down, and then Mr Cobbs would interject: 'There was never any proof for that,' or 'That was only hearsay.'

'Well, that's what my mama told me anyway,' Ms Guynn

would say with a smile, and I would strike her juicy assertion from my notepad.

When the interview with Mr Cobbs was over, Ms Guynn offered to take me to a motel. But in the time it took to get from the front door to the car she had decided that she wanted me as a role model for her son, Justin. And from then on, I was on Planet Guynn – not an altogether unpleasant place, because things always happened there, but a scary one nonetheless, because it had clearly spun from its social axis and was destined for ever to collide with other planets with both impunity and indiscretion, leaving a trail of confusion in its wake.

First we went to Justin's school, Woodberry Hills Elementary. During the five-minute drive, Ms Guynn told me that she was keen for Justin, who had expressed an interest in being a writer, to meet as many positive black male role models as possible. This was particularly important at the moment, she added, because she had recently separated from her husband who had left her for an older woman and then left the older woman to live with his mother.

At the school entrance, we bumped into the headmistress who was just coming out of her office. Ms Guynn introduced us briefly – 'This is Mr Younge. He's a writer from England. He's writing a book about the South. Isn't that great?' – and asked whether Ms Solomons, Justin's teacher, was in. The principal, a small, gently spoken white woman, said Ms Solomons would not be in until tomorrow.

Ms Guynn stamped her foot and made a face. 'Ooohhh, I wanted her to meet Mr Younge. Well, I would still like Justin to meet him,' she said.

The principal pointed us in the direction of Justin's classroom. On the way we met Tracy.

'I want you to meet Mr Younge, he's a writer from England,' said Ms Guynn.

Tracy said hello and I nodded hello back.

'Say Tracy,' ordered Ms Guynn.

'What?' I asked.

'Say Tracy,' she repeated more insistently.

I said Tracy.

'Do you see what a cute accent he has?' she said, and then we were off up the corridor, through a blurry tunnel of children's art and round the corner to Justin's classroom. She knocked on the door and asked the teacher if she could see him for a minute. Justin, a buck-toothed ten-year-old soaked in embarrassment, ambled out and looked straight at his shoes. His mother introduced me yet again.

'I want you to meet Mr Younge. He's a novelist from England,' she said. I wondered whether Ms Guynn would award me a Pulitzer before the day was out. Justin shuffled, and I tried to think of something to say.

'Your mother tells me you want to be a writer,' I said.

Justin said nothing. Ms Guynn took the silence as a cue to make us both feel uncomfortable.

'Justin, you know I want to introduce you to as many positive role models as possible,' she said.

Now we were both looking at our shoes, and shortly afterwards Justin sloped back into his class while his mother took me back to see the headmistress. 'I would really like him to come and talk to the children tomorrow. I think it would be so good for them to meet a writer ... and from England,' she told the principal, who was trying to be tactful but was clearly none too keen on having a runaway parent rearranging her timetable.

'I'm sure they would find it very useful but I couldn't possibly agree without speaking to Ms Solomons first, and she's not here,' she said.

Ms Guynn was not to be deterred. 'But it would be so interesting for them,' she insisted.

The headmistress agreed to nothing but gave me her card with her home number on it and said I should call her that night. Throughout the conversation I stood mute and stupefied, watching my next day being planned by a woman I had only just met. As far as Ms Guynn was concerned, the principal's response represented a done deal. As we walked out, she informed me that she would pick me up early the next morning and take me into school.

Finally she took me to a motel. On the way to the car she patted her head and moaned: 'Oooh look at my hair. I'm a mess. That's why my husband left me.' I assured her that almost certainly wasn't the reason. In the three-minute drive to the motel, she told me that Ms Solomons was beautiful and pleaded with me not to marry her and take her away. Justin had a crush on her, which, she said, was a good thing.

'I'm glad, because that's healthy, and I worry about him just growing up with me and having no father around. In the summer, I send him to stay with my sister and her husband at Fayetteville. You know, my biggest worry is that he'll end up being a faggot. Is that bad of me?' I was spared answering, as we had arrived at the Super 8 motel on Danville's Riverside Drive.

I dumped my bags and went for a walk around the tiny town centre. Danville was the site of the last meeting of the Confederate cabinet before surrendering to the Union army in the dying days of the Civil War, and the birthplace of Nancy Astor, the first woman to sit in the British Parliament. But these were accidents of geography and politics. Danville is just a place where shards of history happened to fall; it is difficult to believe that anyone put them there on purpose.

Still, if you stand at the top of the sloping Main Street, just opposite the Freemasons' headquarters, on a bright autumn day, you can feel the aesthetic clarity that comes with a town surrounded by moulting trees and running water. A few yards down the road, the Internet café, offering comfy sofas, fancy bagels and more than fifty brands of coffee, is the one hopeful sign in a long line of boarded-up shop fronts and cheap clothing stores that better times may come again.

For they have been before, a long time ago when the tobacco and textile barons lived on Millionaires' Row, and the Victorian and Edwardian architecture made the old train station the envy of southern Virginia and North Carolina. But now there are only historic walking tours – strolls through an elegant and opulent past mapped out by the tourist office. One of Danville's few modest claims to modern fame is that, according to one demographic study, it is one of the least segregated metropolitan areas in the United States. But from the conversation in Mr Cobbs's front room, I would never have guessed it.

Sitting in my motel room, recovering from the events of the day and wondering precisely what surprises tomorrow would bring on Planet Guynn, I was thinking about the odd situations having a black skin and an English accent had got me into before. In Britain, where there are fewer black people, and race is rarely discussed, I look foreign and sound local, and everyone tries hard not to notice. In America, where there are lots of black people and race is frequently talked about, I look local, sound foreign and often become an object of curiosity.

A few months earlier, I had been sent to Mississippi to do a story for the *Observer*. I was to write about a high school in a small town called Hernando, where everything was still segregated. There were two principals – one white, one black; two year books – one white, one black; two cheerleader captains – one white, one black. Everything in the school, apart from the classes themselves, was segregated.

When I called the black principal, he refused to be interviewed. There had been too much coverage of this issue already, he said, and most of it was inaccurate. When I called the white principal, he was hesitant at first.

'Where you from?' he asked.

'England,' I said.

'Where in England?' he asked. I have never understood why Americans ask this because they have rarely heard of anywhere apart from London, Liverpool and Manchester.

'Near London,' I said.

'Where near London?' he asked.

I wanted the interview and thought as long as I kept him on the phone I would still have a chance.

'It's a small town thirty miles north of London that I doubt you'd have heard of. It's called Stevenage,' I said.

'Stevenage!' he cried. 'I know Stevenage. I have a friend in Baldock.'

Baldock is about ten miles north of Stevenage. I have been there a few times. I cannot recall why. It's that kind of place. It didn't matter. He invited me over to the school immediately.

When I got there, he was waiting in the corridor. I presented myself to him, and his jaw dropped. I was black. The only thing, it seems, that could possibly be more surprising than meeting someone roaming around Mississippi who had been to Baldock was for that person to be black. To be fair, he didn't appear disappointed or annoyed, just stunned.

After an hour or so of chatting about the A1, the extortionate exchange rate and Kings Cross Station, he relaxed. He discussed the school's idiosyncrasies candidly and suggested I talk to the black principal. I said the black principal had already turned down my request for an interview. He waved his hand as if to say his colleague would talk if he vouched for me.

The black principal came out of his office and warmly shook my hand. The three of us stood there for a few minutes exchanging pleasantries and then the white principal went back to his office.

'Are you the guy that called the other day?' asked the black principal.

I nodded reluctantly, expecting him to tell me that he had already said he didn't want to talk to me and had no intention of changing his mind.

'I am so sorry,' he said. 'When you called I thought you were white. I've had enough of white people coming here and digging up this thing. If I had known . . .' He laughed to himself. 'A black man from England.' He shook his head and took me to lunch.

To understand what went on in that small Southern town, one must grasp just what an antiquated view Americans, of all races, have of England. England, to them, is a land of gents in monocles and waistcoats quaffing port, and chirpy cockneys selling oranges by the roadside. England, to them, is the old country. When I wrote a piece for the *Washington Post* about what it is like to be black and British in the United States, it ran alongside a cartoon of a black man in a bowler hat carrying an umbrella in one hand and a cup of tea in the other. When a cab driver in Atlanta, who had served in England during the war, found out I was British he asked, 'Do old ladies over there still ride bikes?'

'What?' I asked.

'Never seen so many old ladies riding bikes as over there,' he said.

After Divine Brown was found in a car with Hugh Grant she said she had never heard of him. When someone told her he was a famous actor she said: 'He sounded just like that guy, Captain Peacock' – the po-faced floor manager in *Are You Being Served?*.

When I think of British humour, I think of Vic and Bob's *Shooting Stars* or the man on *The Fast Show* who finishes every sketch with 'I was very, very drunk.' When Americans think of our comedy, they recall Mrs Slocombe's pussy.

It is possibly because American images of the English are so outdated that they maintain such a rose-tinted view of what we are like. In most countries, when people hear the word 'England' (and sometimes 'Britain'), they think of arrogant colonialists, crass tourists and leery, beery football hooligans. When Americans hear it they think of *Hetty Wainthrop Investigates*, Lady Di and Sherlock Holmes. The rest of the world thinks we are violent; Americans think we are quaint. And not only does the American image of Britain predate football thugs, but also the significant influx of black people into the country. Even those who have visited in the past few years find it so difficult to match fact and fiction that they tend to stick with fiction. When a man who worked in the Ebenezer Baptist church in Atlanta discovered I was English, he laughed.

'I just came back from London and I didn't see but two black people there. And then I was in Manchester and there were even less.'

'Where in London?' I asked, knowing that you would have to be in a pretty particular part of the capital to see only two black people.

'Oh, all over the centre,' he said.

He was lying. Just like I did when I came back from a trip to East Berlin with the Stevenage Youth Orchestra when I was fourteen and said that everyone looked miserable. That was what I was expecting, what I thought I was supposed to say, and what I thought people wanted to hear. So I said it.

Americans think of black Brits the way that I think of the Cameroonian Orangemen who are devotees of Ian Paisley, or white citizens of Barbados and Jamaica. Anomalies. Intriguing always, entertaining often, but understood and accepted no more nor less than for what they are? Very rarely.

From the motel in Danville, I called the headmistress of Woodberry Hills and tried to explain that, while I did consider myself a responsible adult, I could take no responsibility for what had gone on in the school earlier in the day with Ms Guynn. I said that while I did not want to intrude, I would be happy to speak to the children if she wanted me to.

I had done it before, to a class of six-year-olds in Tulse Hill, south London. They had grasped the fact that I was a journalist but could not understand how I could keep tabs on what was happening throughout the world all the time. When it was time for questions, their hands stretched skywards and they asked me: 'What time do you go to bed?' and 'Do you have an alarm clock?'

The principal said she would call Ms Solomons, Justin's teacher, and then get her to call me. Ms Solomons rang and said she would love to have me come and talk. She wanted me to impress on the children the importance of reading and writing and said it would be useful for them to see someone who made a living from it. Shortly afterwards, Ms Guynn called, unaware of all the arrangements that had been made to sort out the arrangements she had made, and told me when she would pick me up.

'Can you do some shorthand on the blackboard for the children also?' she asked. 'I saw you doing some earlier at Mr Cobbs's, and it would be good for the children to see a black man doing something like that.'

GARY YOUNGE

The next morning, Ms Guynn, dressed in a tartan jacket with shorts to match, took me to the school, and we met Ms Solomons at the front door with three children hanging adoringly on to each arm. She was more handsome than beautiful; a young woman in her early twenties, of medium height and athletic build, who ruled her class of fourth-graders with a firm affection.

By Southern state-school standards it was a very inte-grated class: no Hispanics, no Asian-Americans and no Native Americans – just four or five white children and twenty or so blacks. Along with the regular batch of poems and pictures you find on the walls of a class full of ten-year-olds in most places in the world, there was a poster advertising Spike Lee's film *Get On The Bus*, and two posters of Martin Luther King. Over one set of work on the main wall were the words, WE ARE OVERCOMERS.

The usual classroom pandemonium of shouting, snatch-ing, flinging and poking which I recall starting all of my primary school days was interrupted by a noise from above the blackboard which signalled an altogether unfamiliar set of rituals. At my primary school, all horseplay was brought to an end by the bell for assembly when we would be told a moral fable or hear some Christian wisdom, sing some hymns and then listen to school announcements.

Here the principal addressed the school through the tannoy system located just above the blackboard. First came the awards for pupil of the day (selected by a teacher), followed by teacher of the day (selected by the pupils), followed by the day's birthdays and then a warning for all those who had been misbehaving on the bus that morning. The tannoy clicked off.

Ms Solomons then chose a boy to recite the Pledge of Allegiance. All of the children stood up, put their hands on their chests and turned towards the flag in the corner of the classroom which I had only just noticed.

Unaccustomed to saluting a flag (I do not stand for the Union Jack, as I do not believe that it stands for me), I wondered whether I should remain seated or not. I wondered whether it would be possible to be excused from pledging allegiance every morning if your mother wrote in and said she didn't want you to for moral reasons, in the same way that Jehovah's Witnesses at my school used to be excused from morning assembly whenever it was about religion. I wondered whether, if we had had to pledge allegiance to the flag in England, my mother would have written a note so that I could have been excused. She was no great fan of the flag either. She would recall how, as a girl in Barbados, she had to salute the Union Jack every day before she went home from school. Once, in her eagerness to avoid a playground fight, she had left early, missed the salute and was caned the next day.

I wondered whether my antipathy was to all flags or just the Union Jack. As a teenage Trotskyite, I had risen for the Red Flag and the Socialist anthem, 'The Internationale'. In South Africa, during the country's first democratic elections, I had voluntarily worn a lapel badge with the nation's new flag on it, and even held my fist clenched and upright for the soon-to-be-official anthem, '*Nkosi Sikelel Afrika*'. But now that I thought about it, those were the only times I had felt comfortable doing anything apart from sitting down and crossing my arms in front of a flag.

I wondered. And then I stood. I needed more time and figured that since it was not my flag, it didn't really matter. The children recited their patriotism in the same kind of monotone that I remember using for my times tables. The only difference between this and my tables was that by the age of ten I pretty much understood my tables, whereas I am fairly certain I could not have grasped the concepts contained in the pledge. Nor was I convinced that these children had either.

I pledge allegiance
to the flag
of the United States of America
and to the Republic
for which it stands
one nation
under God
indivisible
with liberty
and justice
for all.

I later learnt that everybody in the country recites the oath in exactly the same way, with the same intonation and the same pauses. But I could not find anyone who knew why or where the rhythm started.

Meanwhile, Justin, who sat at the front of the class near the teacher, was looking upset. He beckoned to Ms Solomons, pointed to me, then to his classmates, stuck his lip out and asked her if she could make an announcement. Ms Solomons pulled an understanding face and nodded. She told the class that I was not Justin's dad and then introduced me.

I told them I was from Britain and asked one boy if he could show me where it was on the world map that hung over the board. He probably would have managed it on his own, but there was a piece of string that covered the island completely and which slightly confused him, so I lifted it and helped him out.

Following Ms Solomons's brief, I told them that I loved

writing because it enabled me to visit lots of places in the world I wouldn't have been able to go to otherwise and pointed out these places on the map. I explained that I was following the route of the Freedom Riders to look at places I had read about in books. But since I was never going to be able to go everywhere in the world, reading was great because it could take you to places in your imagination.

About halfway through they lost interest. I asked if there were any questions.

None of them had heard of the Freedom Riders, so for the first five minutes we concentrated on Lady Di and the Spice Girls. One girl asked if I had heard of the Spice Girls. I said I had and asked her if she could name them. She thought I had asked her to sing one of their songs and, in a moment of pre-teen excitement, she broke out into a rendition of 'Wannabe' until Ms Solomons asked her to stop.

Then came the serious comparative issues.

'What kind of candy bars do you have in England. Do you have Hersheys?'

'What kind of potato chips do you have in England?'

'What kind of bubble gum do you have in England?'

'What kind of cartoons do you have in England?'

Whatever I said, the children managed to validate their position as the centrifugal point around which all matters of importance revolve. If I mentioned something they had never heard of, they would pull their faces into a 'What-the-hell-do-you-have-a-candy-bar-called-Fruit-&-Nut-for?' expression. And if I mentioned something with which they were familiar, they would shrug their shoulders knowingly in a 'Snickers-that's-so-totally-passé' sort of way.

Languages were next.

The previous day I had told Ms Guynn that I had studied languages, and Ms Guynn had told Ms Solomons. Ms Solomons asked me which ones I spoke. 'French, Russian and a little bit of German,' I said. One boy asked me to say something in Russian. I refused – I already felt like some kind of circus marmoset. 'There wouldn't be any point,' I said. 'You would have no idea what I'm saying.'

Ms Solomons was not impressed. She asked me if I had been to Russia and what I had done while I was there. I said I had been to St Petersburg for five months to study, and then she asked me if I could say that in Russian. I did. The class performed that dramatic, wide-eyed, collective intake of breath that children do when they want to exaggerate a sense of surprise and amazement.

'Man, I'm going to study Russian,' said the boy at the front who had asked me to say something in the first place, and I felt churlish for my original, precious refusal. To compensate, I showed a few of them on the board how their names would be spelt in Cyrillic script.

A girl at the back raised her hand. 'How do you say Woodberry Hills Elementary School, Home of the Little Eagles, in French?' she asked as though her life depended on the answer. It was my turn to take a deep breath. They wanted me to show off. If I were not careful the marmoset would be out of the cage and cavorting around the room in no time. I closed my eyes and just said it as quickly as I could before moving on and refusing to take any more language questions.

A few minutes later, it was all over. The class had a test on states and their capitals to do, and I was getting in the way. They gave me a clap, and Ms Solomons offered to take me back to my motel during break.

On the way, she thanked me and said that it was good for the children to hear someone talk from out of town and especially good to hear these things from a black man, since they seldom heard anything from them. She described how she had been slowly edging her way up north over the past few years. Starting from her home town in South Carolina, she moved up to the historically black university, A&T, in Greensboro, North Carolina, and now to Danville on Virginia's southern border. Danville, she said, was a small redneck place full of good ol' boys – 'They don't think. They just know' – and she said she aimed to head further north in the future. 'New York?' I asked. 'Not that far,' she said. 'Maybe northern Virginia.'

A couple of hours later, I was in Burger King, going through the day's events with Ms Guynn and Justin. Ms Guynn was telling me that she was black, not African-American. 'What business have I got with Africa? Uh-uh, I'm black,' she said, as her head went from left to right in time to her words and her shoulders stayed defiantly put.

Then she paused. 'Do you think of yourself as English or American?' she asked.

After all this time and after all the effort that Ms Guynn had put into promoting me as a black Englishman, she still didn't get it. She had seen my skin and heard my accent, but still could not believe the two could co-exist.

'I think of myself as black mostly, but English as well,' I said. 'England is where I was born and where I grew up. That's where my passport's from and where I can vote.' I might as well have said I was from Jupiter but considered myself a Vulcan, since nothing I could say would ever take the bewilderment out of her eyes.

'Oh,' said Ms Guynn. 'That's weird. It's just that you look like us. You just don't sound like us.'

CHAPTER FIVE

North Carolina: Franklin's Moment

'Greensboro, though reputed for its liberalism, was the first city where the color signs started to become the rule,' wrote James Peck. 'The first greetings to our arriving are oversized signs all around the building with arrows pointing to the colored waiting room.' The blacks-only waiting room had been closed a week before the Freedom Riders arrived.

The trip's first arrest came unexpectedly in Charlotte, on the southern tip of North Carolina, after one of the Freedom Riders was refused a shoeshine. Charles Person, a college freshman from the historically black university of Morehouse, sat up in the shoeshine chair and refused to move until a policeman arrived with handcuffs.

The group were thrown into confusion. They had no policy on shoeshines and had to elaborate one fast. They concluded that this provided as good a case as any on which to challenge segregation. It was decided that another black man, Joe Perkins, would stay in the shoeshine chair and wait until he was arrested. Within minutes he was taken away and charged, only to be acquitted a few days later on the basis of Boynton vs. Commonwealth of Virginia *– the trip's first legal victory.*

It's forty miles from Danville to Greensboro. When I arrived, the city's peripheries were humming. Out by the motorways, the motels were almost all booked up, and the restaurants were holding queues around the block and promising at least a half-hour wait. Usually, Greensboro is a quiet place; its downtown area is almost over within fifteen minutes' walk in any direction. Ask a hotel receptionist in one of the few hotels in the centre if there is somewhere nice to eat on a weekday evening, and they will send you at least three miles up the road – even then, restaurants will close as early as 9 p.m. At the weekend it is deserted. At lunchtime I was the only person among the collection of restaurants, plaques, second-hand clothes stores and a bookshop that make up its main road, Elm Street.

By luck rather than judgement I had arrived during a weekend of major festivities. In one part of town there was the fourteenth annual barbecue festival, named one of the top ten food festivals in the country that summer by *Travel and Leisure* magazine. The festival started in the morning with the mayor tucking into a huge barbecue sandwich for the cameras, and ended with some country music in the evening. In between there was a forty-five-minute Parade of Pigs and a huge amount of food.

Elsewhere, Greensboro's main historically black university, North Carolina Agricultural & Technical State, was preparing for its homecoming parade. A&T is part of a tradition of black higher education stretching back around 150 years, which still exists and in many places is thriving. Since the segregation laws existed in the South until the late sixties, and the poverty that has always excluded blacks from higher education remains, the colleges still have a major role to play.

For a few weeks in 1960, A&T was where it all happened. Four young men walked into the Elm Street Woolworths on 1 February, bought some college supplies and then sat at the whites-only counter and asked to be served. The manager shut the store down rather than serve them, and the next day they were back. Within a month, their efforts were being replicated around the nation. Black students (and some whites) throughout the South and beyond were sitting in to desegregate social spaces in an effective but uncoordinated campaign that took the entire country – not least the established civil rights organizations – completely by surprise.

The Woolworths has since closed down. McArthur Davis, a genial former stockbroker, has given up the high life in order to raise money to transform the building into an international civil rights centre and museum. Efforts to draw the cash from the local black community have borne very little fruit. Now he is waiting for 'five minutes with Oprah'.

'Just five minutes with her or Michael Jordan or Bill Cosby. That's all I would need,' he said. 'They could give us the money without even noticing it. The trouble is everybody is after them for the same thing and, since it's for charity, their agents don't get a cut, and you have to get past them first.'

Outside, there are the four footprints of the original sit-in activists, Franklin McCain, Joseph McNeil, Ezell Blair and David Richmond. There is also a plaque, erected on the twentieth anniversary of their action, which says: 'February 1 1960 Birthplace of the civil rights movement. Four students at North Carolina A&T State University conducted the first lunch counter sit-in on February 1 1960 at the Woolworth store.' At the bottom there is a quote, 'Sometimes taking a stand for what is undeniably right means taking a seat', and a picture of the four men looking much older.

If you go around the corner to what used to be called Sycamore Street and cup your hands around your eyes to shut out the light, you can look through a dusty side window and catch a glimpse of the old lunch counter where the sit-in took place. Today it is called February One 1960 Street.

Looking through the window at the broken tiles and other debris on the floor, I tried to recall other places where I had seen dates used for street names and public signs. There is La Corneuve/May 8 1945 tube station in Paris, marking the date of the liberation; no end of squares and streets in the former Soviet Union branded 1917, the year of the revolution; and the 6 May 1973 Street in Berlin which commemorates the uprising in East Berlin which was quashed by the government of the former East Germany. You will find them all over Africa celebrating a great war or the end of colonialism. But the phenomenon, it seems, is confined to countries that either had a revolution or were liberated from an occupying force – places where a major shift in power took place and where it was both possible and desirable to mark that shift with a date.

'This was a revolution,' said Davis. 'This is the first time students stood up and made a difference. This was their act of disobedience and it shook up the whole country.'

But the alumni in town that weekend were not in Greensboro to stake a claim on the past but to have a good time in the present. That, after all, is what homecoming is for, an annual ceremony where former students are invited back to their alma mater to watch a football game and party with their old classmates.

There is a homecoming queen, elected by her peers in what amounts to a campus-wide popularity contest. She is escorted to most official engagements by a homecoming court – a coterie of men similarly elected. In Greensboro that weekend, A&T were to hold a street parade and the coronation of Miss A&T followed by a formal ball. There was to be a step show, a synchronized dance routine put on by the fraternities, and a pre-dawn jam. On Saturday there would be a homecoming football game with Howard University and a homecoming concert with Redman, Rampage and Rare Essence. On Sunday there would be an annual worship service and in the afternoon a gospel concert.

At the tourist office, just around the back of Elm Street, there is a black woman in her thirties who once dated a black British man of West Indian parentage with relatives in Brooklyn, New York, but it all broke up because he was allergic to commitment. I know this because she told me. Twice. The first time was when I had passed through Greensboro on the way to see my aunt in Savannah almost exactly a year before. I remembered her, but she didn't remember me.

'Where are you from?' she said.

'England,' I said.

'I can hear that, I mean where in England?'

I told her I was from a town near London (Stevenage was a secret that I shared with the white principal from Mississippi), and then we were back talking about her ex-boyfriend as though the intervening year had never happened.

With the help of a few maps and some check calls, she recommended a concert on Saturday night or a comedy at the Coliseum that evening. I went for the comedy, and after she had helped me book my tickets, I made my way in a hire car up the highway to my motel.

In the lobby a group of black women, in town for homecoming, seemed to be taking out centuries of indignation on a white receptionist. There was some confusion – one of those 'he said, she said' rows, which appeared to hinge on the fact that the woman who called and made the booking with her Visa card was not the person standing in front of the receptionist wanting to confirm the reservation with another Visa card. Every time the receptionist turned her head, the women, who apparently grew up in the South and now lived in the North, started laughing at her and claiming a racial motive for the problems they were having.

'Man, every time I come back down here I get this shit,' one of them said. 'These people trying to mess you up, "Can't do this, can't do that." Man, just do the damn thing, and then we can all get on with our lives. Know what I'm saying?' Her friends nodded.

The receptionist was going red, not with anger, but with a mixture of embarrassment and helplessness. She found a way to fix the problem (which I think involved starting all over again) and then explained to the women how she had done it. To them this was just simply confirmation that she could have done it all along if she had wanted to, and that without their persistence they would have been shown the door.

To an onlooker the whole episode was utterly depressing. Four against one; black against white; consumer against service provider; North against South; adults against teenager; past against present: all bubbled through an argument about the procedure for booking a room with a credit card. There were no sides to take, no arguments to unravel or truths to disclose. Just noise to listen to and pain to watch until everyone had played out their roles.

Friday night at the Coliseum: the A&T alumni were out in force and looking for laughs. At $27.50 a ticket an almost exclusively black audience strode in, most in couples but some in far larger groups, looking both chic and boisterous. Some had clearly graduated some time ago, but most were in their twenties. The car park boasted a healthy number of Mercedes and Porsches, many of which had the Greek insignia of the black fraternities and sororities stamped on their plates.

I have only been to a handful of comedy shows before and usually come away with mixed feelings. Humour is never neutral – it depends whom you are laughing at and whom you are laughing with. While I was a student, I went to see Gerry Sadowitz, who specializes in the kind of humour invented for the priapic nihilist that I, at one time, found highly amusing. He ridiculed everyone from Mother Theresa to Nelson Mandela – 'Mandela, what a cunt. Lend him a fiver and then you never see him again.' The profane disrespect had me both wincing and laughing. Holy cows were being slaughtered, and I admit, I wanted to watch.

But then he started telling 'Paki jokes'. There were no Asians in the audience – just me and a crowd of white people having their prejudices confirmed. Of course, they could have all been savouring the irony of his comments. But the year before, I had been chased down one of the city's main streets by two white men carrying baseball bats and shouting 'nigger'. That didn't feel very ironic. I didn't particularly like the idea of sitting in a room full of white people, about five minutes from where I was chased, and laughing at other black people.

I tried to explain to a friend why I hadn't enjoyed the show, and he told me my politics had ruined my sense of humour. I told him it was difficult to have a sense of humour and to be offended at the same time. We agreed to differ, but I did wonder whether I could laugh at the Mother Theresa jokes because I'm not a devout Catholic and did not find the jokes about Pakistanis funny because they were partly aimed at me (in Britain if you hate one set of non-white people, then you usually hate them all – it's a package deal). I wondered too whether if the theatre had been full of blacks and Asians, I would have found the same joke funny. This night at the Coliseum would be like laboratory conditions.

The first act was a man who called himself Michael

Blackson, who said he had come all the way from Africa. It was clear after about two seconds that, even though Blackson was wearing a dashiki, he had not come from Africa at all. He even appeared to have his face blacked over. He told jokes about how primitive his village was, how much he wanted to emigrate to America, the number of wives he had and what he liked to do with them. The crowd loved him, and I thought he was repulsive. When his act was drawing to a close, he did something I have never seen a comedian do before. He thanked God and praised his maker for all he had done for him. This earned him his biggest cheer.

After him came a truly enormous and very funny man from Atlanta nattily dressed in a green shirt. A hit with the crowd, he told jokes about male/female relationships, about how black people love to dance no matter where they are, and how they never pay their bills on time.

Then came a man who, judging from his introduction, used to be the anchor for a late-night television show. He took offensiveness to new and dizzying heights. He picked a black guy out of the audience who was with his white girlfriend and started to berate him. 'That's cool. I ain't got no problem with that. Just so long as you know that don't make you white,' he said to resounding applause. Up until there, I had no problem. It wasn't exactly kind, but it is one of the occupational hazards of being in a mixed-race relationship. If you go to a black comedy night and sit near the front, you may well get picked out and be made fun of.

'You just got to know the rules. You got to know that there are going to be places where she cannot go with you.' This was a little tough, not because it wasn't true, but because it seemed unnecessarily vindictive. Had he stopped there I would have been impressed. He had broached a tricky subject, made his point, got some laughs and made me feel slightly uncomfortable. But he was just beginning.

The only reason black men like white women, he said, is because they could beat them and white women would take it, whereas black women – at this point he started to imitate a black woman taking out her teeth, rolling up her sleeves and getting ready for a fight – would always fight back. White women, he said, also like to 'suck dick', whereas black women always made out that they did not, even though they obviously did. 'White women will suck your dick anywhere,' he said – at a traffic light, in the queue for the cashpoint machine or at work. The couple sat through the whole thing. The audience roared. Then he started on people with learning difficulties, whom he took pride in calling retarded.

After the interval, most of the jokes seemed to be about 'retarded' people and white women. There were occasional rays of light – lines about the sort of slow and scary white people that you see in the Waffle House (a fast-food chain frequented mostly by poor whites). About how Jesus could not have been either black, because he would have sought revenge, or Puerto Rican, because his clothes matched. But for the most part, everything grated. The adjectival noun of choice was 'mothafucka'; the favourite, and as I recall only, form of self-definition was 'nigga'.

When I left the Coliseum, I felt deflated. In one of her short stories, Alice Walker wrote: 'Every day taught me something about myself I had always suspected: I thought black people superior people. Not simply superior to white people, because even without thinking about it much, I assumed almost everyone was superior to them; but to everyone . . . it never occurred to me that black people could treat Luna [her white friend] and me with anything but warmth and concern.' Naive though it sounds, I had presumed that too. I thought that black people, after all we had gone through, would have more sense than to turn our ire on the vulnerable. It took me a few days to work out that this was purely my problem. What I had seen was nothing more or less significant than bad comedy. In my subconscious, I had been playing God and handing out lots to people for a secure tenure on the moral high ground. But nobody ever asked for these sacred patches of turf. Now they had chosen not to take them up, and I was angry at them for the poor upkeep of precious land that they never wanted and that wasn't mine to give in the first place.

Black people have the right to be as crass as anybody else. But that doesn't mean I have to like it. What was I expecting? Something raucous, and a little risqué; a few jokes I didn't understand, a few that stretched and challenged me, and a few I thought were beyond the pale. Most of all, I suppose, I was expecting not to be offended. I expected to laugh, and however unrealistic my other presumptions may have been, that was not too much to ask from a comedy night.

At the corner of Laurel and Bluford the next morning, the crowd out to see the homecoming parade was four people thick, spanning the generations from babes in arms to the elderly. All stood in the light drizzle and cheered as representatives of the major fraternities, youth groups and toddlers from local kindergartens came dancing, waving, driving or walking by.

There were brass bands up to one hundred strong in uniforms, carrying sousaphones, euphoniums, trombones, clarinets and bugles, pumping out sounds you could sway to as bandleaders with hatfuls of plumes and cheerleaders in sequinned leotards twirled batons, led chants and conducted their peers. There was the Miss American Society of Mechanical Engineers waving from a Cadillac in a white sash and hugging a bull mastiff, followed by women from the Order of the Eastern Star, the female wing of the Freemasons, clad in black minks. There was a group called Jesus is Lord who got a big cheer just, it seemed, for their name; another called the mighty marching Trojans; and a Mr and Miss Biology Pre-med. For well over an hour, they just kept coming.

Those around me laughed at the lame floats, yelled at the impressive ones and every now and then shouted: 'That's family, that's family,' and earned themselves the right to a personal wave back. The lady standing next to me, who had a daughter who was taking part, had herself gone to A&T. Her mother, who stood next to her, had also studied there. This was the African-American middle class on parade, generations of blacks schooled in autonomy, raised on race pride and infused with self-confidence. I could only envy them as they played their own tunes and strutted to the sounds of their own sweet history.

There was a long queue for the bus to Charlotte, and I got the last seat, right at the back, by a wan white woman with sallow cheeks and dyed blonde hair with black roots who was looking sullenly out of the window.

'Don't ya just hate travelling by bus?' she said as she nodded at a noisy infant a few seats ahead of us. She talked with a languorous drawl, and her breath smelt of stale alcohol. On either side of her eyes were large crow's feet that twitched even when she didn't blink. But she had a nice smile and I soon realized that what I had taken for solemnity was in fact just boredom.

Her name was Pamela. I asked her where she was going, and she told me where she had come from, starting her story right at the beginning.

Pamela was born in California. When she was fifteen she got married to a man called Rich from Jacksonville, Florida, and when she finished school she moved east. 'My parents didn't mind. I think they were glad to hand me over to someone else,' she said.

For the first few years, the marriage went well. Pamela gave birth to a boy, who was now a chubby-faced teenager who lived on a photo in her purse. But she couldn't get on with Rich's family. 'I don't know what I would have done differently now but I suppose I just wasn't used to Southern ways. His folks were always up in my business. It was like I never left home and like he never wanted to ... I s'pose I just wasn't ready for all that yet. I was only nineteen and it was like my life was over already.'

A few years later, the marriage was over. Her husband's family kept her son, and she found herself cut adrift. She stayed in Jacksonville and started getting in with a bad crowd. 'I started taking drugs and then I started selling drugs, although I was always taking more than I was selling. I got involved with this guy. You know, I've always had a thing for black men, and he was real handsome.'

She had another son, who lived on the other side of her purse – a small, brown, curly-haired toddler. She opened up her purse so I could see them both. 'That's my brown sugar, that's my white sugar. That's what I call them,' she said, and laughed to herself in a way that made me think she was about to cry.

She got busted for drugs and went to jail for a few years. Her black son got taken away from her and put in care. 'Can you believe that? That's what gets me about this place. They just can't get over that black-white shit. It's shit. In California there's just so much else going on, man, that they haven't got time for that. Black, white, Hispanic, Asian ... there's just so much going on people don't get caught up in all that shit.' She spat out the word 'shit' as though she had just swallowed some. Her eyes were full of water, but she was not actually crying – it was overflow from ducts that were on twenty-four-hour call. Apart from the inconvenience of not being able to see, she seemed hardly to notice.

She pointed to the picture of her white son, dried her eyes, and smiled again. 'He's just like a brother. You'd like him,' she said. 'He wears his pants real long and walks like this' – she did a poor imitation of a hip-hop swagger with her torso – 'and he got suspended for taking a gun to school. He's my baby boy. Just like a brother.' She smiled with pride.

After that, her stories descended into a confusing jumble. There were men she couldn't get rid of and incidents she mentioned obliquely and then said she didn't want to talk about; plans and promises, vitriol and disappointment – a monologue that quickly lost its narrative structure and descended into a verbal and psychological collage. Just as I was about to leave I asked her again where she was going, since she still had not told me.

'Jacksonville,' she said. 'You should come down there. It's great.'

Sitting in my room in Charlotte and flicking through the cable TV, I waited for Franklin McCain to call. Setting up the interview had been an arduous process. I had called his office. His secretary had asked me to fax my request. I had called a few days after I had faxed, but he was never there. In Danville, I had tried again, and he had picked up the phone. He had asked me to explain more about my project and then, finally, three weeks after my initial contact, he had agreed to meet me one evening in Charlotte, where he now lives and works for a chemical company.

It was worth the wait. As one of the A&T students who staged the original sit-in at the Woolworths in Greensboro, McCain has earned his right to a place in the civil rights hall of fame. The actions of these four young men had set the tone for a decade of student militancy that changed the nature of political protest throughout the Western world – a legacy that felt like both a burden and an inspiration to my generation of students, since many of us wanted to live up to it but, for all sorts of reasons, couldn't.

The sit-in in Greensboro was not the first of its kind, but it was by far the most effective since it broke the mould of civil rights protest in three very crucial ways. Firstly, it was independent, the work of four young men acting under their own steam with none of the tempering influences of bureaucracy. Secondly, it was led by students, rather than Church elders or community spokesmen, with the caution that their years bring. And finally, even though none of the four went to prison, it endorsed conflict with the law in the name of racial equality, and so transformed a jail sentence from a social stigma into a badge of honour.

In most photographic portrayals of the civil rights era you will see McCain. Along with the dog ripping the trousers from a young man in Kelly Ingram Park in Birmingham, Alabama, and the picture of Elizabeth Eckford being followed by screaming bigots in Little Rock, Arkansas, on her first day at school, there is a shot of four good-looking black teenagers with neatly pressed trousers striding past the Woolworths in Greensboro. Second from the left, standing tall, lean, upright and serious, in an army hat and a smart black coat, is the bespectacled seventeen-year-old McCain.

The man who rolled up in an expensive car a few hours later was not one I would have recognized from the legendary photograph. He is still tall but has gained a lot of weight and now looks not unlike Eddie Murphy's Nutty Professor.

As I buckled my seat belt I thanked him for agreeing to speak to me.

'You must do this kind of interview a lot,' I said.

'Well, I couldn't do all the ones that people ask me to do because there wouldn't be enough hours in the day. But given that you've come all the way from England, I thought I should make the effort. The only ones I regret are those where people haven't done adequate research. I often just cut the interviews short if it looks like they want me to go over the same old stuff.'

This was a scary start. I had no idea what 'the same old stuff' might be, but if my first few questions fitted the bill he could turn the car round at any moment and take me right back to the motel.

During the fifteen-minute drive to his house, I asked him if there was anything in his upbringing to suggest that he was going to make history. He took a deep breath and launched into a free-flowing account of his motivation with both clarity and passion, stopping only for breath and more questions for the next hour and a half.

'I was brought up with a major myth. I was told that if I worked hard, believed in the Constitution, the Ten Commandments and the Bill of Rights, and got a good education, I would be successful. For a long time, I held it against my parents and my grandparents as well. I felt they had lied to me and I felt suicidal. I felt that if that is what this life was all about then it wasn't worth it. There seemed no prospect for dignity or respect as a young black man. And all because of this protective pigmentation. I was as angry as hell. Really angry and frustrated. I don't know whether it was happenstance or divine intervention, but all four of us got along quite well. Everybody had the same kind of feelings I had. We were determined to get some relief. We were on a mission.

'I don't think the NAACP or CORE really understood what the driving force was for this movement. We had four kids here trying to address an unequal system. Just four kids who were somewhat introspective. The night before, we had been talking about all sorts of things. We had these bull sessions where we discussed everything from Kant to Spinoza. We gave our parents and our grandparents hell for accepting unequal rights. But then we said, all we've ever done is talk. At least our parents and grandparents had survived. We were just armchair activists. We were hypocrites . . . We were really hard on ourselves too. So we decided to do something.'

At this point we arrived at McCain's house. We walked through a huge, well-lit kitchen before groping our way in the dark down a short corridor into the living room, which was vast. We sat in two armchairs opposite each other.

There were tints of grey in his hair. And only now, with the lights on, did I realize how big he really was. He only just fitted into the chair; his feet only just fitted in his shoes.

He picked up where he had left off. 'We wanted to go beyond what our parents had done. And we had nothing to lose. I thought, they can't touch us. The worst thing that could happen was that the Ku Klux Klan could kill us or we could go to jail. Well, I was none too bothered about going to jail, and I had already contemplated suicide, so I thought, go ahead. I had no concern for my personal safety. It would be different now, because I have a wife and a family, but then it was meaningless. So we kind of goaded ourselves into action.

'We didn't really talk to anybody about it, because seventeen-year-old boys don't trust anybody over nineteen or twenty. If we had talked to adults, they would have said, talk to the management and see if you can't sort this out around the conference table. But they didn't understand the urgency.'

At that time, most adults could not afford the urgency either. They had jobs they could be fired from, and clients they could lose. This economic intimidation goes some way to explaining the dominance of the Church in so many of the conflicts, since clergymen were not reliant on the local white economy for funds, as well as the involvement of a high proportion of shopkeepers, dentists and doctors who could lead many local battles because they were self-employed. But it was also one more reason why youngsters would advance to the front line. They had no stake, no matter how meagre, in the system as it stood.

'We asked two or three other people to join us, but they didn't even believe that we were going to do it. We just thought it was useless waiting for them to catch up. We didn't have the time to convince people.'

While later in the decade students elsewhere would draw their inspiration from Marx and Mao and argue the case for collective action, McCain was motivated by his religious faith, combined with a very definite sense of an individual's role in history.

'We were all Christians by upbringing and we took a lot of motivation from this man called Jesus. He had twelve followers and they weren't even reliable and look how much he achieved. And then there was Gandhi, who kicked the hell out of the British. And then there was Mary McLeod Bethune, who set up a school with nothing but a dream. So we knew that throughout history, any single event that occurred was carried out by very few people.

'Like Christ, the weapon we used for all this was love. I would look at a man with his spit streaming down my face, a man who had just spat at me, and I would point my finger at him and say, "You are my brother, I love you and I forgive you." That just wipes them out. We had to be non-violent because we didn't have the bodies and didn't have the guns. We could not have got the endorsement either, if we had resorted to violence. It worked for Christ, and that's good enough for me.'

He freely acknowledged that his was not the first sit-in, although he had not heard of others at the time. But the crucial difference, McCain believes, was the determination of the four to see the protest through to the bitter end. At times, his comments bordered on the boastful. But McCain is not a braggart. He is a man with an acute awareness of his place in history and a keen wish that it should not be downgraded.

'People needed to believe in it enough to die; they had to walk on the picket line until their shoes wore out. Too many people who started out with noble objectives were not prepared to suffer. We were prepared to do whatever was necessary to succeed. It was an idea whose time had come; it was also in the right city. Greensboro boasted that it was the gateway to the South and to progress – it was a lie, but it was a lie that they had begun to promote, and so they couldn't let too much happen. It was supposed to be a city of openness and progress, so they had to think about how this was going to look.'

On the day itself, he was the last to get out of classes because he had Reserve Officers Training, hence the army hat in the photographs. He knew he was not going to get served at the counter but he was not prepared for any of what happened.

'When we sat down, and the waitress refused to take our orders, there was a policeman behind us slapping his nightstick on his hand. I thought, I guess this is it. But then it occurred to me that the policeman really didn't know what he was doing, and I must say I was greatly relieved.

'Some way through, an old white lady, who must have been seventy-five or eighty-five, came over and put her hands on my shoulders and said: "Boys I am so proud of you. You should have done this ten years ago." That is exactly the sort of person you didn't expect to hear anything from. That woman grew up under separate but equal. It was something I was not prepared for. Then there was the black help in the Woolworths kitchen who told me to get up and leave, saying "You are not supposed to be here." At that time the whites did the serving and the blacks did the washing and helping out. It was only fifteen or twenty years later that I learnt to forgive them and understand them. I was threatening their livelihood. And it was around that time I realized that my parents weren't naive in the cruel lie that they had told me. They lied to me because they loved me.'

The four went into Woolworths around 3.45 p.m. and went back to campus at around 5.15. It was earlier than they had expected because the management, not knowing what else to do, closed the store. The way McCain tells it, that one and a half hours were the most glorious of his life, a truly transcendental experience.

'On the day that I sat at that counter I had the most tremendous feeling of elation and celebration. I felt that in this life nothing else mattered. I felt like one of those wise men who sits cross-legged and cross-armed and has reached a natural high. Nothing else has ever come close. Not the birth of my first son nor my marriage. And it was a cruel hoax, because people go through their whole lives and they don't get that to happen to them. And here it was being visited on me as a seventeen-year-old. It was wonderful but it was sad also, because I know that I will never have that again. I'm just sorry it was when I was seventeen.

'It was the most intense peace within myself and my surroundings. I had no tensions and no concerns. If there's a heaven, I got there for a few minutes. I just felt that you can't touch me. You can't hurt me. There is no other experience like it. And so today nothing excites me. There is no one I feel I have to meet. No experience that unglues me. Nothing.

I'm not moved by them. I'm just a spectator, and you can't excite me.

'I don't go back to that day every day. But I do when I am getting despondent and frustrated and then I conclude that, hey, it's not that important. Life goes on. It's a resting place, a renewal place. I'm not sure I could stand it too much, though. Now I know what it's like I'm not so sure I could go there for any length of time. I think it would be illegal and unlawful for someone to feel that good and that much at peace.'

I wondered if there is ever a good time to go to a 'place' like the one Franklin McCain went to on 1 February 1960. Get there early in your life and you can live the rest of it with a real sense of perspective, but know you have peaked too soon. Get there late and you will have lived most of your life in the dark but finish on a high. I suppose the point is just to get there at all and leave fate to worry about the timing.

I asked him whether at this time and through the years following it – a decade which saw assassinations, beatings and betrayals – he ever questioned his national identity; whether the denial of his civil rights ever undermined his confidence in his desire to call himself an American.

'I never had a feeling that this wasn't my country. Black people are how this country got to be great. The Indians wouldn't work for the whites. They ran away. It was their country and they knew where to run to. But by God, my ancestors worked hard in this country, and I always knew that I belonged. Even with its shortcomings, there is no place that I would rather live than in the US. I've kissed the ground on my return more than once. I come from here. As a citizen and a person, this is where I belong. We have good labor law, civil rights law, the thirteenth, fourteenth and fifteenth amendments. I feel good about my country. It's my country-men I need to convince.'

McCain is an optimist. When I asked him for his opinion on those blacks who claim that segregation was not the problem, just the inequality that came with it, he said he understands where they are coming from but still believes they are wrong.

'Some of this comes from frustration, and it is fine to have some frustration. But I think what we have to do is look at these problems from a historical perspective. One hundred years ago we were property; forty years ago we couldn't ride in the front of the bus; thirty years ago we couldn't eat at a lunch counter. Look at where we have come from. Those who say it was better under segregation must remember the golden rule: he who has the gold makes the rules. In this country, to have power, you have to control the school boards, the schools, the commission, the police and so on, and there is no place in this country where black people control all of that. Most people should have lived long enough to understand that white people will always take care of themselves first. Power concedes nothing. And a lot of these feelings come from nostalgia. People remember how good it used to be. It was hell. Sure there were some advantages. There was the dentist who lived next door to the ditch digger who lived next door to the preacher before economic stratification started to happen. But that's not right either. It's not at all good for someone who has been working hard to get where they are in their profession to be forced to live in a shack. So now we have a choice. If you want to do that you can. But I don't want anybody telling me I should or I have to, because I don't.'

What, I asked him, would he be getting involved in if he was seventeen today?

'I think I would be raising hell in public schools. I would

want to be agitating to make sure that black kids get an equal share and I would be trying to get parents involved with their children. That is our main concern. As a people and a race we need to shore up our love for our children and a respect for learning. We have to show them the link between education and a solid opportunity. What we don't need now is another Martin Luther King. What we need is small enclaves of dedicated people, not someone who can rally a hundred thousand people and give a good speech. Opportunity is not like a revolving door that keeps on coming around. It's like an escalator. If you miss it, it's gone. We have got to get on that escalator. Our kids need to be knocking on that door and getting their tickets punched. It's hard for someone to ride the back of folk who aren't stooped. Because it's not just about giving the white folks hell. Believe me, there is enough hell to go around.'

McCain said he would take me home and carried on chatting in the car. About half a mile from my motel a light turned from green to amber while he was in mid-flow. He paused for a second, then speeded up and said under his breath, 'Go on Franklin, take this one.'

While I was in Charlotte, the North Carolina Governor, Richard Hunt, was hosting a two-day conference on racial reconciliation at the Adams Mark Hotel. The gathering had been inspired by President Clinton, who shortly after his inauguration had called for town meetings around the country to discuss how to bring about greater racial understanding. Most, including those attended by the President, had been a flop. Politeness, not politics, had prevailed. Many blacks had turned up to vent a little anger; a handful of whites (generally not the ones who needed to be there) had aired a little guilt. Everyone had said they should love each

GARY YOUNGE

other more, and then gone home to their segregated neighbourhoods.

Judging by Hunt's vacuous observations, North Carolina's meeting would be no different. 'What we do now is say that racism and discrimination and treating people wrong because of the color of their skin is just wrong in itself, and we've got to speak out about it,' he said. 'In 2000, we can come back as a state and be prepared to report back where we are, where we need to move ahead.'

A story on the front page of the *Charlotte Observer* that day showed just how much still had to be done in the state next door. Under the headline SOUTH CAROLINA OFFICIAL RESIGNS AFTER SLURS REACH WRONG ADDRESS was a story relating how an investigator with South Carolina's state attorney general's office, Tommy Windsor, had mistakenly sent offensive e-mails to the person he was insulting. Windsor had meant to send the messages to a Republican friend who had been the subject of a critical article by Michael Cubelo, a Democratic Party activist. Instead, he had sent them to Cubelo.

Windsor's first message read: 'I'll bet you this guy is a fag, probably a minority. And he has probably never seen the inside of a Baptist church. There is no question that he is a product of the public school system and has to pick his welfare check up every Friday to buy crack and a bottle of Ripple ... We ought to go to his house and beat the shit out of him, hang him from a tree in his front yard and set the cross on fire. The gall of him stereotyping all of us God-fearing Republicans.' Then, not yet realizing his mistake, he sent another one: 'It is obvious that he is not a regular American, that he is one type of immigrant. You know, these foreigners have ruined this great country of normal WASP Americans.'

Windsor was forced to resign. In a statement he said: 'I

116

used poor judgement in an effort to use exaggeration to make a point. This has cost me dearly.' He wrote to Cubelo explaining the mistake, asserting that 'any educated person would not take this seriously'.

In the tiny patch of land that is downtown Charlotte, you can do one of three things: eat, shop or go to the bank. Its sterile centre once earned it the nickname 'White Shirt City' because of all the neatly pressed, clean-cut young bankers striding, as through a washing-powder commercial, from one dull meeting to another. The town, one journalist wrote, has 'the vacant calm of a place where it's always ten thirty in the morning'. So, after I had had my lunch, changed some money I didn't really need changed and browsed in shops stocking nothing I wanted to buy, I decided the cheapest place to spend my remaining hour and a half was in the bus station.

Charlotte's bus station was filled with the sound of people waiting, the dull drone of travellers' torpor against a back-drop of tannoy announcements and revving engines – enough noise to stop you going to sleep, but not enough to keep you fully awake. There were tired people who may have been travelling for more than a day slumped in chairs with their eyes closed and their ears open; children so bored they couldn't be bothered to be naughty any more; old couples with packed lunches; army types with big green bags and crew cuts: all waiting – an essential part of the Greyhound experience, along with late departures (not one of the buses I boarded through the entire journey ever left on time), rude employees and terminals in rundown areas.

The station in Charlotte was more or less what you

would expect. There were lockers, a ticket counter, a customer service centre, toilets, vending machines, computer games, a gift shop and a cafeteria. On some of the seats in the waiting room there were small televisions on which, for a quarter, you could watch fuzzy cartoons and daytime television for fifteen minutes if you were lucky. If you were unlucky you just got fifteen minutes of fuzz, which at least helped you appreciate the quiet when it stopped.

Greyhound travellers are a motley crew. There is the handful of people who cannot drive or hate driving; the millions who cannot afford a car or whose car will not make it long distances and who do not have the price of a plane ticket; and the odd few who are afraid of flying. There are students and army folk – both groups get Greyhound discounts – and people who have been let out of prison, who are given travel vouchers by the authorities which are often exchanged for Greyhound tickets. There are women who do not want to drive alone at night (forty-two per cent are single females), large families and people who live in small towns a long way from an airport. A third of Greyhound passengers travel three hundred miles or more on any one trip; almost three-quarters travel alone; over a half are either unemployed, full-time students or pensioners. More than a quarter earn less than $10,000 and almost sixty per cent take home less than $25,000 (the national average annual pay is $26,939). Just over half are white; just under a quarter are black and little more than a tenth are Hispanic.

Factor in the relative discomfort of travelling by bus, and a clearer picture of the company's clientele emerges – people without much money, who often travel long distances, are not in a rush and have no other options.

The journey across the border into South Carolina and the small town of Rock Hill is a short one. The Greyhound bus station there is a launderette in an ugly place. In small towns like this, Greyhound does a deal with a local business (like a garage or a grocery store) to double up as a station for a cut of the revenue.

The launderette was on Riverside Plaza. The name conjures up images of a Mediterranean square with the warm sea lapping at the esplanade at sunset. It is in fact a small collection of shops opposite a huge textile plant, an enormous, metallic, smoke-belching monstrosity behind large gates. One of the men who got off in front of me went around the side of the building and peed up the wall. I was with him in spirit.

I hauled my stuff into the dimly lit laundromat, dumped it near the door and walked the length of the room to the counter. There were about thirty to forty machines which looked as though they had been bought shortly after the Freedom Riders had come through. In three of the four corners of the room there were drinks machines but only one of them worked. At the back there were a few Hispanic men playing video poker.

I got the woman at the counter to dial me a cab and also asked her what there was to do in Rock Hill.

'To do?' she said looking shocked.

'Yes, you know, are there any good bars or clubs or things to see?' I asked.

She sucked her pen for a short while.

'There's karaoke at the Holiday Inn,' she said with a doubtful smile and then pulled a discouraging face. 'But that's on a Tuesday, and it's already Wednesday. I really don't know, to be honest with you. I just go to work, go home and go to work again.'

I thanked her and made my way to the door. Outside, the textile mill was looking bleak in the dusk, belching fumes into what would soon be sunset. I waited for the cab and thanked God that I had not been born in Rock Hill.

CHAPTER SIX

South Carolina: Surrounded

It was in Rock Hill that the Freedom Riders were first met with violence. The Greyhound station there served as a meeting place for young white men who would hang around the pinball machines. They had heard the Freedom Riders were coming, and as the bus pulled up, around twenty were waiting for them. John Lewis stepped out and started walking towards the white waiting room when two men with DA haircuts blocked his way. 'Other side, nigger,' said one, and pointed in the direction of the 'For Colored' waiting room entrance.

Lewis recited his lines: 'I have a right to go in here on grounds of the Supreme Court decision in the Boynton case.'

The youth looked at Lewis in confusion and after a short pause replied: 'Shit on that.'

Lewis was pushed, shoved and then felled with a punch to the mouth. Bigelow, who was next in line, stepped forward and was similarly beaten. As he fell he took Genevieve Hughes, a white activist, with him. Only then did the police, who had been standing by, step in and break it up. They asked Lewis and Bigelow if they wanted to press charges. The two men refused, claiming that their struggle was against a system rather than individuals. Two hours later, when the Trailways bus arrived, the terminal was closed and locked.

That the Freedom Riders were first attacked in South Carolina is somewhat surprising. It is the Deep South, was the first state to secede from the Union and the last to keep the Confederate flag flying over the state Capitol in Columbia. But with the exception of the police shooting of three unarmed young black men in Orangeburg following a dispute over a segregated bowling alley in 1968, the violent confrontations that scarred Alabama, Mississippi, Arkansas and Tennessee during the fifties and sixties mostly passed South Carolina by. This was not because South Carolina was any less racist – most blacks I spoke to considered it the most redneck state in the South after Mississippi and Alabama – but because a conscious decision was made by those in authority to manage racial conflict in a more sophisticated way than other Southern states.

When black students went to integrate the University of Alabama in 1963, Governor George Wallace stood in the schoolhouse doorway. 'We are God-fearing people, not government-fearing people,' he said. 'We practice today the free heritage bequested to us by the founding fathers.' And he physically prevented a federal official from entering through the front door. Away from the cameras, the two black students were being shown to their dorms under a deal worked out with the federal government. The whole stunt was face-saving theatre for Wallace's racist electorate.

By contrast, when Harvey Gantt became the first black student to go to Clemson University in South Carolina, thereby breaking the segregation barrier there, the outgoing Governor, Ernest Hollings, told the legislature: 'As we meet, South Carolina is running out of courts. If and when every legal remedy has been exhausted, this General Assembly must make clear South Carolina's choice, a government of laws rather than a government of men. As determined as we are, we of today must realize the lesson of one hundred years ago, and move on for the good of South Carolina and our United States. This should be done with dignity. It must be done with law and order.' South Carolina's establishment grudgingly accepted change when it was forced upon them; elsewhere in the Deep South they would continue to oppose it even after it was a fact of life, in the hope that the mob could turn the clock back.

On the other hand, if the Freedom Riders were going to be attacked anywhere in South Carolina, then it is not so surprising that it should have been in Rock Hill. During the nineteenth century, York County, in which Rock Hill is situated, was a hotbed of Klan activity. In 1871, a former Klan member told a court how he, along with a dozen Klansmen in York County, rode into the night in search of a black man suspected of being a Republican (which then meant a radical) called Roundtree. They chased him into the loft and on to his roof, from which he jumped and ran. When they caught up with him, the Klansmen shot him down and then slit his throat.

In 1850 a fifty-six-year-old slave, Andrew Cathcart, bought his freedom. By 1871 he had acquired ninety-eight acres of farmland in York County. On 11 March of that year fifteen to twenty Klansmen, riled by his success, took him from his bed, whipped him and beat him but left him alive as they went to try and burn down the small building that black children used for school.

In January 1871, the Klan punished a white woman who had hidden men they were chasing by pouring a mixture of tar and lime into her vagina and then spreading the rest over her body with a paddle.

In the spring of that year, the Governor of South Carolina asked the US President to send the cavalry to York County to suppress Klan-inspired terrorism, under the command of Major Lewis Merrill. 'He faced a demanding situation,' wrote Tolnay and Beck in *A Festival of Violence: an analysis of Southern lynchings, 1882–1930*. 'Not only did terrorists enjoy broad support within the white community, but the state's criminal justice system also seemed to be in the hands of the Klan or its sympathizers. Merrill reported to Washington that night riders were responsible for three to four hundred whippings and murders in York County alone, and yet the civil authorities refused to prosecute.'

Wandering around Rock Hill, I let history mess with my mind. When I went on school trips to Germany I used to do this – I would find my gaze resting longer than is polite on anyone over the age of fifty-five and wonder whether they had burnt books and scrawled stars on Jewish homes, worked in the concentration camps or beaten up Poles and Slavs. Or maybe they had fled and joined the resistance. I wondered what they had done, or what they might have done given the chance. There was, of course, a mawkish, morbid and arbitrary quality to all this. But there was a point to it, too. The veneer of civilization and order that we grow up with is as fragile as it is glossy. For all sorts of reasons, the person who is giving you a light or helping you to push your car one day can be the person standing at the top of the street and screaming abuse on another. The man who refused to get off the party line when my brother had trapped his finger in the back door helped me make the box for the metronome I submitted for my sixth-form technology project eleven years later, while his wife brought in tea and biscuits. The teachers who lectured about tolerance and discipline at my mother's school were also the ones who refused to lift a finger when kids scratched racist insults into her desk. Just because things look normal it doesn't mean that they always have been or always will be.

Nowhere is this more true than in the American South. Anyone over the age of about forty who grew up in the South is likely to have gone to a segregated school. Most whites of that age were raised to call black men 'boy'; most black men were raised to avoid making eye contact with white women. As recently as 1964, this region of a country that lectured the world on political freedom did not allow black people to vote. It is difficult at times not to stare at pensioners, black or white, having a meal or walking through a shopping mall, and wonder what part they played in the whole drama.

Sitting in his office, surrounded by three walls of certificates attesting to his professional qualifications, Ernest Brown, the head of the local NAACP and Executive Director of the town's medical centre, is lamenting the end of segregation.

'When segregation went, we lost the very foundation of our community. You need your own. When I was at school, the teachers had attitude and commitment. I don't see that towards our children now. We don't have any black teachers, administrators, coaches, class presidents, valedictorians. When I was growing up nobody said you couldn't achieve. I felt fortunate that I went to a black school. I joined the drama society, the choir and was always encouraged to be the best I could be. The equal is the only part I want. When I was at school we used to get the hand-me-downs from the white schools and use their athletics fields when they weren't using them. If we had the same facilities that they had I don't care if we never went to school with them. I want the same buildings and the same kind of resources. I'm not bothered about sitting side by side with them.'

It is a common view among African-Americans, although the fact that it should come from an office bearer of the NAACP, an integrated organization whose greatest victory was the landmark *Brown vs. Board of Education* ruling, is odd. But the logic of it is simple. When there was segregation, the black community had both autonomy and an internal dynamic of its own. You bought food at the black grocer because you weren't treated well at the white stores. You bought clothes in black areas because you weren't allowed to try them on at the white shops. You ate in black-owned restaurants because white ones wouldn't serve you. Regardless of your job or social status, your race was all that mattered, and this provided a sense of cohesion. In short, everyone was in the same boat; it was a rickety vessel that was always taking in water, but you either rowed together or you would surely all drown together.

Then came integration. Black businesses, which had little capital, found it difficult to compete with bigger, white ones. The most promising black students were bussed to white schools; the most successful black professionals moved into white suburbs. The black baseball league collapsed as the best players went into the white teams. As one man in Greensboro put it, 'Some of us thought the water in the Whites Only fountain tasted better.' The community became stratified by economics and, as was the case in Jackson ward in Richmond, things started to fall apart. Given the amount of poverty that prevails among those who were left behind, African-Americans seem to have ended up with the worst of all worlds; they have lost their common sense of identity and yet remain unequal. In Atlanta's former bustling black district of Auburn there is a mural pasted over some run-down businesses, which says: 'When race relations were at their lowest point black business development was on the rise. Racial segregation and repression unified the black community.'

This makes sense. Integration of the races in America was very much like the unifying of the two Germanies after the Wall came down: it ended up being assimilation of the powerless into the world of the powerful. Blacks had to fit in to white society, but white society made few concessions to them. Education provides a good example. The smart black students went to white schools, weakening the black establishments. When they got there, they found few attempts to reflect their history, identity or experience. The best they could expect was to be tolerated – and that was rare. So long as racism has remained prevalent in the white community, blacks have been faced with a choice: integrate into a white society that does not want you, or stick together and make the best of what few resources you have.

It has not been a difficult decision. According to a Gallup poll in 1997, seventy-one per cent of black people attended mostly or all-black churches, forty-one per cent lived in mostly or all-black neighbourhoods, thirty-two per cent belonged to mostly or all-black clubs or organizations and twenty-five per cent had their oldest child in a mostly or all-black school. But to elevate this to a point of principle, that the separation of the races is fine so long as they have equal resources, I felt was depressing and flawed. First of all it is built on a fairly romantic notion of just how solid the black community was before integration and ignores the fact that the races were segregated at gunpoint. But also because it seemed black Americans were moving on to an ideological terrain ill-suited for the battles they were waging.

The only reason racial segregation exists is because racism exists. Take that away, and there is no more point in wanting to live in a black area than there would be in wanting to live in an area where everyone was tall, fat or had ginger hair. But for weeks I had been quizzing African-Americans about their views on segregation as opposed to integration, until someone pointed out to me that I had been asking the wrong question.

Charles Payne, an African-American lecturer at Duke University in North Carolina, explained: 'The issue for black people was never integration or segregation, but white supremacy. The paradigm of integration and segregation was a white concern. That was how they posed the issue of civil rights given their own interests, and that was how the entire issue then became understood. But the central concerns of black people were not whether they should integrate with white people or not, but how to challenge white people's hold on the power structure.'

His comments reminded me of the week I had spent with a family in Alexandria, a South African township near Johannesburg, just before the country's first democratic elections. In the white areas, all most people seemed to be worried about were blacks: blacks and crime, blacks and violence, blacks in government. Since few of them actually knew any blacks, apart from their gardeners and maids, this simply gave them the opportunity to elevate blacks collectively into a huge, imaginary monster. The whites sat surrounded by high walls and barbed wire, worrying about the horrors that a black future held.

In the township, I tried desperately to tease out of black people what they thought about whites, but would always be met with blank expressions. After a few days I worked out that while they were keen to get rid of apartheid, they didn't think about whites *per se* at all. They had more important things to worry about, like feeding their families and keeping their homes under a decaying apartheid regime.

Viewed in this context, what Brown went on to say about his work in Rock Hill made much more sense. 'There are no black people around here in positions of authority. We are not represented at a serious level on any of the boards where we can decide how to expend resources equitably. The last time I checked, there were no black members of the country club, because we know we wouldn't be welcome. I am on the board of directors for the Chamber of Commerce and have two masters degrees. I have an executive position.

But I haven't been invited to any social gatherings that have been going on, and that is where a lot of the decisions are taken. They take the vote at the meeting, but they make their decisions at dinner or over a drink. Rock Hill is a typical small Southern town where the good ol' boy network is still going strong.'

When the interview ended, it was just past 7 p.m., and I was not yet ready to go back to my motel. With history still playing tricks with my imagination, I asked Brown whether it would be safe for me to go for a drive and stop off at a local bar for a drink.

Brown leant back in his chair and after a long pause said: 'I'm not sure that you'd get lynched but I wouldn't know. You don't get black bars around here as such, only white ones. Now, most likely, nothing would happen. But if there's a few white boys in there and they've been drinking beer and they had some bad racial encounter during the day, then all you would need is for some white woman to come on up to you and start a conversation about your accent, and you would be in a whole heap of trouble.'

I went back to the motel.

To get back, I had to drive through the mile-long ode to uniformity that welcomes you at the entrance to all American towns – a discordant symphony of standardized garishness, standing straight and tall, in a long line, leading from the highway past the high street and on into cultural oblivion. They announce themselves for miles on the interstate road signs, informing a motorist that their staples – gas, food and lodging – are only minutes away. There is McDonald's, with its huge M elevated at least thirty feet from the ground; Burger King, home of the whopper; Bo Jangle's, Taco Bell, Popeye's and Shoney's, Hardee's, Arby's, Denny's and

Wendy's. Each one has a Special – as much as you can eat for $5; happy meals, bargain buckets and combos; wings, thighs, breasts and ribs; broiled, baked, fried and grilled.

Then there are the petrol stations and motels: Texaco, Citgo, Amoco and Conoco, Exxon and Shell, BP and Spur; Days Inn, Comfort Inn, Bestway Inn and Sleep Inn, Super 8, Super 6, Holiday Inn and Econo Lodge. Familiar places. Open twenty-four hours a day. Everywhere. Anywhere. For that is where you are. Each one is the same, so you know what you are going to get. Not much, but enough: a meal and a bed in a place that you can easily forget; some petrol in your tank so you can leave. Each is designed to make you feel that you have been there before. Each manages to create the impression that you never left the place you started from.

Their strength is that you know what to expect. You could venture into town and try to find something different but then you never know what you will get or if you will find anything at all. The room might be dirty, the meal might be expensive, the service might be bad and you might get caught on a scary one-way system. Best stick with what you know. But this is not just about filling up your car and your belly and finding a bed for the night. It is about a way of life and a set of values – the most telling illustration of the fact that Americans have a completely different sense of place from most Europeans. And in a country as vast as the US, they have to – the United Kingdom could fit into the United States about thirty-seven and a half times.

The most common means of navigating this huge area is the car. Driving is central to American culture. Many people think nothing of driving fifty miles for a meal. A number of times during my trip, people described a place four hours' drive away as just up the road. Most schools teach driving; in some areas the lack of parking facilities for high-school students is a serious political issue. Along with a passport, a driver's licence is the only universally accepted form of picture ID.

When I first came to America to work, aged twenty-seven, I couldn't drive. When I mentioned this to people they reacted in a similar way in which I would expect people in Britain to respond if I told them I was illiterate – not with disdain, exactly, but with pity, and amazement that I could get through life without such a basic human skill. I passed my test in DC. Within a month, I had written off a car in Wichita, Kansas; within two I had parked another one in a ditch outside a Kentucky Fried Chicken in Harriman, Tennessee; within three I had made a 2,500-mile trip in just over a week.

Cities and towns are generally built with cars in mind. They sprawl over miles, offering nucleii of commercial activity just off the highway and often, as is the case in Los Angeles, they have no centre at all in the way that we would understand it in England, with pedestrian areas, post offices and theatres all within walking distance of each other. In lots of suburbs they don't even bother with pavements.

Weather, time differences and landscape do, of course make a major difference. You know when you are at the foot of the Rockies, in the Arizona desert or around Louisiana's bayous. The sceneries are distinctive, the accents are different and so are the local mores. But, from the vantage point of a car steering-wheel, there are vast tracts in between that all look and feel pretty much the same.

Not all of this can be blamed on the standardization brought about by rapacious American capitalism, the huge economies of scale which undoubtedly make producing millions of identical burgers, fries and motel beds more profitable than having local subsidiaries making different styles for different regions. Its huge size notwithstanding, the US is one country. If you can get John Menzies, Safeway's and

Sainsbury's in Andover and Aberdeen, then there is no reason why you shouldn't find Shoney's and Arby's in Alaska and Alabama. But still, there are times when a sense of place seems to have been swallowed up by the push for profit. It is not uncommon for a local newspaper to have its entire front page filled with stories provided by a wire service like the Associated Press, and for the majority of its columnists to be syndicated from Washington, New York or Los Angeles. This is a country where football and baseball teams can simply up sticks from their home turf and move across the continent – for a price. In 1966 the Milwaukee Braves baseball team moved south and became the Atlanta Braves; four years later the Seattle Pilots went east and turned into the Milwaukee Brewers.

As a result, travelling around the South, with its fair share of soulless malls, out-of-town cineplexes and suburban estates, can feel like travelling around anywhere else in the United States. There are times when you feel the urge to check a map just to remind yourself of exactly where you are, and of the fact that you have travelled a great distance.

That night in a chain motel in Rock Hill was one of those times. There are some basic things you can expect from any chain motel. Near where you check in there are at least two vending machines – one for Cokes and one for cigarettes. A receptionist may ask for your driver's licence, licence-plate number, address, or all (or none) of these things as proof of ID. She may get messages passed on to you, but she may not. Some motels come with swimming pools with little umbrellas fixed on to tables on the side, for those who like to lounge in the sun next to a four-lane motorway. Some have keys for the rooms, and others have little plastic keycards which rarely work first time around. In that case, the person at the desk will give you a demonstration of the speed and agility with which you have to dunk it in its slot and whisk it out, only to find that the reason it isn't working is that they haven't programmed it properly.

When you open the door to your room, you are hit by the smell of newly sprayed air freshener. Inside are the accessories – a Bible, a Yellow Pages, a residential directory, a desk, a bath, a phone with an appendage through which you can swipe your credit card and buy a movie for the night.

After that things get a little unpredictable. Sometimes there are plastic flowers on the desk, and usually there are pictures of sunsets, fruit, or horses galloping around the countryside on the wall. Occasionally you will not be able to dial long-distance on the phone. You may be woken up at nine to see if you want your room cleaned, or you may return at 2.30 p.m. to find you cannot get in because your room is being cleaned. Sometimes there is a little restaurant or bar on the side. Your nightly charge (around $40) will sometimes come with a Continental breakfast which comprises coffee, cereal and a sticky doughnut (I have no idea which continent that is supposed to come from).

There is only so much you can do in a room like this, even if you are supposed to be working. You can read, watch television, go to the toilet or have a bath (after you have done either of those a couple of times they get a bit boring). You can do each one for a short while before the urge just to get up and breathe some fresh air and feel that you are somewhere as opposed to anywhere at all grabs you with such intensity that you will get up and walk around the car park.

If you find that you've forgotten anything, like toothpaste and skin cream, or if you want to dull your torpor with some beer, then you can jump back in the car for a two-minute drive or take a most bizarre ten-minute walk. My pedestrian search for alcohol in Rock Hill took me across the car park and along a grass verge (there was no pavement) to avoid the cars, then across four lanes of traffic.

On my return I settled down for a night's TV. The great thing about American cable television (most of the motels have cable) is the repeats. Among your choice of twenty or so channels there will almost certainly be some programme that evokes fond memories of childhood. The Friday night relief after a hard week at school when the A-Team title beckoned; the Saturday evenings after the football results when the Dukes of Hazzard appeared; the Sunday afternoon before *Weekend World* when Fonzie would show up on *Happy Days* – bad programmes which you used to love and which, with twenty-four hours of programming to fill, cable channels are only too happy to rerun.

But otherwise, with the notable exception of gems like *Seinfeld* or *ER*, you have the choice of watching something that is so terrifying you are scared to go to sleep or being sent into a slumber by something completely inane. News and current affairs programmes flag their items with lines like, 'Can any child ever be safe from sexual predators?' or 'Who eats more healthily, your children or prisoners?' An hour later there will be an interview with a sexual predator in jail saying he would definitely re-offend and has never been so well fed.

Sitting in my room in Rock Hill surfing the channels for five minutes the following programmes appeared:

Kids competing for the title of Swamp King in what looked like the Florida Everglades, by paddling in shallow water surrounded by tall reeds.
An offer to join the Pay TV movie channel.
How to curl your hair like Chelsea Clinton.
A sitcom called *Legal Eagles* which appeared to involve lots

of tough, professional-looking people giving it to each
other straight and getting stressed out in the process.

A 1950s war film.

A trailer for a news programme saying, 'Minutes after this
video was taken, the surfer was bitten by a shark – and
lived – coming up next.'

The English detective programme *Hetty Wainthrop
Investigates*.

A sitcom called *Mama's Family*.

It takes five minutes because there are so many ads. There
are ads between the title sequence and the beginning of the
show, three more breaks in thirty minutes and then more ads
between the end and the credits. Bored, I dozed off only to
wake up in my clothes just after midnight just in time for a
Jerry Springer programme. One day someone will write a
thesis about why people go on these shows and bare their
miserable souls. And across the corridor one of their colleagues will examine why people who think they know
better cannot help but watch them. After about twenty
minutes, I went back to sleep.

The next day was Halloween. A Ms Bennie Long walked
into the town's medical clinic and emptied the contents of a
.357 Smith & Wesson into the body of the clinic's regional
director, who died instantly. She was, it appeared, upset by
something that had happened in a staff meeting earlier in the
week.

Rock Hill was getting scary. I left the following day.

I was about to head off the route of the Freedom Riders in
order to see my aunt in Savannah, Georgia, and pass through

Orangeburg. I got my luggage ticket from the woman at the ticket counter (it had taken me a while, but I was learning) and handed my Ameripass to the driver.

'Two months, man,' he said. 'That's a lot of travelling.' And he ushered me on.

When I changed buses in the state capital, Columbia, the driver told me I needed a new ticket. I told him I didn't because I had an Ameripass. He told me I still needed a new ticket. I thrust my Ameripass at him as though it were some kind of invincible weapon. 'Listen, I've gotten from DC to here on this. I really don't need one.' He told me I did again. I was about to get huffy when he stopped me with a smile and a question.

'You from England? My wife's from England.'

He had met his wife, who was originally from Grenada, when he was serving in the US Army in Chicksands, Bedfordshire, and she had moved back with him to South Carolina.

'Don't sweat it, brother. You need a Carolina pass to get all the way there. You don't have to pay for one; if you show them that ticket they'll give you one,' he said.

I went to the counter to get a ticket for what I assumed to be one of Greyhound's partner companies, but there was a long queue. Fearing I would miss my bus I went back and told him it was taking for ever. He promised not to leave without me. I went back and took my place in the queue.

After about twenty minutes he came to the counter himself, told the woman doing the ticketing that I was his 'main man from England' and asked if they could please hurry up.

He came over to me and smiled again.

'So you went to England and came back with an English wife,' I said.

'I prefer to say a beautiful black woman,' he replied, as though the two were mutually exclusive.

I was the last on the bus and it looked full. I went to the back and found a seat next to a black woman. As I put my laptop in the shelf overhead, she gave me such a hostile stare that I took it down and looked around for somewhere else. At the front there was a seat behind the driver with his hat and coat on it. I asked him if I could move them. He was delighted. 'So my home boy from England is sitting up beside me now,' he said, relishing the captive audience he would now have for the next couple of hours.

He was a talker. When he had completed the regular spiel over the tannoy he embarked on a detailed explanation of how the air vents and chair recliners worked. When he had finished he asked me why I was sitting up at the front. I told him about the stare the woman at the back of the bus had given me.

'Man, all you got to do is lay some of that English accent on them and you would be fine. The sisters love that.'

I asked him what he thought of the Confederate flag flying on the state Capitol. He said it didn't bother him, given the number of black soldiers who fought for the Confederacy during the Civil War – a fact he said that white Southerners often chose to ignore. 'Every black person should have a Confederate flag. It's our heritage too,' he said.

This was a slightly creative interpretation of history. After the Confederate troops fell at Vicksburg and lost at Gettysburg and were riven by internal squabbles – just, basically, when the South was running out of options – slaves were conscripted. Most were kept away from both weapons and the front line. 'We are forced by the necessity of our condition', one newspaper stated at the time, 'to take a step which is revolting to every sentiment of pride, and to every principle that governed our institutions before the war.'

But for the driver, who also insisted that Barbados had once been an American state, these were irritating facts that got in the way of his expansive world view, which made him sound like a combination of the Dalai Lama and Pol Pot.

'There is not enough love in the world,' he said. 'I don't care if you don't like me and I don't care what you think about me. We got to live together. But if you touch me, I'll kill you and I'll kill your family. We need more love in the world and less hate.'

Our conversation, if you can call it that, continued in this manner. I would ask him a straightforward question, like, 'Which is your favourite part of the country?' He would start to answer it with some broad-brush statement – 'I don't have any favourite states because all of the states are beautiful' – but would end up with an excited polemic – 'When people say "I come from America," I say, "The hell you don't. America is a continent. You come from the United States of America – that's your country."'

By the time we drew in to the Orangeburg depot, he had worn me out. After days without any social contact, I was ready for another week of solitude. Which was just as well, because nobody would talk to me in Orangeburg. The two contacts I rang told me to call other people who were either not in or referred me back to the person who had referred me to them.

It was Saturday afternoon in a small Southern town, and I had time on my hands. I asked the receptionist for some advice. He sucked his bottom lip for a short while: 'There's a strip bar up the road if you're into that kind of stuff and then you know where route 21 meets 178, well there's—'

'I'm not driving,' I said.

'Oh.' He sucked his lip a little more. 'Well, I can't think of anywhere you could walk to.' And that was that. In the rural South, I was discovering, you pretty much have to make your own entertainment.

Orangeburg was the closest I had yet come to the image of the South I had before I left. This majority-black town of around 13,500 has a main square watched over by a statue of a Confederate soldier and looks a little bit like a South African *dorp*. Just down from the square is the main street, Russell Street, where the bright colours of the old shop fronts have long since faded, and the pharmacists, cobblers and barbers are peppered among stores selling household clutter. The sun was shining, people were walking slower than normal and everything looked a shabby, ageing shade of poor. In the back of one of the largest shops, Freese's, there was a lunch counter, where the waitresses seemed to know everyone who came in, and the food was served hot enough to burn a hole in the polystyrene plates.

The lady serving me in Freese's thought my accent just about the funniest thing she had ever heard come out of a black man's mouth. So funny in fact that she very nearly spilt my lemonade all over my burger and fries. With little else to occupy my mind I turned my efforts to hamming up my English accent to see just how long I could keep her laughing. Since Orangeburg, a few miles from the motorway, could not have had too many non-student visitors from out of town, let alone out of the country, I figured this would give her a tale to tell for a few weeks. Whenever she brought me a new glass of lemonade, some cutlery or came to take my plate away I put on my best impression of a toff English accent and said: 'Splendid,' or 'First class.' Not wishing to offend, she would suppress her laugh until she had returned to the kitchen, where I could hear her noisily sharing the joke with her colleagues. Then she would return to serve another customer and look over at me and shrug her con-

siderable shoulders in a the-things-you-see-in-this-job sort of
way.

When I left Freese's I went down the road for the barber
visit to end all barber visits. I decided that since nobody
knew what I was talking about when I asked for a two-one,
and nobody knew me in South Carolina, I would ask for a
haircut that both I and they understood. I got it all shaved
off. It was easy. I went into a tiny, ramshackle hairdressers
and asked him to take it all off. He asked me why. I said I
was tired of it. He asked if I was sure. I said yes. And fifteen
minutes later I came out with the sun on my scalp.

From there I went to the All Star Triangle Bowl across
town. In 1968, the owner, Harry Floyd, swapped his WHITES
ONLY sign on the entrance door for a sign saying PRIVATELY
OWNED to keep the alley segregated but legal. When blacks
asked him if they could use the bowling alley just one night
a week, Floyd refused. Even though other parts of Orangeburg were already integrated, he thought he would lose
white customers if he let blacks bowl there. He said he did
not cater to 'tourists' and did not use goods or machinery
covered by interstate regulations, so he did not have to
comply with federal law.

The bowling alley, which sits only five blocks from the
historically black South Carolina State College, became a
focal point of discontent among students. The row on the
night of 5 February 1968 started after a group of black
students tried to enter the alley and Floyd refused to admit
them. Demonstrations outside the Bowling Alley led to
confrontations with the police which in turn led to a stand-
off between police and students outside the campus. Fires
were lit and objects thrown. A banister hit a patrolman and
knocked him out, feeding a rumour among other patrolmen
that he had been shot in the head. A squad of highway

patrolmen then opened fire, and three young men – Delano Middleton, Henry Smith and Samuel Hammond Jr – were killed. A further twenty-seven were wounded, 'all but two or three from the rear or the side,' wrote Jack Bass and Jack Nelson in *The Orangeburg Massacre.*

Floyd was later forced to open his doors to blacks, yet for several reasons Orangeburg never made it into the major anthologies of the civil rights years. 1968 was a big year for news. There was King's assassination in April, the Paris uprising and the Prague Spring in May, Bobby Kennedy's assassination in June and the election of Nixon in November – all of this against the backdrop of the Vietnam War. The bloody events in a small town in South Carolina had little claim on the resources of major news outlets or the public's attention. And the events in Orangeburg took place in a very different political context to the civil rights struggles that had occurred in the early part of the decade. The year before there had been riots in Detroit, Michigan, Newark New Jersey, Watts, California and other urban areas of the North and West – young black men and women in Afros quoting Mao and shooting back at the police alongside urban youth rebelling against the lack of jobs, poor housing and police harassment. The debate on race in America was changing, becoming more national and less centred on the South, more about class and less about race. The casting of heroes and villains was also becoming more complex.

'The media largely misrepresented the Orangeburg events because these events were out of tune with the times,' writes Thomas Pettigrew in the foreword to *The Orangeburg Massacre.* 'Had it occurred three or four years earlier, the Orangeburg massacre would almost undoubtedly have achieved considerable notoriety.'

On the tenth anniversary of the shootings, Floyd told a *Washington Post* reporter things were going fine. 'Never had a bit of trouble since that one time . . . Not one black has come along and made a smart remark or anything. No trouble from the whites either.'

The bowling alley still stands there, tucked into the corner of an L-shaped row of tumbledown shops offering what looks like charity bric-à-brac and cheap clothes. Inside, past the trophy cabinets with bowling paraphernalia on one side and local newspaper clippings of when All Star made the news on the other, lies a huge vista of bowling lanes. The entire room was empty, bathed in a painfully bright artificial light. And I was handed my bowling shoes by Harry Floyd himself, a small, poorly shaven man with a cigarette and a brown jumper. As I took the shoes to my lane I was at a loss as to what to do. I had not counted on his being there thirty years later. I understood that he was still alive. But I would no more have expected him to be working at the scene of his own crime than I would have expected to be walking through the Alabama Capitol building and see George Wallace at his desk.

Professionally I know the right thing to do would have been to go up and ask him for an interview. Politically it would have been the right thing to do, too. I could have asked him if he had a conscience and, if he did, were the lives of three young black men on it? I could have asked whether he had ever thought to apologize to the families of the men who had died. If Nelson Mandela can invite his former jailers to his inauguration, then I can try to exchange a few words with Harry Floyd. 'Forgive, but never forget,' was the slogan they used in South Africa during the transition. But personally, I could not stomach it. The fact that he was still there denoted a lack of progress for me. I know why he did what he did, and to my knowledge he has never apologized for it. The 'punishment' for his obstinacy was to allow black people to boost the profits of his bowling alley.

I didn't want to talk to him. I wanted to yell at him, spit in his face and trash all of his vending machines.

And since I couldn't do that either, I turned around, put the shoes on the counter and walked out of the door.

Out on the street the light was fading. I was told Earl's BBQ was in walking distance, but my request for directions was being met with strange stares which I assumed were to do with my accent but soon discovered were probably related to my mode of transport. I walked through dusk and into dark, along a main road and across railroad tracks. I stopped to ask directions at an off-licence and was offered some drugs. And just when I was about to give up hope I smelled it — a rich, warm waft of barbecue sauce, mixed with the scent of beans and broiled chicken.

On one side, there were cars waiting at a hatch for their takeaways. Around the corner was the front door which opened on to a room that looked not unlike my school canteen. On the tables there were jugs of iced tea and loaves of white bread. Around the side of the room was a queue leading to the service counter at the front. Most of the people inside were white, many of the men were in their hunting gear, a green camouflage jump suit and a hat. I asked the woman at the counter what one of the dishes, which looked like a part of a farmyard animal that I had never eaten before soaked in red sauce, was called.

'You telling me you don't know what barbedeediddlydo [I couldn't understand what she said] is?' she asked incredulously.

'No, I don't,' I said and she laughed so forcefully that she forgot to explain.

Despite the presence of some unknown bodies on my plate, the food at Earl's was so good and so filling that I had to unbutton my trousers and just sit there for about twenty minutes before I could even think about walking back to my motel.

The most segregated hour in the Southern week is eleven o'clock on a Sunday morning. That is when blacks and whites put on their best togs and go to separate buildings to worship the same God. Religion, throughout the United States, is more segregated than housing, work or socializing, and nowhere more so than in the South, to the extent that in small towns churches will often stage pulpit exchanges – attempts to cement racial understanding, where the white preacher will deliver his sermon at the black church and the black preacher at the white church: cultural exchanges in towns of no more than three or four thousand.

Paradoxically, religious belief is also one of the main things that unite blacks and whites in the South. Almost two-thirds of Southerners are Protestant compared to less than forty per cent of the rest of the country, and the bulk of those are Baptists. They are also more fervent and consistent in practising their religion than the rest of the country. Polls show that, in any given week, Southerners are far more likely to attend church, read the Bible at home or pray away from the church than those in the rest of the country. Almost half identify themselves as Evangelical or born-again Christians. More than eighty per cent believe both the Devil and angels are real.

It is not at all uncommon to go into an office and see a Bible on someone's desk, or a framed piece of scripture on the wall. From foul-mouthed comedians to national politicians – both President Clinton and Vice-President Gore, both Southerners, both Baptists, start their weekly meeting with a prayer – religion is as much a part of Southern life as fried chicken and Confederate statues.

In the Yellow Pages for the Rock Hill area, churches covered eight pages – three times more than the amount for plumbers. In a phone book that serves around a hundred thousand people, there were more than 200 churches listed under the following denominations: AME (African Methodist Episcopal), AME Zion, Apostolic, ARP, ARP – Assemblies of God, Baha'i, Baptist, Baptist Free Will, Baptist Southern, Catholic, Christian, Church of Christ, Church of God, Church of God in Christ, Church of Jesus Christ of Latter Day Saints, Episcopal, Evangelical, Evangelical Free Church, Foursquare Gospel, Holiness, Independent, Independent Fundamental, Interdenominational, Jehovah's Witnesses, Lutheran, Lutheran ELCA, Messianic, Messianic Judaism, Methodist-United, Mormon, Nazarene, Non-denominational, Pentecostal, Pentecostal Holiness, Presbyterian-PCA, Salvation Army, Seventh Day Adventist, United Pentecostal, Unity and Wesleyan.

For someone who has had as little contact as I have with the Church, this very public and pervasive affirmation of faith came as quite a shock. My grandmother in Barbados is very religious. She is a Seventh Day Adventist. My mother told me what that meant once, and I forgot, although I do remember that they don't do anything on Saturdays and can't drink tea or coffee. Every present I have ever bought my Gran, who still goes to church every week that she is able, has in some way been tied to helping her continue her faith: a new hat for church, a handbag big enough to put her Bible in, or the Old and New Testament on tape when her eyes got too bad to read the large-print Bible my brother had bought her.

Not much of this was transferred to my mother, who was the kind of believer who never attended church but sang along very loudly with *Songs of Praise*. Mum, who definitely believed in Something, embraced a credo that went like this:

'There are lots of bad people who go to church and lots of good people who don't. So long as I stock up on my fair share of good deeds and live my life with integrity then the rest will take care of itself.' By the time these tenets were handed down to me, any sense of religious affiliation had been diluted to the level of indifference. Not that I had any problem with other people being religious. But I had my own keen sense of right and wrong, and a home-grown spiritual compass which I had no desire to honour with a name. If I ever gave the matter much consideration, I suppose I would describe myself as an atheist. Since I never do, I usually prefer to say agnostic. I suppose I'm a lapsed agnostic – I used to not know, but it's a long time since I really thought about it.

Still, every Sunday during my journey I shook the creases out of my smartest, rucksack-packed clothes, put on the one tie I had brought with me and stood among the faithful. I actually started to look forward to it, not because the message was beginning to sink in, but because the music was usually good, the oratory was impressive and it was a slice of life I had never tasted before.

The black churches varied in size and wealth. Some were tiny, with a congregation of maybe fifty which would come together in the kind of small wooden building that looks precarious in a strong wind. Others were huge. One, in Atlanta, had policemen outside directing the traffic, and television screens inside for those that did not make it into the main hall. At the first kind the collection plate would come around jingling with quarters and, at most, five-dollar bills; at the second the faithful wrote out cheques.

In Greensboro I walked in to the sounds of 'We will all be wearing a crown to the New Jerusalem' from a gospel choir. At the door I was usually spotted as a visitor and given a card, distributed to all newcomers, asking me how many children I had and how long I would be staying in the area. Sometimes the ushers were older men with white gloves; sometimes they were young girls in frilly party dresses. Inside, the preacher was always male, and the congregation was always made up mostly of women and small children; there were very few single people under the age of thirty, and those that were were also usually female.

Most churches, no matter how small, had a decent-sized, well-rehearsed choir which accompanied the congregation at hymns. More than once, when the gospel singers were very good, I would marvel at the sight of a row of black women in their fifties standing in front of me swaying their shoulders and clapping to the music. They looked as though they were at a soul concert that happened to be taking place in the middle of Sunday afternoon.

Once or twice, someone would 'get the spirit'. At a church in Alabama, a woman in a red dress started shaking uncontrollably, the flowers pinned to her breast flapping while her feet performed some impressive dance steps and her head flopped from side to side as the two men either side of her jumped up to try and stop her hurting herself. Another time, further down in South Carolina, an old lady in a grey suit started doing something that looked like a cross between a moonwalk and the South African *toyi-toyi*, prompting the choir to assist her with a verse of: 'You know, Lord, whether I'm right or wrong.'

Then, when the notices had all been read out advising people of NAACP fundraisers and church socials and calling on women to go for mammograms and smear tests and everyone to go for blood-pressure tests to detect hypertension, came the bit I always dreaded, the time when the minister would ask the visitors to stand and introduce themselves. Everyone stood up together, and a few of the ushers, usually equipped with microphones, would dart around the church to let people announce themselves. There would be those who had come to see family or friends, and others who had moved in from out of town. Every now and then, somebody who had grown up in the church and was returning for good or just to visit family would make a small speech. 'I have no secrets from the Lord or anyone here,' said one woman in Greensboro who had recently returned from Florida. 'I had to lose everything to know just what I had. I have been clean from alcohol and drugs for a year now,' she said between her tears, and the congregation clapped and said Amen.

Somewhere around this time I would say my piece. I had to. Given the scarcity of other young men of my age in the church, I stuck out already. If that had not given me away then it would only have taken one question to blow my cover.

'My name is Gary Younge and I am visiting here from London, England,' I would say. In the quiet of the church, my Stevenage accent sounded flat and grey, but to the worshippers it was as though I had just filled the font with champagne. They would all turn around, nod and make faces similar to those I had seen in the classroom in Danville when I spoke Russian. Shortly after the introductions everyone would stand up, turn to their neighbour, give them a hug or shake their hand and say, 'Jesus loves you and so do I.' Once, in Oxford, Mississippi, I was told to write down where I came from so that the preacher could read it out. When the time came, he asked me to stand up. 'We have a stranger in our midst who we would like to welcome. A Mr Gary Younge from Saint Evenage.'

Then came the sermon, which was usually the dullest part. I'm not sure what I had been expecting – certainly not a shaft of light to come through the stained-glass windows and strike me with its righteousness, but something at least that I couldn't have come up with myself. But most of the time the preacher would spend half an hour illustrating that you 'just have to believe in God and he will help you', or that 'even when things are going badly God will still be on your side'.

But even if the message was fairly dull, the oratory was engaging. Every now and then the preacher would punctuate the sermon with catch phrases like 'C'mon and help me,' or 'Can ya hear me?' to which the congregation would say 'Preach it,' or 'That's right.' In one church in Georgia the preacher said, 'God is good.'

'All the time,' the congregation replied.

'All the time?' the preacher returned, slightly raising his voice.

'God is good,' concluded the faithful.

But for the most part the preachers would just spew forth one breathless tirade. Sentences without full stops, rhymes without reason, a demagogy of fluent patter all wrapped up in scripture and anecdote and delivered with forceful intent, their voices rising and falling, screaming and then whispering, stopping for dramatic pauses as they wiped their brow with a white hanky and then off again like a galloping colt.

One sermon, which was all about how we should thank God for everything, not just those things that we want and enjoy, went something like this. 'Just because your wife burnt the cornbread and you got your mouth set on some good sweet cornbread and when she takes it out of the oven and brings it to the table it's all black and burnt and feels like a rock you don't start shoutin' and a hollerin' . . . YOU DON'T START COMPLAININ' AN' CURSIN' . . . you must say, "Thank you Jesus."'

After the sermon came the tithes and after the tithes came the chance for new members to come forward. Usually there was at least one: someone who was new in town and had been trying the church out for a while. Sometimes, in the bigger churches, as many as twenty would come forward. Occasionally, as was the case in Atlanta, they would try to threaten you into joining. The preacher cited the recent stick-up in a local fast food chain and another drug-related murder as evidence that you never knew when your life was going to end and you had to make peace with God before it did. At the front two large men stood with white gloves ready to catch anyone that came forward. Nobody did.

All of those Sundays I went to churches which were either exclusively black or had just one or two white people in them. They were not difficult to find. Ask any black person on the street where the local black Baptist church is and he or she will tell you. Otherwise, you could drive around (or walk on the few occasions it is feasible) at around ten thirty until you see a throng of black folks dressed up, and just follow them.

But all of that takes planning and foresight and on the Sunday morning I woke up in Orangeburg I had none of those. I had overslept and risen at ten thirty, just enough time to find a clean shirt and then wash and go. I asked the receptionist, a white woman, if she could direct me to the nearest Baptist church. She pointed to a place just around the corner.

As I raced down the road and panted up the steps, I realized that she had answered my question as though the issue of race had never existed in the South. She had sent me to a white church.

This wasn't all bad. I had planned to go to a white church at some time, not for some Sidney Poitier-style grandstanding but just to see what they were like. I had been hoping to choose the day myself, but now the day had chosen me. I wasn't exactly annoyed with the receptionist. But as the man at the front door gave me the first of many sideways glances, I wondered why she would wilfully put me in such an awkward situation. Was it that my English accent had made her forget I was black? A pathetic attempt to show that she could not 'see race'? Or was it simply that she didn't care?

I nodded a hello to the man at the door as though I go to white churches in the rural South all the time. He nodded hello back as though he knew that I didn't. As I walked in heads turned and stayed turned. The choir was singing the 'Adagio' from Organ Sonata No. 5 by Rheinberger. I wanted to leave, or at least plonk myself on the back pew, but the usher was having none of it. He walked me down about three aisles and made me sit in the middle.

Those few feet seemed to take for ever, and when I sat down I checked to see that nobody had slipped a bone through my nose and a leather thong around my hips since I entered. That is what it felt like. From every angle, I could feel eyes on me – from the balcony, from the left and the right and even from behind, eyes that bored into my melanin and stripped me of everything that did not pertain to my race. I have never felt so black.

I have been stared at before – while I was studying in Russia (every day for five months), on holidays in Turkey, rural areas in the UK and Ireland and on work trips to Finland, the Czech Republic and Switzerland. But these were places where locals had rarely seen black people except on television. They stared, for the most part, because they were curious and didn't know any better. Then there are the stares you get at theatres, swanky stores and expensive restaurants in most Western cities, the can-you-pay-the-bill glares from people who see black people often but don't know any and don't want to. And then there are the plain hostile stares you get from skinheads and their ideological offspring – looks of hatred at the fact that you exist from minds plotting for the day when you won't.

The eyes that besieged me that morning in Orangeburg betrayed elements of all of those but could be summed up by none of them. Orangeburg is sixty per cent black, so the fact that black people exist was hardly a surprise. While the stares were not friendly, nor were they downright hostile or suspicious. Whatever else I felt, I did not feel threatened or in danger. It was Sunday afternoon in a church. How hostile could they be? These were the pathetic and angry eyes of frustration and confusion. These were eyes that said: 'What are you doing here? You know the rules. Everybody knows the rules. We don't go to your churches, and you don't come to ours. Why are you doing this to us? What do you want?' If my blushes could show from a distance, I would have looked like a traffic light stuck on red. I felt not only self-conscious and uncomfortable but a little bit guilty – like an intruder on a local ritual.

Aptly enough, the theme for the sermon, by Reverend Bill Coates, was 'Surrounded'. He talked about his walk through a graveyard where his father and mother were buried as well as his Sunday school teacher and the man from the local store – a graveyard that I presumed had once been segregated and possibly still was. He was explaining how all of our values, and all that we know, stem from all of those that have gone before us, and the values that come after we have died will be the sum of what we have inherited plus whatever we have added.

I thought about how that related to the South and its past, the whiteness of this church and my discomfort. I realized that many of these people grew up in this church, and their families had been in it for generations. It was an integral part of their social and spiritual life. They were no more likely to change their place of worship than I was to vote Conservative or join the police. It was the way they had been brought up. Segregation, in this sense, was not so much about the systemic exclusion of one race or another but a habit. A bad habit, but a habit nonetheless.

I recalled a paragraph from James Jackson Kilpatrick's *The Southern Case for School Segregation*. From what is otherwise a hopeless justification for racism emerged one lucid point: 'For three hundred years the South has lived with this subconsciousness of race. Who hears a clock tick, or the surf murmur, or the trains pass? Not those who live by the clock or the sea or the track. In the South, the acceptance of racial separation begins in the cradle. What rational man imagines this concept can be shattered overnight?'.

My thoughts were interrupted by a near disaster. My morning ritual returned: I started to sneeze. In my rush to find a suitable pair of trousers, I had left all things that could have served as a handkerchief behind, and the more I tried not to sneeze, the more it felt like I would. Now I was sitting in fear that I might pebbledash the neck of the woman in front at any minute and, in so doing, set the cause for the integration of churches in Orangeburg back by decades. I imagined two white churchgoers discussing my visit a few years hence.

'We had a nigra in here a way back. A bald fella. Damn near sneezed the place down he did. Ruined the collar on Mrs Wallace's dress.'

In the name of racial dignity, the next couple of potential eruptions that made their way to my nostrils I managed to keep down.

Up at the pulpit the reverend continued. But this sermon was not interrupted by any 'that's rights,' or 'Say it, preacher.' There was no opportunity to stand up and introduce (or in my case explain) myself to the congregation, although we did all get a collective welcome. The organ music was beautiful but not moving. There were no drums or swaying. It was sedate and as classical as the organ's silver pipes and the white pillars around which the music reverberated.

When the sermon was over I rose with the intention of leaving as quickly as I could when a hand caught my shoulder.

'Welcome. I'm so glad you came,' said the woman behind me in an eager tone, as a hundred other eyes waited for my reaction.

'Thank you, I'm glad to be here,' I said, and her face relaxed a little.

'You're not from here are you?' she said.

'No, I'm from England,' I said and heard my words repeated all around me. 'He's from England.' 'He's English,' I could hear people muttering as though my presence there had finally been explained. I was English. I didn't know any better. Within seconds there was a mini-stampede of people coming to shake my hand vigorously and thank me for coming.

As I made my way back to my motel I wondered what they would have said if I was from Orangeburg or if I had come in with five or six black friends – if I had, in fact, done anything to threaten the racial cohesion of their church.

As I climbed the steps to my motel room the receptionist ran from behind her desk and called after me. 'Did I send you to the right church?' she asked.

'I think so,' I said, not wanting to embarrass her.

'It's just that right after I told you where to go I was concerned that maybe that wasn't the kind of church you wanted,' she said rather awkwardly.

'Well, I wouldn't know,' I said, keeping up the lie to spare her blushes. 'I'm not from around here.'

On Monday morning the US Army called. I had been trying to organize a visit to Fort Bragg military base in Fayetteville, North Carolina, to interview some black soldiers. They rang to say I could come the next day.

On the day I first called them, some three weeks before, the British Army had launched a campaign to recruit black soldiers back to England. They had adapted the famous poster of Lord Kitchener, with staring eyes and a handlebar moustache, pointing his finger and barking, 'Your country needs YOU.' The new one had a black officer in the Royal Artillery in the same pose with the same mad eyes and the same message, although thankfully the designer had dropped the whiskers. 'Whether we like it or not, there is a perception that the army is a racist organization,' said the Chief of the General Staff, General Sir Roger Wheeler. Underneath his quote, an article in the *Guardian* gave several examples of where this 'perception' might have come from.

When Mark Parchment joined the Royal Marines in 1988, his instructor told him that since he was black his weapon would be a spear. He was made to clean his spear every day and take it on manoeuvres. When he joined a commando unit in Scotland, a special initiation for 'niggers' involved tipping a bucket of urine over him and trying to shave his genitals.

After Prince Charles called for more black soldiers at the Trooping of the Colour, the Household Cavalry recruited Richard Stokes in 1990. Stokes left after receiving hate mail and having a fellow soldier throw a banana at him during a rehearsal.

In 1994, Mark Campbell joined the mounted ranks of

the Life Guards, the first black person to do so. His bed was soaked in urine, and someone left him a note saying: 'There is no black in the Union Jack.'

These are just some of the cases that we heard about. In general, blacks go into the British armed forces as if through a revolving door. They join. They are abused. They leave. Unemployment in Britain's non-white communities is very high, particularly among those of African-Caribbean, Pakistani and Bangladeshi origins. In London, around sixty per cent of black men under the age of twenty-five are unemployed. Yet few will join the army. Less than one per cent of the armed forces comes from ethnic minorities, compared with 5.6 per cent in the population as a whole.

The 'perception' that the armed forces are not for 'us' seems to be widespread. In my upbringing it formed one of my mother's two favourite mantras. One was: 'Any woman who comes in here and says she's pregnant for any of you is coming in, and you are going out. I will look after her and the grandchildren myself.' The other was: 'Murder, steal or maim, you will still be my son. But if one of you joins the police or the army . . . Tchaa. If I wanted you dead I would kill you myself.'

That was it. At the age of twelve the likelihood of me doing either was pretty remote. I didn't get my first kiss until I was fifteen. And I hadn't even heard of these horror stories about racism. But I didn't need to. I 'perceived' them. My gut reaction when I did hear them in later years was not surprise but, 'Well, what do you expect? That's what the army's like, isn't it?'

Only some of this was to do with the armed forces themselves. If you walk around generally feeling so little for the nation you were born in that you find it difficult to support its football team or stand for its flag, then the chances that you are going to want to lay down your life for it are pretty slim. I didn't feel like it was my country, so how could they be my armed forces? So it always intrigued me that, whenever I saw the US Army on television during one of its numerous invasions/peacekeeping roles, or when I went to Germany and saw American soldiers, so many of them were African-Americans. Almost every black male I met during my time in the South who had been to England – including Oliver Hill, Louis Cobbs and the bus driver from Columbia to Orangeburg – had been there with the army. Here is a country with a recent racial history that is far more ugly than Britain's, with far more entrenched racial problems and which is far more segregated. And yet, with a few exceptions – like Muhammad Ali who was a conscientious objector during the Vietnam War or James Farmer, who refused to fight in the Second World War – black people have been signing up to die for it in their droves.

This is partly because African-Americans clearly feel far more American than black Britons do British. One black sergeant-major who went to Somalia during Operation Restore Hope in 1992–3 said: 'I deployed as an American and I'll come home as an American. This talk about our ancestors coming from here has it wrong. My people are from east Texas. I learnt a lot about race the hard way back home. But in the army we should all be brothers in the same Church.' The army also subsidizes people through college, a major incentive for those from working-class backgrounds. But the reasons African-Americans join the military, I discovered, are not just rooted in national identity or career development, but in history as well. The right to fight for America has, at times, become a focal point of many crucial debates about race and citizenship in the US.

At the beginning of the American Revolution, George Washington forbade blacks from enlisting to fight the British. The British offered blacks their freedom if they fought for

King George – ironic given the comparative state of race relations in the two armies now – and only then did Washington allow blacks to enlist. Almost a hundred years later, during the first few years of the Civil War, Union forces refused to enlist black soldiers on the grounds that it was 'a white man's war'. Black abolitionists fought hard for the right to take up arms against the South. Said Frederick Douglass: 'Once let the black man get upon his person the brass letters, US; let him get an eagle on his button, and a musket on his shoulder and bullets in his pocket and there is no power on earth which can deny that he has earned the right to citizenship.' Only after 1863 was his wish granted.

The white generals' reluctance was understandable. It is one thing denying people their basic human rights when they are in chains. But once you give them loaded guns and teach them how to shoot, it is not long before they will force you to reconsider your views on their place in civil society. In both the revolution of 1776 and the Civil War, it was neither arguments about citizenship nor freedom that convinced white leaders to allow blacks to fight. It was not an abstract notion of liberty, but a pragmatic desire to win the wars they were waging that tipped the balance. But still, from 1863 until after the Second World War, blacks who were allowed to fight did so in segregated regiments. It took a threat by Philip A. Randolph, the head of the Brotherhood of Sleeping Car Porters, a black union for those who worked the railroads, to change all that. In the spring of 1948, Randolph threatened to stage a march on Washington and a nationwide campaign of civil disobedience unless President Truman agreed to desegregate the armed forces. Truman obliged.

By the time of the Korean War of 1950 – before Brown, before the Montgomery bus boycott and while King was still at college – blacks and whites were fighting in formally integrated units. Today, twenty-seven per cent of all US personnel on active duty are black – more than twice the proportion of African-Americans in the nation as a whole. They make up twenty-four per cent of the lower enlisted ranks, thirty-five per cent of non-commissioned officers and twelve per cent of commissioned officers. The first black man to look like a serious contender for the American presidency, Colin Powell, came through the army. The few times I went to the campuses at historically black universities I saw both students and soldiers strutting around in military uniform, and several posters calling on blacks to join the armed forces.

It remains for me one of the country's great paradoxes that an institution that plays such a reactionary role on the world stage can be so progressive in its internal workings. It is one of the few areas where black people feel confident that they can get on. In the civil service, black employees are nearly two and a half times more likely to be sacked than whites. In the army they are twenty per cent less likely to suffer the same fate.

'One major American institution contradicts the prevailing race paradigm,' write Butler and Mokos in their book, *All That We Can Be.* 'It is an organization unmatched in its level of racial integration. It is an institution unmatched in its broad record of black achievement. It is a world in which the Afro-American heritage is part and parcel of the institutional culture. It is the only place in American life where whites are routinely bossed around by blacks. The institution is the US Army.'

And yet there are still problems.

James H. Burmeister II wanted a spider's web tattoo. On 7 December 1995, the twenty-year-old from Thompson, Pennsylvania, who was stationed at Fort Bragg, had joked about getting one all night. But he had to earn it, and the skinhead badge of honour did not come cheap. To get it, he had to kill a black or a gay.

That night, after he finished his dinner, he went for a drive into town with two of his colleagues from the 82nd Airborne Division. At the wheel was Randy Lee Meadows Jr.; the third man was Burmeister's friend, Malcolm Wright. Wright already had his tattoo; Burmeister had a 9mm Ruger pistol. They went into a bar and drank some beers.

After they left the bar, they cruised around looking for blacks to harass and attack in the African-American area of town, but did not have much luck. Then they spotted Jackie Burden, twenty-two, and Michael James, thirty-six, two black people walking down the street. Wright asked Meadows to stop the car and told him to stay there and wait for them.

The next thing Meadows heard was gunshots. Six of them. He got out of the car to check that his friends were all right but could not find them. Minutes later, police found Burden and James dead in a pool of blood. James had been shot in the head; Burden in the head and back.

Wright and Burmeister never did go back to the car, choosing instead to catch a cab back to Burmeister's trailer, where they went to sleep. When the police caught Meadows near the scene and arrested him, he gave them a statement and led them to the trailer. There they found white-supremacist literature, a bomb-making manual and pamphlets on Hitler and Nazi Germany. At the trial of the three men, photographs were produced showing Burmeister performing the Nazi salute in front of a swastika. His ex-girlfriend said he had become involved in skinhead activities earlier that year and liked to listen to songs like 'Third Reich', a white-power anthem about killing blacks and Jews.

The case sent shock waves through the armed forces. An institution that prided itself on racial tolerance had racist killers in its ranks. Burmeister, Wright and Meadows had already been discharged along with others who actively participated in groups which shared their views. Burmeister and Wright were sentenced to life while Meadows was released after testifying for the prosecution. A community forum was convened at the behest of the local NAACP chapter, whose officials were allowed to tour Fort Bragg and question soldiers about racism and extremism. But an investigation into white-supremacist activity found little evidence of widespread organized hate groups in the army. Even so, the army toughened up its policies to prevent them taking root.

In a prefab in Fort Bragg I interviewed three black soldiers – Sergeant Jacqueline Stewart, First Sergeant Debra Brown and Private Momulu Soine – all dressed in khaki with huge leather boots. One of their superiors, Major Thomas Moyer, who arranged the interviews for me, was also in the room.

The drive up from Orangeburg to the base had been straightforward, although finding Major Moyer's cabin took a while. Peculiarly, there was nobody to check me coming on or off the base. Among all the construction work and the identical World War Two type bunkers dotted around, I had to stop a few times and wander into an office to ask directions to Major Moyer. Without being asked for a press pass or letter of introduction, I would be pointed on my way. I was impressed by the openness but wondered why the Hezbollah or Zapatistas had never tried this.

After a coffee and a chat about the relative merits of British and American media relations and journalism, Major Moyer took me to meet my three interviewees. All had come to the army via very different routes. Stewart, twenty-eight, a slim woman with a Caribbean lilt, grew up in Jamaica and moved to the Bronx, New York, in 1991. She joined the military in 1993 because she likes travelling, and so far has been to Korea, Texas, Missouri and South Carolina. First Sergeant Brown, a gregarious woman who loves to laugh, grew up in Tampa, Florida, and joined the army in 1983. She joined to get 'a different perspective on life' after a year as a teacher's assistant back home. Private Soine, a baby-faced teenager with halting English, had recently arrived from Liberia. He joined the army after he saw an advertisement in a magazine. 'The opportunities just weren't there [in Liberia]. When I came to America I read something and then got some brochures. I thought it would give me the opportunity to go to school,' he said.

All of them claimed never to have suffered any racist abuse in the army. Only one of them, Stewart, would admit there was any racism in the military at all: 'I know it's there. It's just never come directly to me,' she said.

All emphasized that they have to work closely with white colleagues to get their jobs done. 'If they are your superiors and they say jump, you jump,' they say. 'If they are your colleagues then you will have to rely on them in your time of need.' Army folk, it seems, are too busy to be prejudiced.

But do they socialize with white people? 'No. Work is work,' said Stewart. 'After work, people stick together.' Even though there is a large African-American population outside the base, the soldiers rarely go into town. 'The military is much safer. If somebody does something to you, you can track them down,' says Stewart. 'They will rob you down town in the drive-thru line,' adds Brown.

Even a mention of Burmeister, Wright and the racist murders that occurred two years earlier fails to tease out any thorny issues. Brown said she received worried calls from her parents. 'For a while, Fort Bragg was the ugliest place in the world just because of one or two incidents. There is a process now to monitor and weed out those people. There are tattoo checks, and equal opportunity officers have gotten involved. Fort Bragg is OK.'

Clearly, one cannot read a whole lot into interviews like these, especially when the interviewees have been picked by one superior and another one is sitting in the room. But coupled with conversations I had had with other African-Americans, I think some things can be said with confidence.

None of the interviewees saw a conflict of interest between being black and joining the army before they enlisted. Whatever else they 'perceived' the army to be, they did not 'perceive' it to be racist – or at least no more racist than anywhere else, and probably a lot less. Being black in the US Army was not a very big deal to them. And even when I got them to concede the hypothetical existence of racism in the army, all were convinced it would not be tolerated by those in charge if it came to light. Those factors in themselves set the US Army apart from Britain's.

Major Moyer took me to see Sergeant First Class Stephanie Gerami-Henderson, who is involved in anti-racist training and personnel work. Ms Henderson, whose mother is Native American and whose father is Italian, grew up in Texas during the oil boom but 'wanted to do more'. All but one of the five children in her family joined the army. When we walked into her room she was wading through a report on extremist gangs. 'They try and get young soldiers to join because they are vulnerable and have access to weapons. Not many of them, but enough for us to keep a close eye on,' she said. Any further explanation was cut short by a knock at the door.

A tall, well-built black man, Colonel Porter, walked in with an armful of stripes and a chest of medals. Everybody in the room, including me, jumped up. Moyer and Henderson saluted. I nodded. Porter had a brief conversation with Sergeant Gerami-Henderson and then left.

A black man walks in. A white man and a woman of Italian/Native American descent jump to their feet and salute him as their superior. Then he walks out. Simple as that. Only in America. And even then, only in the military.

CHAPTER SEVEN

Georgia: Somebody's Son

The Freedom Riders stopped in Georgia for two nights and one day of rest. While they were there, Martin Luther King invited them to a prestigious black-owned restaurant where he shook each of them by the hand, praised their efforts as non-violent direct action at its best and generally lifted their spirits. The one thing he didn't do, as Farmer ruefully observed, was pay for the meal.

After the dinner, King took the Ebony *and* Jet *reporter, Simeon Booker, aside and warned him: 'You will never make it through Alabama.' Booker tried to laugh it off and told King he would stay close to the corpulent Farmer — 'He's the only one I can outrun.'*

During the previous week, Farmer's father's health had been deteriorating rapidly. He had pleaded with his son not to venture into Alabama, for he feared for his life. That night, he died, and his son granted him his last wish. Farmer left the Ride for his father's funeral in Washington. His troops started their journey into Alabama, the Freedom Ride's most dangerous terrain, without him.

The sunset was seeping through the Spanish moss as I made my way down Savannah's Victory Drive to my Aunt Judy's. On the right stood large Georgian houses, to the left tennis courts, on both sides palmettos danced to a soft, cool breeze.

Five minutes in Savannah is all it takes to know you could not be anywhere else. It looks as though someone took Edinburgh's architecture, Cape Town's weather and Naples' café culture, injected Berlin's decadence from the thirties and then plonked it on America's south-eastern shores. Among its twenty-one shaded squares there are places where you can sip coffee, read papers and dissolve into comfy sofas. You can go for walks through the old town or along the riverside and stop off to browse in bookshops or drink in bars – simple pleasures that I had not been able to enjoy since I was in Richmond.

The town's beauty is now legend thanks to what locals call the 'Book', John Berendt's *Midnight in the Garden of Good and Evil*, a work of non-fiction which has transformed the town from a minor outpost of Georgian eccentricity into a living cultural artefact. Since its publication in 1994, visitors to Savannah have doubled in number. The 'Book' has been translated into eighteen languages and broke the longevity record for the *New York Times* bestseller list after more than three years in the top twenty. The 'Book' has created several hundred jobs and sent property prices in the historic district rocketing. But having basked in a few years of fame, Savannah's natives are restless, tired of the tourists clogging up the pavement and crowding out their favourite bars.

Driving past the historic district, which is where most of the Book is set, over two bridges, past a long line of video stores, fast-food joints and garages, you arrive in suburbia where my Aunt Judy, the youngest of my father's sisters, lives with her son Ajani and husband Charles.

During my childhood, Aunt Judy lived in an out-of-focus picture that my mother must have taken in 1974 when we went to Barbados for six weeks. Wearing an impossibly short miniskirt and impossibly long Afro, one foot neatly placed at an angle in front of the other, she was a tall, beige, shapely figure on a beach. Her hair is shorter now, and tinted red, but she is otherwise a more mature version of the original.

I was given a welcome fit for a nephew. Judy approved of my haircut – 'You look like somebody's son,' she said; cooked coconut bread and souse in my honour; and lent me her washing machine to relieve my clothes of their traveller's whiff. It was a welcome change from motel life. I was fed until I could barely walk unassisted to the sofa, where I watched TV with her and Charles while the heavens wept outside. I told her tales from my travels, and she laughed an indulgent, aunt's laugh. We talked about me, her, family and life while Ajani, a lanky thirteen-year-old, did things I couldn't understand on the computer in the back room.

Judy has been in America for around fifteen years but goes 'home' every few years and often sends Ajani to Barbados to stay with family. By the time she was ready to leave the island, much of the immigration to Britain had dried up, but there were still many opportunities in America. She started out in Texas, then moved to Virginia and a few years ago came down to Georgia, an honorary citizen of the former Confederacy.

On balance, her life appears less stressful than those of her generation who went to Britain. While other aunts of mine, who are nursing in London, are struggling with restructured NHS grades and waiting to pay off their mortgages and retire, Judy, a contract nurse, is paid a premium for her flexibility and the lack of security that allows her to fit her working life around her own needs.

While issues of race are important to her – she walked out of a film not so long ago because she thought it was racist – she has bypassed, apparently unfazed, those aspects of the South's racial labyrinth that she finds most egregious. She lives in an integrated area; Ajani goes to an integrated school; she calls churches before she attends them to check that they are not segregated.

When I told her about my book and the Freedom Riders, she sighed and said it must be tough being an African-American. 'When you think of all they went through and how recently it was. And right here in their own country. I mean, at least if I don't like it I can go home. They don't know anywhere else. And they would sit there with people beating them and protest peacefully. I don't know that I could have gone through all of that. Not in my own country.'

Similarly Ajani appears to have far less trouble navigating his national identity than I did at his age. I was eighteen before I would ever admit that I was British. Before then, depending on my mood, I used to either dodge the question with a shrug and a surly 'dunno', insist that it didn't matter, or say I was from Barbados, even though I'd only been there for six weeks when I was four.

But when I went to work as a teacher in Sudan, none of these responses really worked. I was teaching Eritrean refugees with three white boys, and local people would come up to me and start speaking Arabic, expecting me to translate for them. When it became clear that I didn't have a clue what they were saying, they would ask where I was from. Saying, 'Dunno,' would have made me look simple. And most people had never heard of Barbados. I learnt from a Sudanese friend how to say, 'I was born in England but my mother comes from Jamaica.' I'd never been to Jamaica and, given island rivalries, my mother would have boiled me alive if she knew I had cast her as a Jamaican. But thanks to Bob Marley, the Sudanese had at least heard of the place. It was a fudge I could live with, but I knew it was time to come up with something more convincing. The fact that I was working with Eritrean refugees simply rubbed my face in my dilemma. Here I was, among people who had a very strong sense of national identity but no country because it was being occupied; I had two free countries to choose from, complete with passports, borders and national sports teams that the whole world recognized, and still I couldn't make up my mind about where I was from.

The breakthrough came after the general election of 1987 when one of my Sudanese friends came up, thrust an Arabic newspaper in my face and congratulated me on the election of my 'compatriots'. Four black MPs had been voted in. Before then my insistence that I had been born and raised in Britain had been ridiculed by most Sudanese, who simply didn't believe me. Now there was not only proof but congratulations. Black Britons did exist. I was not just making it up.

This was not an epiphany. I knew I hadn't been making it up. But it did provide the basic ingredients for a different flavour of fudge. I was British, but not like the guys I had come to Sudan to work with. That was evident, not just in the stories we would tell about our lives back home, but in the local market, where, so long as I shopped on my own, I would be offered local prices because people thought I was a local person. And it was clear from Western tourists, who would often wave me away in the belief that I was 'just another Sudanese' coming to bother them for money and cigarettes.

Identities suffocate if trapped in the narrow confines of a definition for too long. But everyone needs a working title. From then on I decided I could be black and British and anyone who wanted to challenge my claim to either of these could expect a ferocious response. I saw none of this confusion or defiance in Ajani. Ask him where he is from, and he says America. He wouldn't deny his Bajan heritage, but it does not intrude on his sense of being American. This intrigued me because Ajani, and my other American cousins – I have about six or seven – are my peers. Like my mother, their parents left Barbados and had children abroad, and those children are growing up as second-generation immigrants. It is the closest thing you can get to laboratory conditions for looking at the different ways that America and England affect your sense of racial identity.

In my daydreamy moments, throughout my trip, I had wondered what my life would have been like if my mother had come to America. I imagined myself in a parallel universe, with a Brooklyn accent, a New York attitude and hip hop style. The possibilities in that life seem endless. I would have grown up with a choice of anyone from Michael Jordan to Henry Louis Gates Jr. as role models, whereas in Britain we had to pick between Frank Bruno, Lenny Henry and Trevor McDonald. But despite that I was glad that she had moved to England instead. America is hot on success but tough on failure, and the chasm between the successful and the failures is wide and scary. If I had grown up as a young black male in America, I would have been more likely to go to college and get a decent job than I ever was in Britain. But if Ajani had grown up in Britain, he would have a longer life expectancy and be less likely to end up in jail.

It sounds like a facile juxtaposition – you can be educated and wealthy in America or alive and out of prison in England – and in many ways it is. But growing up as the child of an immigrant, I inherited a distinct sense of precariousness and vulnerability in Britain. My mother arrived in a 'host country' and therefore was often treated like a 'guest'. If she overstayed her welcome or questioned the host's hospitality, she might be denounced as an ingrate and shown the door. Some of that got passed down to me – a feeling that I was being tolerated, there on sufferance, and that, regardless of my degree or professional track record or anything else, I could at any moment be driven to some rundown area, dropped off and told: 'This is where you belong, now stay there.' I felt, in the words of black British author Andrea Levy, 'Never far from Nowhere'. And Nowhere, in America, without a welfare state and with an endemic gun culture, looks like a much more scary, chilling place than it does in Britain.

After four days of being washed, fed and generally indulged by Aunt Judy, I made my way to Atlanta. Atlanta is where the money is and where the black people are. At the airport car rental offices the queues were winding back on themselves, mostly black people aged between twenty and forty, in classic corporate shirts and blouses, all wrapped up in woollen three-quarter-length coats and carrying briefcases so shiny they looked as though they had been polished.

The airport, the second busiest in the world, is the hub for Delta Airlines, which dominates the Southern skies. If you die and go to hell, goes one Southern saying, you will probably have to change in Atlanta. While you are alive, Atlanta is Buppie heaven.

Look in your fridge, on your TV or in your post box and you can probably find something bearing the mark MADE IN ATLANTA. It is home to the headquarters of Coca Cola, CNN and the courier company UPS. In 1994, 420 of *Fortune*'s 500 top industrial companies had offices in Atlanta. The city has been transformed from what used to be thought of as a provincial backwater into a cosmopolitan, fashionable and lucrative metropolis. In the 1970s, there was one sushi bar in the entire city. With 150 Japanese firms in town, it now has thirty.

But the biggest change has been in the suburbs, where qualified middle-class blacks have been swarming in for the past twenty years, areas like Decatur and Stone Mountain, where clipped lawns and two cars in the garage come with an acute sense of racial awareness and high expectations of professional achievement.

Atlanta is the capital of what they call the New South, a place renowned for low wages and weak unions, which needed stability and well-educated workers for capital to come flooding in. So long as segregation was maintained, this was never going to happen. But as racial barriers started coming down, the investors started rolling in. This was the South's reward for swapping racial bigotry for a place in the global economy, shedding its dependence on the rural and unskilled labour in favour of high-tech manufacturing and service industries.

During the post-war years, the mechanization of cotton picking forced impoverished blacks up north in their millions. For many, the choice was not difficult. You could pick cotton amid viciously enforced segregation on a plantation for $2 a week, most of which went back to the landlords in rent; or you could make seventy-five cents an hour in a factory up north, where race relations were believed to be better.

Black people voted with their livelihoods. In 1940, seventy-seven per cent of black Americans lived in the South, and forty-nine per cent were rural. By 1970, black America was only half Southern, and seventy-five per cent lived in cities.

But now, they are coming back. Every state in the former Confederacy has shown a year-on-year increase in its black population since 1990, according to the US census bureau. They are pulled by low living costs, better career prospects and a warmer climate; pushed by the North's more frantic pace, cold ways and a realization that the racism there is just as bad as in the South, simply better hidden. The most segregated city in the country is not Jackson, Mississippi, but Gary, Indiana. With the exception of the lynching in Jasper, Texas, in 1998, the racial outrages that have defined the nineties have emerged not in the South but in the West (the beating of Rodney King by policemen in Los Angeles and the riots that ensued after a predominantly white jury exonerated them) and in the East (the Haitian man who had a plunger stuffed up his rectum by a policeman in New York). The only person capable of organizing and promoting the Million-Man March, Louis Farrakhan, is based not in the South but in Chicago.

During the civil rights era, white Southerners were keen to point out to pious Northerners that whites in the rural South had more contact with black people than urban white Northerners ever did. White Southerners were often raised and even breast-fed by blacks. Those who could not afford separate slave quarters lived with blacks. In the North, blacks lived in areas segregated by the custom and practice of discrimination rather than by law. Within these self-sufficient, autonomous communities, some amassed considerable wealth and power, but few were ever accepted in white society. 'In the North, it doesn't matter how big you get, just how close,' the saying went. 'In the South, it doesn't matter how close you get, just how big.'

For the past twenty years the South has been swollen with smug self-congratulation for how far it has moved on since the turn of the century. In 1938 President Roosevelt branded the South the nation's number one economic problem; today if the eleven states of the former Confederacy were a separate country it would be the fourth largest economy in the world. But a quick look at the census figures shows just how incomplete a picture of the South this is. The

South has the top five states for infant mortality, four of the top five for teenage pregnancies, and three for both violent crime and the proportion of people who live below the poverty line. Meanwhile it has three of the bottom five states for median household income. Only one of them, Virginia, which has the eighth highest level of median household income, is in the top ten for anything positive.

You can see these statistics pushing prams in South Carolina, sitting on porches in Mississippi and in the crime pages of newspapers in Alabama. A disproportionate amount of this poverty, ill heath and social meltdown is concentrated in black communities.

This does not mean that the South is not changing. In some areas it is changing fast. It is radically different from the way it was thirty or forty years ago but, a bit like Tony Blair's New Labour, the New South is a mixture of PR jingle and political construct – it has made a definite break from its past but is still defined more by what it has abandoned than what it actually is.

Atlanta provides the most explicit illustration that there is a lot of wealth, as well as a lot of poverty, in black America. You can see it in the black magazines. In *Ebony* and *Emerge* there are adverts for prestige products like Cadillacs and Rémy Martin. Most ads in Britain's black newspaper, the *Voice*, are for jobs in local government.

Some of this has to do with time. African-Americans, as so many of the people I spoke to throughout my trip were keen to emphasize, are one of the oldest ethnic groups in the country. They may all have come over in the same boat as slaves, but the past hundred and fifty years have given them time to go their separate ways. Having landed on the moon, sat on the Supreme Court and led their country into war, there are not that many barriers, the White House excepted, that black America still has to break.

Some have risen through America's class structure to emerge rich and professionally successful in government, business, entertainment and academia. Others have sunk below it, descending to the very bottom, where welfare, drugs, violence and prison are just a way of life. And then there are the vast numbers in between, with pension plans, car pools and regular jobs, who march in time with, although to a different tune from, the rest of mainstream America.

There is not one black America, but several. Enough to split up into different classes and for one class not really to know, and at times be unable even to recognize, another. So much so that when I arrived in Washington DC, African-American colleagues at the *Washington Post* told me to be careful when going to certain impoverished black areas. They did so for a good reason: they were dangerous places with a record of high and violent crime, where so few people visited that a stranger would easily be spotted and robbed or worse. Still, the warning made me uncomfortable because I felt like I was being told to look in the mirror and be afraid. I have never felt this in Britain because we have not been in the country long enough to develop such disparate experiences.

Our parents' boats docked far more recently. Most have been in the country in any significant numbers for only forty years or so, and most arrived with a lot in common. They were abroad, had very little money and were hired to do similar sorts of jobs – low-paid public-sector work in health or transport. Back home, their island differences felt huge, but in Britain, their black immigrant experience bound them fast. They enjoyed similar sports (cricket, racing and dominoes, which becomes a sport when West Indians play it) and listened to the same kind of music (calypso, socca). So, in Britain, the black community is only beginning to stratify.

Our parents had a shared experience; my generation shares experiences. Our parents were pioneers to a different land; we are pioneers within our own country. We are seeking out new classes, tastes and places to work, rest and play; we are constantly finding ourselves the first to arrive.

In the United States, groups of wealthy black people occupy entire suburbs, not just in Atlanta, but around Washington DC, Charlotte, Houston and Chicago. There are enough of them to fill a fairly expensive restaurant, a night club and a couple of dinner parties all on the same night with not a white person in sight. They have moved a great distance from where their ancestors started out, and have had a long, long time to get there.

I doubt we will ever see this in Britain. But this is not only to do with time; it is also to do with numbers. Not that there aren't a significant number of black people in the UK who earn a decent amount of money. But there aren't enough, nor will there ever be, to create an entire, self-sufficient, social scene with the purchasing power of the black American middle class. And class in Britain is far more rigid than it is in the States. There, you can earn your way into a class. Go to college, get a good job, move to the suburbs, and you are middle class, regardless of what your parents did or what school you went to, what accent you have or where you grew up. To be middle class in America is a badge of honour. But in Britain you are born into a class. And regardless of how much you earn or what you have achieved, your die has already been cast. Say dinner instead of lunch, go out for a meal that is anything other than Indian or Chinese, or drink bottled water, and people will start to make assumptions about how you vote and what you do on a Saturday night. Class in Britain is not just about salary and social standing — it's a badge of authenticity. To describe someone as middle class is almost an insult. It comes between 'typical' and 'wanker'. Working-class people can be proud that they have made it through life without any privileges. Upper-class people can be bullish about the fact that they have lots of privileges. But middle-class people – black or white – are in an ugly and rootless no-man's-land.

After queuing for almost half an hour at Atlanta airport, I was told that I had a choice between a 'soccer mom' seven-seater minivan and a luxury car which cost twice as much. I took the van and drove off to look for somewhere to stay.

Driving in Atlanta is a scary thing – you can be doing seventy on a slip road, and it will not feel as though you are going fast enough. You can be doing sixty in the slow lane, and the cars behind you will still make out you are holding them up. The week I was there, a man was shot by another motorist for overtaking.

I drove to the district of Auburn, formerly known as Sweet Auburn, the area where Martin Luther King was born, where his father preached, and where he was laid to rest with the words *Free at last, free at last, thank God Almighty, free at last* engraved on his granite tomb. When it was Sweet, Auburn was home to Atlanta's black middle class, the Southern Christian Leadership Conference (SCLC) which organized much of the protest during the fifties and sixties, and the Top Hat Club which hosted Duke Ellington and the Supremes.

At the top of Auburn Avenue, near Peachtree Street, there are portraits hanging from the lamp-posts of the black entrepreneurs who ran the area in the past. As you walk down the hill and into its present, it becomes clear how long gone those days are.

Five minutes away, beneath the underpass where the traffic roars overhead, stands a plaque:

Pause and look up at this massive overpass. An entire block of black-owned businesses were destroyed to construct it. The highway's curving ramps drove a concrete wedge through the Auburn Avenue Community, separating businesses from customers and one from one another. Today the overpass ... pays tribute to the black-owned businesses, shops and restaurants that closed their doors forever in this section of Auburn.

As you start to climb another small incline you come to the office of the SCLC, which is still in its original place. On the doors there is a picture of King, with tears pouring down his face, hovering over a crowd of black faces. Underneath is a picture of Joseph Lowery, the recently retired Chairman, and the message, *Stop the killing. End the violence. Let us turn to each other, not on each other.* Further up the hill are some good record shops and fast-food places, a police station and several tramps. At the top is the civil rights district, where I spent several hours. Within a few hundred square yards stands King's tomb, Ebenezer Baptist church, where his father used to preach, the house where King was born, and a civil rights museum preserved by the National Park Service. There is also a popular soul-food establishment, modestly called The Beautiful Restaurant. At the counter is the famous picture of King and Malcolm X on the one occasion they met. Over the top is the message: *Dine with freedom in mind.* I did.

That evening I had an appointment to meet Ken Reid at Denny's Restaurant, just off the Old National Highway. Reid is the publisher of Atlanta's Black Pages, a telephone and Internet directory of black-owned and -run businesses and other companies looking either to contract or serve African-Americans in the area. Reid is the man who sells black

Atlanta to other black Atlantans, and some white ones, too. I was looking for someone with a bird's-eye view of what commercial black Atlanta is doing. What I didn't know, when I called his office to ask for an interview, is that he was born in Liverpool.

Reid's Jamaican-born father is an American citizen. His mother is English. He spent most of his childhood and adolescence in Liverpool, but came to Queens, New York, to see his father in the holidays. Toxteth was his home; his accent is a curious hybrid of Southern and Scouse.

Reid was the first English person I had interviewed on my trip. When Reid said football he meant football; eleven men with no helmets, a round piece of leather, two goals and a referee. For the first time in a long time I heard words like two-tone, mods, poll tax and Finsbury Park, and not having to add context to every last detail and anecdote made me feel both comfortable and a long way from home. No more convoluted explanations: I could use shorthand. Here I was, wandering around the South trying to deconstruct the building blocks of my racial identity, and now drooling over these small and random links with Britain. Home, it seems, is wherever you're not.

We drove to a bar and drank some beers as Reid told me his story – a tale of taut bootstraps and rugged individualism with a Toxteth twist. Reid, a bearded, witty man whom you could just about imagine not wearing a suit, but only just, grew up in a multiracial area of Liverpool, home to Britain's oldest black community. It contained a mix of ethnicities which existed in very few places in the country during the early sixties. 'My school was like the United Nations. There were Africans, Chinese, Indians. You name it. You were lucky in my school if you learnt English, let alone black history.'

He was raised at a time when England prided itself on separating the 'achievers' from the 'stragglers' before their teens. 'I liked school but it wasn't particularly important to me. I didn't pass the eleven-plus. In those days, if you didn't pass those exams, the likelihood was that unless you got a trade of some sort then your options would be severely impaired.'

When he left school he wanted to join the merchant marines but was turned down. 'They told me point blank that they didn't take blacks here,' he recalled. His father made him come to America in 1967, when he was seventeen, although he says he had no real desire to.

'I was a messenger for a photostat company. I used to have to pick up the rush jobs, but I learnt quite a bit about the publishing trade. Then I went to university and was an accountancy and finance major.'

The combination of his experience in the publishing trade and his commercial studies guided him towards Black Pages and Atlanta. 'Whenever you ran into people they would say that Atlanta is the place. New York was getting claustrophobic. Everything that you can think of has been done already in New York, and it's too large a market to penetrate with something like this. I thought about Denver, Houston and Atlanta. I needed the open spaces. I counted out Colorado because it was too cold. Here you get more bangs for your buck and the cost of living is low.'

African-Americans in Atlanta have a lot of bucks. That is why Reid believes that, as well as providing a service, he is helping to democratize the local economy. 'To every action there is a reaction. Every time you spend a dollar it's like casting a vote. You are saying, "I like what you are doing and what your company is doing." But ninety-five per cent of the black dollar is spent outside the black community. You can't blame white people for that. Sometimes black people should look in the mirror.'

Reid believes that Black Pages could work in Britain but

doubts he would ever have been in a position to launch it. 'I don't think I would have made it the same way. It would have been more difficult.' It wasn't just the combination of race and class prejudice that would have stood in his way, he says, but more importantly an attitude.

'If you had an idea in those days in Liverpool then it would be ridiculed. When I went back they'd say, "What are you doing now?" And I would say accountancy and they would say, "You don't have the brains to do that." It's difficult to find encouragement and to move forward; either you have to move together with everyone else, or people start resenting you. The British class system is so stifling.'

Reid is not a blind devotee of America's greatest myths and Britain's greatest failings. But he is a black businessman in a country that reveres business and in a city that celebrates its blackness. When he does return to England, it is to visit his mother, who now lives in Crewe, and to go in search of the heady times of his youth, the nights when he and his friends DJ'd in clubs, playing soul, reggae and some ska. Invariably he returns to America disappointed. 'The fondest memories of my life are from my childhood in England. But when I go back I usually just find desperation and confusion. If you're doing better than your mates are in England, they think you think you are better than they are, which could be true but usually isn't. America did have something to do with my success. It's more proactive here. It's a young country. It's like work in progress.'

As I walked into the Richard B. Russell Federal building, a rectangular block of cement in downtown Atlanta that would have done Stalin's architects proud, there was a man offering pens, a red, white and blue sweet and a ribbon of the same colours to pin on my lapel.

In the basement, it looked as though a wedding was about to take place, to which relatives from all over the world had been invited. Excited chatter in many tongues filled the room, as did babies in prams, dads with cameras, old folk with sticks and women in heels. Most of the people were not white, but of Hispanic, Asian or African descent. Most were wearing ribbons, and absolutely everyone was clutching a sheet of paper.

On the sheet was the pledge of allegiance to the American flag and the oath of citizenship. On a grey, overcast morning in the Deep South, 222 people from fifty-five countries were about to be sworn in as US citizens.

It is a ceremony that would never happen in Britain. Britain is not good at ceremony. Britain does pageantry very well – chariots of gold carrying women in crowns, old men in wigs with staffs and cloaks of ermine, or long nuptial trains for blushing brides in tiaras. But ceremony? No. Not like the Americans, anyway.

My memory of the last days of secondary school is one of sweeping out beer cans from my locker, handing books back to teachers and going for drinks with friends in between. The actual last day is in there somewhere, but I cannot remember it. In America, every Rubicon is marked, every new stage noted. In some places, children 'graduate' from kindergarten. When they get older, there is homecoming parade, the high school prom and graduation. Some of these are borderline compulsory. Americans are about as likely not to turn up to their high-school graduation as they are to miss their own wedding.

So in England, your nationality comes in an envelope and lands on your doormat. In the United States, you get togged up and go and declare it in a room full of strangers.

For the people in the basement that morning, this was the end of a long process. To be eligible for citizenship, you must have been a legal permanent resident for at least five years (or three if you are married to an American); have undergone a fingerprint check by the FBI; have taken an oral test to check your English proficiency; and have passed a written test which demonstrates your knowledge of US history and government.

The number of those trying to jump through these hoops has rocketed over the last decade. Applications for citizenship have leapt from 233,843 in 1990 to 1,482,951 in 1997 – that is more people in one year than in the entire decade from 1911 to 1920, an era characterized as one of massive US immigration.

The rate at which immigrants, be they citizens or not, are coming into the US is transforming the landscape of the racial and political debate. Until the early eighties, when people talked about race relations and diversity, they were referring to blacks and whites. In that regard the South was the most diverse region in America, given that it was the area with the lowest proportion of whites. But the influx of immigrants from Mexico, Latin America and Cuba, particularly to states in the West and Southwest, and the high birth rate among Latinos, is changing all of this. In less than a decade there will be more Hispanics than blacks in America. By the year 2020, whites will be in the minority in California, Texas, New Mexico, Arizona and Nevada as well as Hawaii; Florida will not be far behind. When people talked about immigrants in the past, they could have meant anybody – Poles, Irish, Caribbeans or Italians. Today, they mean Hispanics, and many, black and white, do not speak of them fondly. In a country which once prided itself on opening its doors to the world's poor, the number of those who want to lock them again and throw away the key is growing rapidly.

Xenophobia is not new to America. In the 1850s, opposition to a huge increase in immigration mostly from Ireland

and Germany found a political expression in a group called the Know Nothings. This group of native-born Protestants, formed into secret and select Orders, were anti-booze, anti-immigrant and anti-Catholic. When anyone asked members for information about it, they were supposed to say, 'I know nothing,' hence their name. In the early part of this century an Italian envoy was despatched to Mississippi after pogroms against Italian migrant labour there. But the latest wave of anti-immigration feeling that has swept through the West has taken on a new intensity. In California there have been several referendums on excluding immigrants from welfare and ending bilingual education. Many have already been passed. But in the South, where ethnic tensions are still between English-speaking Americans of different colours, both of whom have been in the country for centuries, these debates hardly ever surface.

Listening to the man welcoming the crowd in the basement of the Richard B. Russell Federal building, you would never guess such tensions existed anywhere. He was greeting them to the America of old, inviting them into the melting pot or the salad bowl or whichever culinary metaphor for diversity is now in vogue.

'We welcome more new citizens than all the other countries in the world combined,' he boasted. 'You have all chosen this country. You have shown an ability to read, write and speak English. You are all different. You come from different parts of the world, you speak different languages, you belong to different religions, you have supported different governments – or maybe you didn't and that's why you are here.' Everyone laughed. 'This is a time of opportunity not only for you but for your family. The opportunity for education. You have the opportunity to vote. And in many ways, that counts twice, because half of the people don't vote. So use your vote wisely.'

He recalled the words of Roberto Goizueta, an immigrant who became the head of Coca Cola, who said there are three main obligations that come with opportunity. 'First of all you have to seize it. Secondly you must live it and carry it with you. And thirdly you must defend it. Opportunity is ours to seize, live and defend. If you don't we will lose it. Please stand.' They stood and took the oath. He thanked and congratulated them. They were free to go.

Leaving the ceremony I was filled with the thrill of someone who has just been to the circus, seen a great magic trick or a gymnastic display. The swearing-in ceremony is patriotic theatre. There is no more need to get 222 people in a room every two weeks to pledge an oath of allegiance together than there is to get everyone whose name begins with D to come to the local council in a certain week and pay all their parking fines. And the stuff about 'Land of Opportunity' comes from the same place that says that anyone who works hard enough in the United States can make it – the implication being that anyone who fails does so because they didn't work hard enough. And yet there was something terrifically impressive about the whole charade. Here was a government official standing up and pounding a lectern, welcoming new citizens and calling on them to take advantage of everything the country has to offer. If there must be rhetoric, and it seems that when it comes to immigrants there must, then let it be that.

America is a land populated by relatively recently arrived immigrants, a country where people champion their heritage from overseas. Almost everybody in America is originally from somewhere else, even the white ones. From Monica Lewinsky and Quentin Tarantino to George Stephanopoulos and Matthew McConaughey, non-Anglo-Saxon names are common currency. Of course, most Brits could lay claim to a heritage from elsewhere – Celts, Norse, Danes and the like – if they wanted to go back far enough. But they don't, and Americans do. So almost everybody in America lays claim to another identity. Almost everybody is entitled to a hyphen – Italian-American, Irish-American, Hungarian-American, African-American – and the hyphen qualifies their American identity but does not undermine it. That is why American politicians, from John F. Kennedy to Newt Gingrich, can go to Ireland to seek out their distant roots. The voters like it.

No British leader would ever do that. People would get suspicious if a prime minister went halfway across the world looking for genealogical sustenance. The punters want people to be British. Foreign names and trips abroad? The voters wouldn't like it. That is why a 'black Briton' does not come with a hyphen. They are two separate words relating to two very distinct and often conflicting identities.

There seemed to be only two things the British establishment wanted to do with my national identity. The first was to threaten me with it. It's an attitude best summed up in an interview with the Tory Party Chairman, Norman Tebbit, in 1990. His test of a true Brit? Who do you support when England is playing cricket? If it is Pakistan, India or the West Indies then maybe that is where you belong. 'Which side do they cheer for?' he asked, referring to black Britons of my generation. 'It's an interesting test. Are you still harking back to where you came from, or where you are? I think we've got real problems in that regard ... you can't have two homes ... Where you have a clash of history, a clash of religion, a clash of race then it's all too easy for there to be an actual clash of violence.' The message here was clear. Back England and renounce the land your parents came from or prepare yourself for a beating.

There are lots of things I would gladly back Britain over:

the NHS, the education system, the welfare state (all of which Tebbit did his best to dismantle); the music scene, *The Fast Show*, the *Today Programme*; the fact the police don't carry guns, the most popular national dish is curry and we don't have capital punishment. Now that I have travelled a bit, and can put the country I grew up in in context, I cannot think of many places I would rather live.

But I remember the first and last time I ever supported England. It was the European Cup quarter finals in 1996, and I went to Wembley with a couple of friends to watch them inflict a shock 4–1 defeat on the Netherlands. It was a great night. But when the game was over and we were making our way out of the stadium a group of supporters started singing 'No surrender to the IRA'. To get the country in the mood for semi-finals against Germany, one newspaper put Gazza and Stuart Pearce in World War Two helmets on the front page with the banner headline: LET'S BLITZ FRITZ. Maybe there is a way to wave the Union Jack and cheer for England and not be associated with all of that. But if there is, I have yet to find it.

The alternative to Tebbit's threat was for people to deny my claim on Britishness altogether. At university I was the student union representative on university court, the highest decision-making body in the institution. At my last meeting an old man, with an accent that would not have shamed an earl – a man to whom I had never spoken before – asked me where I was from.

'Stevenage,' I said.
'Where were you born?'
'I was born there.'
'Well, before then.'
'Well, there was no before then.'
'Well, where are your parents from?'
'Barbados.'

'Ahh, you're from Barbados.'

'No, I'm from Stevenage.'

'I was in Ghana, you know.'

I am not making this up.

'That's a long way from Stevenage and Barbados.'

'Ghana...' he said wistfully. 'Beautiful country ... couldn't last of course ... You're a languages man, aren't you?'

'Yes, I do French and Russian.'

'Know any Twitwe?'

I think he meant Twe but the point had been made. In Britain when people ask you where you are from they often mean one of two things. Either, 'Please tell me you are not from here,' or 'You are from here and here only and don't try to deny it.'

That is the choice. With those two options – threats or denial – you can either submerge yourself into a racist culture or be left out of it altogether. The message from the basement of the Richard B. Russell Federal building was: 'You can make a difference to this country. You are part of what makes this country great.' In Britain the message is: 'Our tolerating you is what makes this country great. Don't spoil it.'

As I left the building, there was another man giving out pin badges showing a Statue of Liberty standing firm against a billowing Stars and Stripes. Underneath was the inscription: 'Give me your tired, your poor, your huddled masses yearning to breathe free.' Mistaking me for a brand-new citizen, he offered me his congratulations: 'Welcome to America, sir.'

I left the couples taking pictures and made my way to Sylvia's Soul Food Restaurant. If evidence were ever needed that Atlanta had made it as a new black metropolis, then it is Sylvia's. The original Sylvia's is in Harlem, where pictures of the black American *beau monde* – James Brown, Jesse Jackson, Ron Brown – hang on the walls. You name them, they have been to Sylvia's, if not for a meal then for a mutually advantageous photo opportunity. Soul-food snobs and New York natives will tell you Sylvia is living on her reputation now, and maybe they are right. Fortunately for her, her reputation, like her portions, is big.

Recently, she sent her daughter south to open up on Central Avenue in Atlanta a more modern-looking place than its Harlem cousin, with a slightly more upmarket but no less distinctive menu. It includes 'smothered pork chops, just like your mama's', 'Sylvia's world-famous talked-about BBQ ribs', 'Sylvia's chocolate decadence' and 'light as a butterfly home-made cornbread'. As the descriptions suggest, soul food is not for the faint-hearted or the picky eater. Each serving is a gut-busting, belt-loosening sin against the waistline, an illustration of why Southerners have the least healthy diets in the nation and of why so many people, seeking refuge from America's body-fascists, love the South so much.

I needed about half an hour and a family-pack of serviettes after every soul food meal just to rid my fingers, face and even clothes of the mixture of sauces and grease in which it was cooked. Rich in taste, and large in quantity, it had more or less the same effect on my insides, as though the entire dish had been covered in Velcro so it could stick to my stomach and lie there as a heavy, permanent reminder of my indulgence. I loved it.

Before I had come to the South, I had been under the impression that soul food was synonymous with black food. I'm not sure where I got that impression from – I probably got it confused with soul music and then had my misapprehension compounded by seeing Aretha Franklin serving fried chicken and singing 'Think' in *The Blues Brothers*. I found out the hard way that it was simply Southern food during a trip to Mississippi a year earlier. The place I was directed to looked nice enough from the outside, but as I walked in I heard the clanking of cutlery stop and conversation fall away – not for long, just for the time it takes an entire room to look up, see a black face, wonder what it is doing, assess the risk, decide it is minimal and look down again. It is the same momentary silence a black person will hear in any rural English pub and in several urban ones, too, the short period where the dart hovers at the dart board, and the beer remains suspended between the tap and the glass. It is a pause just long enough so that everyone notices but short enough so that anyone could claim you were imagining it, a tiny stretch of time which lets you know that you are on trial.

Everyone was looking at me. Everyone else in the room was white. And the wall was covered in Confederate flags. I could have left, but since nobody had done anything to me I walked uncomfortably through the silence and stares, took my seat, ordered my meal and waited to see what would happen. What happened was a very tasty meal. As I got ready to leave, priding myself on having handled the situation so calmly, the waitress, a white elderly woman, came to deliver the bill. 'I bet that's the fastest meal you ever ate,' she said, smiled and then walked off to get my change.

Soul food, just like the Baptist faith and social conservatism, is one of the many things that unite blacks and whites in the South. It originated in the plantation kitchens of the seventeenth and eighteenth centuries, when Africans prepared the food and made dishes from ingredients, like okra, black-eyed peas and watermelon, that they were familiar with. Not that everyone ate the same kind of meal. Slaves were given the things white people wouldn't eat – pigs' intestines, which they used to make chitlins; pigs' ears and feet, with which they made souse; and the cuts of beef and pork that white people didn't want, like ribs. Since slaves didn't have ovens, they usually fried their food or boiled it. They also had to make sure it was filling and nutritious, hence the popularity of potato salad, creamed spinach and green beans.

But the same basic culinary techniques that kept the bellies of the slaves' children full also kept the master happy. When former President Jimmy Carter, who is from Georgia, moved to Washington, one of his staff asked the White House cooks whether they could prepare his favourite kinds of food. 'Yes, ma'am,' said the cook, 'we've been fixing that kind of food for the servants for a long time.'

Dean Carter made me feel like a stalker. I had called him at Morehouse College, one of the oldest, largest and wealthiest historically black colleges in the country, to ask if I could speak to him about the role these institutions played in modern, post-civil-rights era America. My experience of higher education had been so white that the very concept of a black university intrigued me.

Studying in Edinburgh at a time when I was becoming increasingly race conscious had made me feel like a racial cross-dresser. There were very few black Britons there, and not many of those were interested in racial politics. By day I would sweat away over a hot French or Russian prose and attend linguistics classes like everyone else. But by night I would turn into a *Viz*-like character, 'Black Militant', campaigning for black sections in the Labour Party, reading Malcolm X and C. L. R. James and involving myself in anti-racist work in the city. So the idea that you could get an entire college full of black people in a majority-white culture just about blew my mind.

But Dean Carter really didn't want to talk to me. 'I'm really sorry,' he said. 'I don't mean to be rude but I have so many requests of this kind, and if I agreed to all of them I would never get anything done. They are ruining my life.' I said I didn't want to upset him, let alone ruin his life, but wondered if there was someone else I could speak to. He suggested Professor Barksdale, who agreed to an interview, arranged a time for me to meet him at his office and then almost remembered having done so when I knocked on his door at the agreed hour.

Were it not for the pictures of Malcolm X and Martin Luther King and the cartoon of Mount Rushmore full of the great and good in black history hanging on his wall, Professor Barksdale's room could have belonged to a history professor almost anywhere in the Western world – groaning bookshelves, papers strewn haphazardly over his desk, and a computer tucked away in the corner near the window making wild shapes with its screensaver.

Professor Barksdale explained how most of the black colleges sprouted in the immediate aftermath of the Civil War and the passing of the thirteenth amendment which formally abolished slavery in 1865. By the early twentieth century, the end of the Reconstruction era – a brief period when troops and administrators from the North made some attempt to remove official racial barriers from black advancement in the South – government funds for higher education for blacks, as well as the spate of black college building, came to an end.

Today, there are 103 historically black colleges in America, from Lewis Business College in Michigan to Xavier in New Orleans. Most are in the South. Almost every Southern town of a reasonable size has at least one – Greensboro has two; Orangeburg has two; Atlanta has six, including Morehouse. Some receive federal funds, some get money from the United Negro College Fund (UNCF) which funds thirty-nine colleges and their students, and others are purely private. While some of the smaller colleges are struggling to survive, as a whole their record is impressive.

So long as segregation continued these colleges catered exclusively to black people, but over the past thirty years, they have accepted a growing number of whites, hence their rather clumsy title of historically black colleges and universities (HBCUs). Nationwide, thirteen per cent of students in these institutions are white – up fifty per cent on twenty years ago. A handful are virtually indistinguishable from the mainstream white colleges. At the HBCU of Bluefield, West Virginia, white students now make up ninety-three per cent of the student body.

For the most part, however, they provide the starting point for young black Americans' long march to the top of corporate, administrative and academic institutions. Their role in swelling the ranks of black professionals is breathtaking. According to the UNCF, HBCUs have produced seventy-five per cent of black Ph.D.s, eighty-five per cent of black doctors, eighty per cent of black federal judges, and seventy-five per cent of black military officers. Morehouse's alumni include Martin Luther King Jr., film maker Spike Lee and the former US Ambassador to the United Nations and Atlanta Mayor, Andrew Young.

'Most of the people who come here are middle class and suburban or even upper class and suburban,' said Barksdale. 'Bill Cosby's late son came here. But most are middle-class kids who grew up in the suburbs and went to predominantly white schools. Most of Morehouse students don't even come from the South. California is the second largest state that we take from, after Georgia. Often, their parents know they have had a white experience where they have grown up, and will be going out into a white world – because there aren't that many black lawyers or doctors. So they want to make sure that they have that black experience.'

Later, as I roamed around Morehouse's verdant quadrangles, I found myself at an unfamiliar intersection between race and class. Black students in baggy jeans and designer tops were darting in and out of the halls of academia, framed by their portentous turn-of-the-century architecture. From the dorm windows I could hear rap music, rhyming tales of the hard and bloody life in the projects. And on the roads, flashy cars rolled by bearing the Greek insignia of the black fraternities and sororities.

Professor Barksdale had a dinner party to go to and courteously and firmly thanked me for my time. I went to a common room and had just struck up a conversation with a student when two strange things happened one after the other. First of all Spike Lee walked past. I didn't see him at first. One of the students who was crashed out on a sofa shouted, 'Look!' The guy I was talking to, one other person and I turned around just in time to see him stroll through the corridor. The others remained slumped in their chairs as though Spike Lee walks through their college every day.

Shortly afterwards, a tall man with the shiniest shoes I have ever seen and a chest full of medals strapped to an army uniform strutted in. 'Either of you guys want to see a black astronaut speak?' For someone just to come up out of the blue with an offer like this on a university campus was, for me, the equivalent of being asked if I wanted to see a bearded lady tame a lion on a tightrope. I followed the man with the dazzling shoes.

The astronaut was a small man with a pleasant manner and big ears who looked like a black Ross Perot. He had drawn a crowd of about forty or fifty. His advice to the students sounded like a sequel to the speech I had heard at the swearing-in ceremony earlier that morning.

'You've got to study hard, work hard, and you cannot be afraid of failure. Most of the time we stop ourselves from doing the things we want to do. We are afraid that we are going to fail, that someone is going to laugh at us or someone is going to say no to us. That is between you and the Maker. The only person who can stop you doing something you want to do is you.'

It is at times like this that I wonder whether I am a cynic, a realist or one of those whiney Limeys who would have kept Ken Reid (of Black Pages) from achieving his ambitions in England.

The astronaut went on exhorting the students to do the right thing, mixing the philosophies of Dale Carnegie and Chairman Mao with ease. 'You must remain involved in your community. You got to go home and help the kids who are struggling,' he said.

Then he showed slides of people with guns and said he had a 'good time in Vietnam'. It was all very weird and the weirdest thing was that, if facial expressions are anything to go by, nobody thought it was weird apart from me.

In between came questions.

'Of all the branches of the military, it seems the one area where African-Americans have not excelled is piloting. Why is that?' asked one student.

'Good question,' said the astronaut. 'Partly because black people are principally motivated by money, and to be a pilot takes a lot of training when you are not going to be making a lot of money.' Everyone nodded. 'Also, if you stand on the outside and wonder why there's problems there will still be problems. You cannot solve a problem from the outside. You have to get in to solve it.'

Just after that I left. The lectern-thumping enthusiasm of the swearing-in ceremony earlier had been enough for one day. I felt one more rallying call would push me over the edge. I walked back from Morehouse campus to the centre of town. Halfway there, the dark, pendulous clouds which had been scowling at the city all day lightened their load. With no obvious shelter in sight I decided to abandon myself to the elements.

By the time I got back to my motel, I was soaked. I hung my drenched clothes over the radiator, had a hot bath, dialled out for a Chinese meal, took a soggy trip out to the vending machine for a drink and settled down for a night of bad TV. As the rain beat at my window I longed for my image of crickets chirping in fields full of magnolia.

At the Atlanta Greyhound station at six thirty in the morning, a weary mix of fatigue and poverty made everybody move in slow motion. There were people emerging from night buses with blankets over their shoulders or hugging pillows. Others were sprawled across the floor, resting their heads on huge boxes bound with string, waiting for journeys that would take them at least a day. Their heavy steps and haggard faces made them look like refugees fleeing some awful famine or tyrant, people who kept going because they were afraid to stop.

We drove in tired silence through Georgia and back in time (there is an hour's difference) to Alabama. I got off at Anniston and went straight to the toilet. A man's voice came over the cubicle. At first I couldn't really understand what he was saying. It was a very thick, Southern accent. I could hear each individual sound, but putting them all together into a language I understood I found problematic. In the end I worked out that he was warning me the bus had just arrived. I told him I had just got off it: 'You comin' into Anniston? I'd just get back on that bus while you still got the chance and move on 'cos there's nothing to do here,' he said.

CHAPTER EIGHT

Alabama: Michael's last walk, Henry's last meal

When the Freedom Riders stopped in Heflin, just inside the Alabama border, drivers heading eastward warned the Greyhound driver there was trouble ahead at Anniston. Less than two hours and a car chase later, the Freedom Riders were firebombed.

The campaigners were taken to hospital, but the racists still did not give up the chase. Hospital staff, fearing reprisals from the crowd outside, refused to treat them and ordered them to leave. The Riders called Fred Shuttlesworth, Birmingham's civil rights leader, and asked for assistance. Not long after, a convoy of armed clergymen were on their way to help them.

When the Trailways bus arrived in Anniston shortly afterwards, eight white youths got on and started physically to move the black Freedom Riders to the back. When Peck and Bergman tried to stop them, they were beaten up. When Bergman's wife begged them to stop beating the old man they called her a 'nigger-lover' and carried on. The blow to her husband's head left him partially brain-damaged.

From there, the bus made its way to Birmingham, where, after a vicious beating from the Klan, the original set of Freedom Riders abandoned their campaign and were replaced by the Student Non-Violent Co-ordinating Committee, led by Diane Nash. Two days later, they were in Shuttlesworth's house ready to take the five o'clock to Montgomery, and after they finally found a white driver who was prepared to take them, they were off again.

John Lewis was first out of the bus in Montgomery, arriving to a still calm he was sure could not last. 'And then,' he said, 'out of *nowhere, from every direction, came people. White people. Men, women and children. Dozens of them. Hundreds of them. Out of alleys, out of side streets, around the corners of office buildings, they emerged from everywhere, all at once, as if they'd been let out of a gate. To this day, I don't know where all those people came from.'*

The next evening, in a besieged First Baptist church surrounded by violent racist protesters, Robert Kennedy asked King to ask Farmer, who had flown down from DC, if he would stop the Rides for a cooling-off period. Farmer refused.

'My objective is not just to make a point but to bring about a real change in the situation. We will continue the Rides until people can sit wherever they wish on buses and use the facilities in any waiting room available to the public. Please tell the Attorney General that we have been cooling off for three hundred and fifty years. If we cool off any more, we will be in a deep freeze.'

It was early, and the streets of Anniston were still empty when I went out in search of breakfast. The only person I could see on the street was a tall black guy who walked with a stick and a limp. I asked him if he knew where I could find something to eat. He said his favourite spot had been torn down. 'This place, damn, they should have put it in the mothafuckin' incinerator years ago, man. There ain't nothing here.'

This seemed a little harsh. While you wouldn't think of heading to Anniston for your second honeymoon, it wasn't that bad. It is surrounded on all sides by the hills of the Talladega National Forest, and its main street has a cinema, a few restaurants within walking distance of downtown and at least two night clubs.

But it had a reputation. When I had told people in Atlanta where I was going next, they sucked their teeth and winced. 'Anniston? Well you make sure if you're driving that

you stay within the speed limit. The cops there can be a little
... well ... kind of particular when a black man is driving,
if you know what I'm saying.' And then they would shake
their heads. 'Anniston?' they would say in a well-I-never kind
of way.

About half an hour after Roosevelt Parker, the local
spokesman for the NAACP, came to pick me up at my motel,
I understood why. I asked Parker if he could put me in touch
with people who remembered the day when the Freedom
Riders came through.

Parker, who was seventeen at the time, remembered the
day but did not actually see the bus burn. 'We were having a
Mother's Day program at the church and it was interrupted
when the priest heard the news. He dismissed the congregation, and we went home to find out what was going on. The
first thing that came into our mind at the time was that the
enemy was attacking us. You see, the Klan used to ride up
and down 15th Street all the time. The older people started
getting their guns out. The atmosphere was real, real tense.'

We drove up to John Morris's service station. He recalled
the day, but was too busy to go to the freeway and see what
was going on. 'I couldn't get up there on account of the Klan
was shooting at my garage, so we were just stuck here trying
to defend the place,' said Morris. 'They were trying to burn
us down.'

Parker laughed. 'Yeah, whenever the Klan were around,
you could never find the police. Because the police *were* the
Klan.'

Up the road at the Mount Zion Baptist church, Reverend
Cleveland Jones did not remember seeing the bus either, but
he recalled that the news of its burning did not surprise him.
Following Reverend Jones's conversation was not easy. The
ninety-year-old clergyman would wander off into the faraway land of reminiscence. In his small room, full of musty

air, papers, pictures and an old typewriter, he called me closer so that he could hear my questions. 'There were a lot of things that people did at that time that I wouldn't know that they would do. A few times they tried to shoot my window out. Every place in the South was dangerous then. I tried to be prepared, because we were always afraid that they were going to attack the church or my house.'

From the church we went to see the former State President of the Alabama NAACP, Gordon Rodgers. Rodgers was President of the Organization when the state of Alabama banned it in 1958. Now he is retired – an old man with a pony tail and cords. Once he was at the forefront of the fight against segregation in one of the most racist states in the country; now he is teaching himself astronomy and Greek mythology. If the bus was going to be burnt anywhere, he said, it was going to be Anniston.

'Anniston was strictly segregated. It was laid out to make it easy for segregation to exist. The railroad tracks here were like the Mason–Dixon line. The east is white and the west is black and that's just the way it has been, is and probably always will be. There were white folks who lived on this side of town, but they didn't count. They were poor. White folks have a way of discounting each other, I think.'

When we left, Parker took me for a tour of the small area reserved for Anniston's black middle class, homes of doctors and lawyers growing increasingly huge as we rolled down the hill.

'Anniston used to be a model city. That's what they used to call it. It was the best city for work around here,' he said. 'We used to make cast-iron pipes and ship them all over the world, but then in the late seventies the world stopped wanting cast-iron pipes, and things dried up.'

We moved on to Blue Mountain, the poor white area which was once a Klan stronghold. An old man, who looked like Uncle Jesse from *The Dukes of Hazzard*, sat on his porch, rocking in the shade. Parker looked up at him: 'See, for all we know, he could have been one of them Klansmen, too. That's just it. You really never know. Poor whites are the worst. They ain't going to do nothing with their lives, and they don't want you to do something with yours. Sometimes in this town it was like a powder keg and you just never knew when it was going to erupt.'

There was one more thing Parker wanted to show me before he dropped me off – the place where it all happened. He started just outside the Winn Dixie grocery store where there is little more than a patch of concrete. 'That's where the old bus station used to be, and that's where all the Klan were waitin' and where they slashed the tyres,' he said, and then took off up Route 21.

'Now, they were driving in this direction. And the Klan, they were just right behind 'em. Just right up on 'em. Who knows what was going through those Riders' minds then? 'Cos the tyre was out, so they knew they weren't going to be going fast. Right up there was Klan territory also, although there was no way they could have known that.'

And then he pulled over, opposite some mobile homes, on to a patch of derelict concrete. 'This is where they stopped. Right here.' It was once a gas station. I could see where the gas pumps had been pulled out. Grass was growing through the concrete, and broken glass was scattered over the ground. This was the setting for this small town's moment of international notoriety. The day John Morris, Reverend Jones, Mr Rodgers and many others stopped suffering racial attacks in complete silence. The day the cameras came and showed the world that what a lot of people in this town thought was normal was wretched and wrong. The day history caught up with Anniston.

Inside the abandoned gas station, it looked like the

owner had recently gone on holiday and some youngsters had broken in, had a party and left abruptly. There was still a sign on the door saying that the owner would card you for cigarettes. By the window were cans of beer left unopened, brewing up in the heat of the late afternoon. And next to the cans sat a cardboard advertisement that made me laugh. 'Crackers,' it said. 'Four for a dollar.'

There are moments which have a significance all to themselves. Quite what triggers them is difficult to say. The event in itself may not be important, but it will engrave a mark on your psyche that you will never be able to shift. It is about you, a time, a place, and a shiver that does not, whatever the clichés say, go anywhere near your spine: it feels as though a colony of frozen ants have been unleashed between your flesh and your muscle and are running wild around your torso. They will crawl all over you and then disappear as quickly as they came.

They used to come to me on the second floor of the Stevenage library whenever I turned to a certain page of a book about the Holocaust. There was a black and white picture of a Jewish Dutch girl, who looked about sixteen, standing at a Nazi transit camp, looking out into space. She wore big boots, like Doctor Martens, and had her coat folded over her hands which she clasped in front of her. On the next page there was a picture of a pile of emaciated dead bodies, their eyes bulging, mouths open, hip bones poking out of their middles and ribs pushing through their chests. And then I would flip back to the picture of the girl. And that was when the ants came. Because I knew what would happen to her.

They came not long after my mother died. We hired a skip to throw away all the bits of cloth and curtains she had been saving for the day that would never come, the day when she would have enough time, energy and money to pack them all up and send them to Barbados. One day, Mrs Stilling came out as I was throwing some stuff away. She held my hand and said it wasn't fair, Mum dying when she was still young. And then we both cried and, as she walked me back into the house, the ants arrived and danced their dance.

And they came in South Africa on the campaign trail with Nelson Mandela, standing in a ramshackle stadium in a town which during apartheid never even appeared on the map because only black people lived there – people who had seen Mandela's face only on a poster, people who had travelled more than fifty miles in a truck for a glimpse. In the distance, you could see the dust rise from his cavalcade, and the local official started the campaign song, '*Sekunjalo Ke Nako*', which means now is the time. And the old and toothless and young and barefoot started dancing, women began to ululate, children cheered and the ants ran amok.

The Civil Rights Institute in Birmingham breeds frozen ants. Through artefacts, video footage and clippings from the civil rights era, I was submerged in the images of pain, cruelty and resistance that characterized the times and left me with a sense of unease that did not evaporate once I had moved on. The ants were there when I watched footage of Martin Luther King making his 'I have a dream' speech, and of the funeral of Dick Chaney, the black volunteer who was murdered along with his two white colleagues, when Dave Dennis, urgently, desperately, hissed his eulogy – 'Don't ... bow ... down ... anymore. We want our freedom now' – while Chaney's younger brother sobbed uncontrollably. They were there in the photograph taken on Edmund Pettus Bridge when the police baton-charged protesters and knocked down a middle-aged black woman with a shopping bag; and in the smile of Emmett Till, the fourteen-year-old boy from Chicago who was killed for saying, 'Bye, baby', to a white woman in a grocery store.

'When we were setting it up, there were questions asked among the white community about why should you open up old wounds?' said Odessa Woolfolk, the President of the Institute's Board of Directors. 'It was Mayor Arrington [Birmingham's first black mayor] who said that if we can take something that has been part of our past and put it in a museum, then that is to say that it is really in the past.

'The idea came after a visit to Yad Vashem in Israel, but the story really starts with the mayor. He said, "I want to invest in this part of town." The business community supported him in general because they believed in his goals for the city as a whole. This was a run-down area, but now, a few blocks from here, there are four major banks and Alabama Power.'

Anxiety about the project was not confined to the white community. 'Many black people were concerned with whose history was going to be dealt with and whose history was going to dominate. They wanted to know what story was going to be told. They asked, "Are you going to give proper credit to the real people who got involved in the struggle but whose efforts were never recorded?" That is why we decided to have an oral history project, so that people could be recorded in a proactive manner. There was also concern about whether there would be enough documents and articles to justify having a separate facility.

'We said, "Are you going to say that everything people are saying about this place is right? When CBS, ABC and NBC are only showing the dogs being set on children? Are you going to allow us to be defined by our negative past?" We said we shouldn't run away from civil rights any more than we do from civil war. We have grown from this particular past. Hopefully we have learned from it. Let's not repeat the kind of miscalculation that led to those days. There is something positive in looking at the past. We can be inspired by the past and have a vision for the future. That became the slogan for the Institute.'

I came out of the Institute unable to shrug off one of the protest songs. On that Saturday night, there was no wind. Birmingham was completely still. The only sounds were the humming of traffic lights and my croaky rendition of: 'Woke up this morning with my mind set on freedom.'

When Birmingham was founded they called it the Magic City. It was a company town run by US Steel that at one stage rivalled Atlanta as the South's premier city. But the town's largest employer now is not the steelyards but the University of Alabama. A short drive in most directions will take you past what remains of its heavy industry, the slag heaps, smoke-belching factories and abandoned railroad lines that lead from derelict buildings and head out into industrial wasteland.

Halfway back to my motel on that Saturday night, I met an old man dressed all in purple – purple fedora, purple trousers, purple jacket, purple shirt and purple winklepicker shoes.

'How you doing today?' he asked, his voice sounding loud in the vast silence of an empty city.

'Fine,' I said. 'How are you?'

'Me,' he laughed, as he carried on walking without turning back. 'I feel good all the time.'

Right outside the Institute is Kelly Ingram Park, the park where the police turned hoses and dogs on young children in 1963. At the entrance there are four broken columns, erected as a memorial to the four girls who died when Klansmen bombed the 16th Street Baptist church. Four sculpted ministers kneeling in prayer and set in ragged stone are there to greet you. Engraved in the small wall that surrounds them are the words *Place of revolution and reconciliation.*

Then comes the Freedom Walk, a tribute to those who risked their lives in 1963 to end segregation on that very turf. Going from left to right, your eyes are first assaulted by three vicious dogs, jaws at eye level, teeth bared, cast in blue metal and restrained by leashes. Shortly afterwards, a bronze policeman holds a black youth by his shirt collar while a dog tries to attack him. Then come the children, the boy in short trousers and the little girl in plaits, in prison, at the bottom of their statue the words *I ain't afraid of your jail.* Then the statue of Martin Luther King stands over the inscription *Yes, if you want to say that I was a drum major say I was a drum major for justice: say that I was a drum major for peace* ... Finally, there is the statue of water cannons aimed at two teenagers, a boy bent over and a girl with her back turned and her hands over her chest. In the middle there is a circle of water, cut in four quads so that you can walk right through it and watch the small eddies circulating from below.

In 1963, the 16th Street Baptist church was mission control not only for Birmingham's black community but for the entire Alabama civil rights movement. The commander of this besieged centre was the church's preacher, Fred Shuttlesworth. When the NAACP was banned in Alabama, it was Shuttlesworth who launched the Alabama Christian Movement for Human Rights which took its place. When Martin Luther King wanted to go to Birmingham, he had to ask Shuttlesworth first. There is a street named after him in

Birmingham and, in the Institute, several pictures of him, standing tall, lean, handsome and clean-shaved, preaching in Montgomery on the night when the worshippers and Freedom Riders were locked inside the church and threatened by a baying mob.

In 1972 Shuttlesworth left the church and moved to Cincinnati, Ohio, where I interviewed him a few months later, and he told me about the day the Freedom Riders came to town.

'Nothing at that time would have surprised me about Alabama – it was just Mississippi moved a little to the east. White people there used to do things first and then think about it later. Even the most liberal white people there supported segregation. It wasn't just a way of life. It was the law.

'I knew the Freedom Riders were coming but I don't remember how I knew. I didn't know there had been any trouble at the bus station until just about the time when I dismissed the service on that Mother's Day. The first time I ever saw a human skull, it was Peck's. I took him to the hospital. By the time I got back, I heard that there was trouble in Anniston. I wanted to go and try to pick them up, but some other people went over there in the end.'

Shuttlesworth says he gave Peck a quarter and told him to call him when he was released. 'They had intended to turn him over to the Ku Klux Klan. We went out that night to pick him up, and I said to the guy driving, "Don't you drive over fifteen miles an hour," because they would put you in jail for that right there. In those days if the Klan didn't get you then the police did, and if the police didn't get you the courts would.'

By that evening, the Shuttlesworths' house was like an emergency room with the bandaged and beaten Freedom

Riders from both Anniston and Birmingham licking their wounds and plotting what they should do next.

Throughout his recollections, Shuttlesworth was rarely more than a sentence away from invoking the deity. Why was he arrested at the Birmingham bus station after the students from Nashville took up the Freedom Rides? 'God was watching over and protecting me.' Did he not ever fear for his personal safety? 'God was with me and I never sensed danger.' Was he surprised by the speed at which integration came in the South after the legal barriers fell? 'It was God's plan and God has a timetable for the universe.'

By the time the Nashville students had arrived, the Freedom Riders were national news. The day they boarded the buses to Montgomery, Shuttlesworth tried to go with them but he was arrested at what he believes to be Robert Kennedy's behest. Kennedy, he says, feared that if any of the major players were severely injured or, worse still, killed, then an already tense situation would veer completely out of control.

A few days earlier Kennedy had called him and pleaded with him not to board the bus which was ultimately heading through Mississippi.

'Do you have to go to Mississippi?' asked Kennedy. 'We can arrange for you to go to New Orleans without stopping in Mississippi.'

Shuttlesworth said the Lord had work to do in the Magnolia State.

'But the good Lord hasn't been in Mississippi for a long time now, Reverend,' Kennedy replied.

'Well, that's why we've got to go,' said Shuttlesworth. 'To make sure he gets there.'

Shuttlesworth was determined to get to Montgomery, so as soon as he was released he rushed home to get changed. He was in such a rush that he slipped with his razor and shaved off half of his moustache. 'I was so hurried I just got rid of the rest of it right there and that was the first time for a long time before and since that I was without a moustache. And that was the day the cameras were there,' he says laughing.

As he reflected on his role during those heady years, it was clear he was disappointed by the fact that his contributions had not received greater acclaim outside his home city. 'Martin Luther King was the man who symbolized the movement. He could articulate what the masses wanted. He was the one God chose to be the charismatic person for that age, and you can't argue with what God wants. But his name never would have become immortal if it had not been for Birmingham. People are just beginning to discover about others of us who were involved.'

The victory in Birmingham during 1963, two years after the Freedom Riders came through, would never have happened, insists Shuttlesworth, without him. He was one of the few people who stood up to King at a crucial juncture during the campaign. At one stage, he says, King had agreed with Kennedy to call off the demonstrations, because they were hampering negotiations with local white businessmen over integration. While the deal was being done, Shuttlesworth was in hospital recovering from a fire-hosing.

When he heard that King and Kennedy were going to hold a joint press conference announcing the postponement, he was furious. 'If you and Kennedy say that, then I will get out of my sick bed and start the demonstrations right up again. They might be calling you Mr King now but they will be calling you Mr Shit when I've finished,' he told King. King backed down.

Recalling the time he went to the White House after the demonstrations he told Howell Raines in his book, *My Soul is Rested*: 'Kennedy used these words: "But for Birmingham, we would not be here today." "But for Birmingham", I think that ought to be remembered. That's a good title. The only thing is, I'm a lazy writer. I'm not a writer. I'm a fighter.'

Shortly after Mrs Rosa Parks had been thrown off the bus, jailed and agreed to be a test case to challenge the seating arrangements on Montgomery's buses, Mr E. D. Nixon went home and got out his ruler. It was Mr Nixon, a union leader for the Brotherhood of Sleeping Car Porters and NAACP activist, who had persuaded Mrs Parks to put herself forward. Now he had to do the planning.

'I went home and I took a sheet of paper and I drew right in the centre of the paper. I used that for the square and then I used Hunter Station, Washington Park, Pickett Springs, all the different areas in Montgomery, and I used a slide rule to get an estimate,' he told Raines. 'I discovered nowhere in Montgomery at that time that a man couldn't walk to work from if he wanted to. I said, "We can beat this thing."'

That is how small Montgomery was in 1955. If you stand on the marble porch outside the front door of the State Capitol you can see most of the places where the events that made the South what it is today took place. You are actually standing on three of them. For it is just there, right outside the Capitol, that Jefferson Davis walked out, stamped his foot and declared an independent Southern Confederacy on 11 February 1861. It is also the place where those who had marched the sixty miles from Selma, demanding the right to vote, handed over their petition in 1965. This is the spot that Alabama Governor George Wallace referred to during his inaugural address in 1963 when he said, 'Today I have stood where Jefferson Davis stood and taken an oath to my people ... In the name of the greatest people that ever trod this earth, I draw the line in the dust and toss the gauntlet before the feet of tyranny, and I say: segregation now, segregation tomorrow, segregation for ever.' Over the road, down Dexter Avenue, you can see the stop where Parks got on the bus – she was arrested two stops down, just around the corner and out of view. A little nearer, up the same road, there is Dexter Avenue Baptist church, King's first church and the centre for the organization of the bus boycott in 1955, a display of collective strength which not only thrust King into the public eye, but marked the beginning of the civil rights era as a time of mass peaceful resistance.

By the time I had checked into my hotel, I was already forty-five minutes late for my appointment at the Southern Poverty Law Center. I had been expecting a tiny place, tucked away in a back street, with posters on the windows and half-drunk cups of coffee left on untidy desks where underpaid, highly stressed political staff worked long hours to put the world right – the sort of place where nobody knows where anybody else is and messages don't get passed on. The Southern Poverty Law Center – it sounded like a Hackney community rights office in the sun.

The Center actually looks like something from *Deep Space 9*. It is a huge spaceship of a building with tight security and gates that appear to open and close all by themselves. I presented myself to a guard who, without taking his eyes off the several TV monitors in front of him, asked me for my driver's licence and then radioed Mr Potok. Mr Potok's voice came through a walkie-talkie, giving the guard the go-ahead to show me through. I was ushered in by a small black man with a barrel chest, who had been married to an English woman from Kings Lynn and was now divorced.

Potok was incredibly kind but rather rushed – he had a child to pick up and a Geraldo Rivera show to prepare for. He gave me some written information on the work the Center had done on various hate groups, apologized profusely and then passed me on to his colleague, Penny Weaver, who runs the Center's Website. On her wall there is a signed picture of Rosa Parks, and on her desk a black and white shot of her walking out of what looks like a court as a young woman.

Before long we were swapping recommendations about books, Penny was advising me of somewhere to eat that night — there was the brewery or the Thai place that had been recently built into the old railway station — and had invited me out to lunch the next day.

It was the beginning of one of the most enjoyable weeks of my trip; a week of being fed, talking politics, watching films and hanging out with great company in bookshops, restaurants and bars; a week when it felt like Islington came to Alabama, bringing its restaurants, lefties and mavericks with it but leaving the toffs and pretentiousness behind.

The two people Penny advised me to start with were Barbara Edwards, a trade union organizer, and Gwen Patton, an activist who had been in town when the Freedom Riders came through. Patton's line was constantly busy. Edwards told me to come over the next day and gave me directions to her house — a curious route that started on a motorway and ended on a dirt road. 'My house is all in red and then there's another place being built next to it. You can't miss it,' she said.

Edwards lives in the buckle of the Black Belt, a swath of land about a hundred miles thick which starts on South Carolina's Atlantic shore and stretches all the way to Houston, Texas. It derives its name not from the skin colour of many of the people who live on it but from the land on which they live — fertile black cotton-growing land.

First to the door was Josh, her small, white-haired, very friendly and very deaf dog. Edwards, a tall, well-built woman in her early fifties, soon followed and invited me in. On the chair next to her was a large book about Che Guevara; on the wall were several African and Caribbean wall hangings and sculptures.

Edwards was born in central Pennsylvania but moved to the South in the mid-seventies. As a young woman she was active in the Black Panthers. Nowadays she is involved in the local black church, the youth club and a literacy programme. Some people have accused her of being something of a black nationalist, a political punch she takes on the chin. She says she couldn't imagine living anywhere but the black community. 'I have chosen to live in comfort rather than educate the whites. They are just not like us. Their worship is different. Their food is different. Their whole value system is different to ours and I just know that this is where I belong.'

Edwards is white. If you closed your eyes you would know that from her accent. But otherwise you would have to keep your ears tuned for the few times when she slips from 'us' to 'they' when referring to the African-Americans. A white woman, whose home is on a dirt road in rural Alabama, living and thriving in the heart of the local black community. How did that happen? Almost inevitably, the answer begins in the sixties.

Edwards was living in Gary, Indiana, in the mid-sixties when it went from being a majority white to a majority black town. She did not move there as a highly politicized woman. 'If anything I was quite naive. I never had discussions about race in my family. My parents never talked ugly about black people or anything, they just didn't mention them at all.'

While she was in Gary she got to know some black people and through them got involved with the Black Panthers. 'Things were really revving up there at that time, and I just wanted to be involved. I knew something was wrong. The Panthers were saying they wanted "to get at the people that are on our necks and then start over", and that sounded sensible to me. I used to run a few guns across the state lines for them. I was a white girl and had a nice car, so who was going to stop me? They were doing something. I wasn't allowed to go to some of the meetings, but I understood why that was.'

A few years later, she started a relationship with a black man, who had nothing to do with the Panthers, whom she met at a cosmetology course. In 1971 she gave birth to Jim. Some of the black women in the Panthers resented her because she had a black son. Others were supportive. The relationship with Jim's father broke up. She moved down South and took her boy with her. 'I don't know what drew me here. Maybe it was the blood in the soil, but it was where I wanted to be.'

That was when the problems really started. In Martinsville, Virginia, local whites hung her kittens and wrote 'nigger lover' on her trailer. 'They scared me, but I didn't let them see that. To them I was sport. They did everything but kill me.'

She went further south into rural Georgia. At the time, she had a big red Afro, and many in the black community decided that she wasn't white, but a very light-skinned black woman. White people, she said, never cut her any slack. She was continually harassed by the police. 'When Jim was six, I got arrested for hooking up the lights of my trailer illegally so that I wouldn't have to pay my electricity bill. That was a joke because I didn't even know how to do that. I wouldn't know how to do that now.'

She kept getting taken to jail, and every time she was hauled off it was the black people who provided support. 'It was black people came to my place to look after my son.

Even if they didn't like me that well they were always there for my child – but often for me, too. They are my people whether they like it or not,' she said.

After Edwards was run out of one town in Georgia and moved to another, where things were not much better, she began, she said, 'to live a different kind of life'. She went on welfare. The constant hounding at the hands of local law enforcement officials forced her to seek legal aid. She was at the legal aid office so often that they gave her a job as a paralegal. Now she works for the United Auto Workers union, representing lawyers, paralegals and secretaries across the south-east of the country.

It was at this point in her story that Edwards's 'black identity' started to make sense. Not that I now thought of her as black. Edwards is white. There is no meaningful way in which she could be called black. But Edwards is very much part of the black community. For the sake of her son's welfare, she has had to be. She takes her responsibilities as a member of that community seriously. The half-built shed next door is to be a home for African, Haitian and local folk art as well as 'all kinds of other crazy stuff' which she is paying for with some inheritance money from her late mother. To try and boost literacy among young children in the area, every now and then she dresses up like Mother Goose, only in a big African skirt, and reads them stories. She helps run a local youth club, and there are always black kids around her house learning how to use the computer or waiting to be ferried to a social or church event. Now that her son has grown up and moved away, she has no desire to go back to a white world which turned its back on her in her time of need. All of that makes sense. It still does not make her black.

And despite many of the things she said that made me believe otherwise, Edwards does understand this. 'When I came into the black community I made a lot of people feel uncomfortable. They would wonder what I was doing here. People would make a remark about white people in a particular discussion and then turn around and say sorry. But I know where that is coming from and it doesn't bother me. White people were lynching black people around here thirty years ago, and that makes black people uncomfortable. I understand that.'

She even jokes about it. A few days later I came back for dinner. There were three black women there. Edwards was arguing the case for black nationalism, which she clearly had some sympathy with. 'Black nationalists want to have an area of the country just for black people and kick all the white people out,' she explained.

'Well they'd kick you out, too,' said Fanny, one of her guests, and they all started to laugh.

'I might have to go,' admitted Edwards with a smile. 'But I reckon they'd give me like honorary privilege and let me stay. In the Panthers they used to say that all the white people that they wanted to stay could wear a special white glove or something like that, and they would recognize us because we would have one of these gloves, and that would save us. I never did believe them.' And the laughter – honest laughing from the belly – continued.

At dinner she broke the news that her daughter-in-law was pregnant. The lady over the road had a dream that there were two big fishes swimming in clear water which, in black Southern folklore, means Edwards was about to become grandmother to twins. The conversation turned to what shade the twins might be.

Fanny said, 'I just hope they come out the same color.' Edwards argued it wouldn't matter what shade they were because she knew her boy would bring them both up the same way. Everybody at the table shook their head. Nobody doubted Jim's potential as a parent, but all agreed that, given the pigmentocracy in the black community, it would be difficult if one of the children were much lighter than the other.

We were putting on our coats when Edwards shouted something at Josh. Josh paid no attention.

'Poor Josh,' she said, patting the dog. 'He's hearing-challenged.'

Fanny laughed so hard it looked like she was going to have to sit down.

'That dog ain't hearing-challenged,' said Fanny. 'That dog is deaf. Why can you never call things what they are?'

The spokeswoman for a PR company charged with improving the image of the town of Dachau, site of a Nazi concentration camp, once lamented that visitors were reluctant to spend money there after they had seen the crematoria. 'No one is really in the mood to bite into a sandwich after that,' she complained.

Selma has never had that problem. A man in a bed and breakfast there told me it had taken a long time to convince the local Chamber of Commerce that the bloody struggles that took place in the town around 1964 would draw people to it rather than scare them away: 'But, heck, this is the most famous town of its size in the world,' he said.

The local businessmen were won over in the end. There used to be a large billboard on the main street, boasting: SELMA: HOME OF CIVIL WAR AND CIVIL RIGHTS. I wondered of which era the town was most proud: the days when it fought to preserve slavery, or the days when black people rose up to protect their rights. But it was not about history. It was about marketing.

The day that terror put Selma on the map was Sunday 7

March 1965. Around six hundred people lined up two by two and set off to march the fifty miles to Montgomery to demand the right to vote. A few weeks earlier, a young man, Jimmy Lee Jackson, who had seen both his eighty-two-year-old grandfather and his mother beaten with police sticks, had fought back and been shot dead. Now black people in Selma, and civil rights activists throughout the country, were more determined than ever. The cameras were in Selma. The world was watching.

But the Alabama Governor didn't care. When the marchers reached the apex of Edmund Pettus Bridge, they met a sea of Alabama state troopers wearing gas masks and carrying billy clubs. John Lewis, veteran of the Freedom Rides, was leading the march. When he ignored the order to disperse, the state troopers moved forward, knocking demonstrators to the ground, while those behind them tried to scramble to safety. Then came the tear gas, the horses, the clubs and the outrage. More than fifty people were sent to hospital. They called it Bloody Sunday. Three days later, they set out again and marched all the way to the capitol in Montgomery, facing nothing but taunts.

At the foot of the bridge, there is now a plaque, erected by the Alabama Historical Commission, bearing witness to what happened on that awful day. It says:

On Sunday March 7, 1965, 600 people led by Hosea Williams and John Lewis began a march to Montgomery to take their quest for voting rights directly to Governor G. C. Wallace. At the Edmund Pettus Bridge they were met by state troopers who used horses, tear gas and billy clubs to break up the march. On March 9, demonstrators led by Martin Luther King met the troopers at the same place and turned around without incident. The federal court ruled the march was legal, and with federal protection 4,000 began the march to Montgomery on March 21. Camping along the road the protestors reached 25,000 in number by the time they reached the state capitol. National news coverage of these events secured widespread support and led to the approval of the Voting Rights Act on August 6, 1965.

Standing at the plaque, at the foot of Edmund Pettus Bridge, I began to see how it is possible for African-Americans to join the army, salute the flag and sing the anthem, and why I could never do the same in Britain. Because, seven years later, four thousand miles away, there was another Bloody Sunday, on the Bogside in Derry, Northern Ireland. There, on 30 January 1972, The 1st Parachute Regiment of the British Army opened fire on a group of unarmed protesters demonstrating against internment. They killed thirteen people, and many others were injured. There are murals and a monument to the dead, erected by local people to honour those who perished. But there are no common markers that stand 'above' the conflict, mourning the end of innocent lives. There has been no official apology; no admission of any wrongdoing by the British government. There has been only a statement of regret – and even that took twenty-five years – that in any way acknowledges that whatever you think of the war in Northern Ireland, whatever you think of internment or Republicanism, these people should not have died.

When it comes to its past, the United States has an ability to sacrifice several parts in favour of the whole. All around the South you will see admissions that some wrongdoing took place; that some awful act of brutality or bigotry happened that needs to be recorded. They do not just do this with race. They honour American soldiers who turned their guns on American soldiers during the My Lai massacre, too.

Throughout my journey I had run across many of these

public acknowledgements – Kelly Ingram Park and the Civil Rights Institute in Birmingham, February One Street in Greensboro and the Martin Luther King Center in Atlanta. The underlying benefit of all of these *mea culpas* is credibility. It suggests that the political culture of the United States is underpinned by a notion of right and wrong which lies above that of partisanship. By admitting to having been wrong, it maintains the ability to claim it has also been right. That leaves enough political space for African-Americans to join in the national project.

This doesn't make Americans more honest in how they deal with their history. Nor does it mean the racial wounds in these societies, once scarred by racial hatred, have healed. There were campaigns, arguments and local battles, usually led by the black community, that went behind erecting plaques like the one at the foot of the Edmund Pettus Bridge. Most of the markers in the South have only been up since the early 1990s. And while it was often moral issues which got the matter raised, the final decision was usually a commercial one – people will come and visit and spend their money here, but only if we give them something to look at. But the fact is the markers are there, and while they might not make American history more morally acceptable, it does make it more believable. It is when a nation never admits it is wrong that an impasse is reached: either you believe in the whole or you reject the whole. You cannot take it in parts. You cannot think that what happened on Bloody Sunday in Derry is wrong and wave the Union Jack with any real sense of pride. There is no constitution to which you can refer spelling out what the flag is supposed to stand for. So all you can do is look at who has waved it in the past and where it has been waved from and draw your own conclusions. That is why you do not see lefties in Britain burning the Union Jack. What would be the point? Nothing was ever demanded of it in the first place.

The Stars and Stripes is more flexible. It is the flag they waved when the US bombed Iraq and the one they stand and salute at school in the daily regime of patriotic indoctrination. But it is also a version of the flag that blacks looked to for the abolition of slavery during the Civil War and that is underwritten by a promise of equality under the constitution. As fireworks boomed over a July 4th celebration in Washington DC one year, a public address system broadcast the voices of great American patriots. The two loudest cheers were for John Wayne, a right-wing racist, and Martin Luther King. In the vast cultural space between those two icons there is enough room for flag wavers and flag burners. It covers a myriad interpretations of right and wrong, which may concur or more likely conflict, but will do so with reference to their own flag.

The next day I finally got to meet Gwen Patton, the activist who was in Montgomery when the Freedom Riders came through.

I arrived a little early. Shortly afterwards, she rolled up from a quick shopping trip and handed me a large box of beers to carry into the house. She is a small woman with one leg considerably shorter than the other; she wears a shoe with a huge sole which compensates but still leaves her with a limp. She has a big seventies-style Afro and was wearing a T-shirt which said: *It's great to fight for people and win.*

It was the first of many slogans I saw that morning. On the fridge was a small child's picture, along with childish lettering saying, 'Robert is proud to be an American.' In her study there was an entire wall filled with badges: 'Jesse for President', 'I'm a grass root', 'Fight Racism, Fight Zionism'. And there were awards for distinguished black women from the Southern Christian Leadership Conference (SCLC) and something to show she was part of the presidential task force from the Democratic National Committee. While I stared at her political conscience plastered over the wall, she prepared a Southern feast: pig's trotters, pickled boiled eggs, carrots to dip and fresh tomatoes. 'I love to have tea parties, but I've eaten already,' she said. 'I'm just going to put another plate down there so you won't feel you're eating by yourself.'

Patton's radical streak seemed genetic. 'It was always a given that I would get involved. My grandparents on both sides were involved. My paternal grandmother was a citizenship counsellor and a teacher so she used to try and encourage people to vote. My mother's side have been here since the Emancipation and they had always been involved.'

Her grandfather was an independent contractor, one of the small businessmen that made up the South's black middle class. Her father worked with him for a while but gave it up and moved to Detroit during the great migration. 'My father couldn't tolerate Jim Crow ways. He was a maverick and quite urbane, quite suave, and he didn't see any future for himself down here. So he moved from being middle class in the South to being working class in the North. He got a job as a welder working for Cadillac and he said he would always drive a Cadillac. Since he made them he figured he had the right to drive one.'

Wherever you are in a conversation with Patton you are never too far from hearing about class. It is a curious contradiction for someone so clearly dedicated to fighting for greater equality that she should invoke the hierarchies of high birth and social standing in the way that she does. Recalling the time she was verbally attacked by one of her political opponents – at one stage or another she seems to have fallen out with most people in Alabama Democratic Party politics but still commands a great deal of respect – she said: 'I told them: "I am the authentic middle class bourgy here. Your grandchildren might be my peers, but they are snivelling nouveau wannabes. You need to be washed through. There have got to be two or three generations before you come anywhere near me."' En route to a classless society, it is people with no class who seem to irritate her most – 'The sort of people who go to Paris and then spend their time looking for fried chicken. The sort of people who spend a lot of money on diamonds. Actually, I probably have more diamonds than anyone else in Montgomery of my class.'

As a child she often used to come down to Montgomery from Detroit during the holidays but did not really notice the segregation. 'We always used to like riding on the back of the bus anyway because it was more fun.' And when she was confronted with discrimination, she reacted like a child of the North. 'I remember going into one department store and asking for some water, and I was served it and I sat down to drink it, and the woman said I couldn't sit there and called me a pickaninny. So I poured the water on the table and left.'

When she was fifteen, her mother died, and she moved back to Montgomery to live with her aunt because her family felt she needed a woman's influence. By then, the black community was buoyed by the victories of the bus boycott, and Patton soon became heavily involved in local politics.

She remembers the day the Freedom Riders came to town because it sparked a major row with her aunt. 'They had broke the bus up in Anniston and attacked them in Birmingham, so we knew that something was going to happen in Montgomery. When the Freedom Riders came, I naturally wanted to meet them. But there was news coming in that they had been beaten up, and my aunt would not go down town with her car.

'I went down there anyway and when I got there I

invited some of the Riders to my house. One of them was a white boy from Alabama. When my aunt came home and saw them there she said, "Did you let that white boy in here? Did he come through the front door? I hope he didn't. I couldn't go through his front door, could I? So I don't want those people coming through my front door." And that shocked me, because for me the whole thing up until then had been about fairness. It was so hypocritical. She loved it when I spoke at the churches, and I was under the assumption that she loved the movement, but she didn't.'

The night when mobs surrounded the First Baptist church she was in there with her grandparents. 'We were singing freedom songs. It was somewhat tense, but we would pray and then sing some more songs. We were prepared to die. While we were trapped in there Governor Patterson sent sandwiches and food, but we threw it out because we thought it was poisoned.'

Patton attended Tuskeegee University and then went on to New York, where she did a masters and adopted a child who was about to be taken away from his alcoholic mother. She came back to Montgomery soon afterwards. 'My grandparents were getting old. My brothers and uncles were everywhere – LA, Las Vegas, Gary and Detroit – and they weren't coming back. So I came back to take care of my grandparents.'

She returned to find a black political leadership which she felt had lost its intellectual edge and replaced it with careerism. 'There is no Sartre, no Camus, no Kierkegaard, no existentialism, no introspection. Most of the black politicians have no concept of democracy. They have reduced politics to a job. Of course it's not a job. It's there to facilitate democracy.' But her continued activism, obdurate nature and political tenacity were soon to bring her into serious conflict with possibly the most powerful living symbol of the entire civil rights era, Rosa Parks. The story of this row is fascinating, because it illustrates both how history can be wilfully distorted, and the deep-seated conservatism within the African-American community during the civil rights era.

The most popular version of the tale that launched the struggle for equality in the South depicts Rosa Parks as a woman who got on a bus after a hard day's work, refused to stand up when she was told to, was arrested and so sparked a defining moment in the history of American civil rights. At the Martin Luther King Visitors' Center in Atlanta she is described as 'a victim of both the forces of history and the forces of destiny. She had been tracked down by the Zeitgeist – the spirit of the time.'

The story of the Montgomery bus boycott is represented as a completely spontaneous act which came about as a result of the defiant actions of a non-politicized woman who wanted to preserve her dignity. It casts Rosa Parks as Everywoman, a middle-aged lady who was tired of injustice. It is a beautiful version of events but misses out some inconvenient detail.

Rosa Parks was not just a casual bus traveller but an NAACP activist who had long campaigned against discrimination. 'I had almost a life history of being rebellious against being mistreated against my color,' she has said. Nor was she the first to be thrown off the buses. Three other people were arrested prior to Mrs Parks. But the local black leadership felt that any black person who was going to be put forward as a test case had to be beyond reproach. So when Parks, a churchgoing, upstanding, married seamstress was arrested, they knew that they had found their woman. This should detract not one iota from the bravery of Parks's actions. To confront the segregation laws in the South at the time took a great deal of courage, and to follow it through demanded immense resolution. But it does show them in a different light.

The movement would make a great deal out of the unblemished nature of Mrs Parks's character, and helped to create the myth that the boycott had emerged by happenstance. At a meeting at the Holt Street Baptist church on 5 December 1955, Martin Luther King said, 'Mrs Rosa Parks is a fine person. And since it had to happen, I'm happy it happened to a person like Mrs Parks, for nobody can doubt the boundless outreach of her integrity. Nobody can doubt the height of her character, nobody can doubt the depth of her Christian commitment and devotion to the teachings of Jesus.'

But the process had left some by the wayside. One such person was Claudette Colvin. On 2 March 1955, Colvin, a fifteen-year-old, described as 'an "A" student, quiet, well-mannered, neat, clean, intelligent, pretty and deeply religious', was dragged off a bus after she refused to give up her seat at the back to a white woman. She was pushed into a police car and charged with misconduct, resisting arrest and violating the city segregation laws and put in jail until her pastor came to bail her out.

But the civil rights activists did not trumpet her case. Why not? The common belief was that it was because Colvin was pregnant, and as an unmarried teen, she would have been a liability. But Patton claimed that Colvin did not become pregnant until the summer after her arrest, and Colvin herself believes it was because she was poor. Her father mowed lawns for a living. She lived in the King Hill area, the poor part of town even for blacks. 'We weren't in the inner circle,' Colvin said in an interview with *USA Today*. The middle-class blacks didn't want us as a role model ... I figured [the boycott] was a middle-class thing, I let it go.'

Her case simply faded away. Patton is still angry about it. 'I respect my elders but I don't respect what they did to Claudette. For a while there was a real distance between me and Mrs Parks over this. Claudette was a kid. I don't think it was just about her being pregnant. I think it was partly because of her color' – Colvin was very dark – 'and because she was working poor. She lived in a little shack. It was a case of bourgy blacks looking down on the working-class blacks.

'I have no problem with them not lifting up Claudette in 1955. I have a problem with them not lifting her up in 1970. Rosa Parks could have said many times since then, "And there were others."'

Colvin's story blurred my rose-tinted vision of the civil rights era. Whether they dropped Colvin because she was pregnant or because she was poor, my image of this struggle as a clear-cut battle between right and wrong had been shattered. It was guided by political pragmatism and informed by prejudice within the black community. Then, as now, the South was a socially conservative place where an unmarried pregnant teen was probably not the ideal figure-head for a movement. But it was not just the white establishment who felt that. The civil rights leaders clearly did, too.

Dropping Colvin felt like a slap in the face for all the unmarried black mothers who walked for thirteen months during the boycott and made so many other sacrifices during the civil rights years. It said, we need you to follow us, but if it ever looks like you might lead us we will drop you like a hot brick.

I was sorry to leave Montgomery. But after a week of socializing, it was time to head off route once again. Instead of heading west for Jackson, Mississippi, as the Freedom Riders had done, I was going south, to Mobile.

It was in Mobile, on the evening of Friday, 20 March 1981, that nineteen-year-old Michael Donald walked around the corner to buy some cigarettes for his niece, who was about the same age. A full moon hung over the coast of the Gulf of Mexico. On his way, he was stopped by a couple of strangers asking directions to a nearby night club.

That night, a three-foot cross was burnt on the lawn of Mobile's court house. The next day, Michael Donald was found hanging from a full-crowned camphor tree in a side street. When the police laid the white sheet on the ground before they cut him down his feet were touching the ground and his head was bent to one side. There were multiple injuries to his head, face, scalp and hands. His throat had been slashed three times. A nylon rope cut a two-and-three-quarter-inch furrow into his neck. It was tied in a classic hangman's noose with thirteen loops.

The man who performed this lived just over the road from where the body hung. Henry Hays was twenty-seven and all he had ever wanted to do was please his father. But his father, Bennie Jack Hays, was a difficult man to please.

'To know Henry Hays and to understand the murder of Michael Donald, you've got to know Bennie Jack,' said Michael Wilson of the *Mobile Register*. 'I don't think it would have happened without the father.'

Bennie Jack Hays was born poor and white in a small town in Arkansas with the name John Henry Houston. He picked cotton, spent time in prison and always claimed that he signed up for the army with an 'X'. He was jailed for nine years for cattle rustling, released on parole and then went back in again after he was caught forging cheques.

During his second stint in prison he escaped on horseback,

met a woman called Opal Grace Frazier, embarked on what his daughter claims was his eighth marriage and changed his name to Bennie Jack Hays to avoid being traced by the law. He and Opal moved to Missouri and had two children, sons they called Raymond and Henry. Three years later the police tracked Bennie Jack down, and the next six years were spent in a prison in Arkansas. While he was inside his wife picked cotton and had another child, a girl called Gail, by a man who is believed to have run off with her sister.

Bennie Jack came out of prison in 1961, the year Michael Donald was born and the Freedom Riders came south. He travelled all around the country working on the railroads. He was an abusive father and beat his kids hard. He once cut off his dog's front paws and covered them with tar because it kept digging up the back garden. He was also a bigot, an officer with the United Klans of America who, despite his Catholic faith (the Klan is staunchly anti-Catholic), rose rapidly to the rank of Klan Grand Titan and ran Mobile's Klavern. Tired of his father's tyrannical ways, Raymond, the eldest son, left home to join the army. Henry, who was having trouble holding down a job, also joined the army but was discharged after he was found in bed with a couple of teenagers. After that he returned home and tried to please his father. When his father said join the Klan, Henry joined the Klan.

The Monday before Michael Donald was killed, Henry Hays and his friend and fellow Klansman, James 'Tiger' Knowles, had had a 'casual conversation' with Bennie Jack Hays about lynching a black person in Mobile. They discussed it in more detail at a Klan meeting in nearby Theodore on the Wednesday. On Friday a mistrial was declared in the case of Josephus Anderson, a black man who was accused of killing a white policeman in Birmingham.

That night Henry Hays and Knowles went out in search of a black man and found Michael Donald walking to the petrol station to buy cigarettes. They stopped and asked for directions. He stopped to help them. When Donald leant into the car, Knowles pulled a gun on him and forced him in.

They headed for Baldwin County, where they beat him over one hundred times and, as Donald fell to the ground, they put a rope around his neck, strangled him, and cut his throat three times. Shortly after midnight, Knowles and a friend who used to be in the Klan went and burnt a cross on the lawn of the county court house as a diversionary tactic. A few hours later they took Donald's body to Herndon Avenue and hung it up over a camphor tree.

Knowles confessed to his part in the crime and turned state's witness, testifying against his friend and accomplice, in return for life in prison. Henry Hays was on his own. The jury, eleven whites and one black, found him guilty of capital murder. They sentenced him to a life sentence without parole. The judge overruled the panel and sentenced him to death. At one minute past midnight on 3 June 1997, Henry Hays went to Yellow Mama, Alabama's electric chair. He refused a last meal and died aged forty-two, still loving his father and protesting his innocence.

Days before he was put to death Hays told Wilson: 'If Michael Donald could be brought back by killing me, fine. If there would be no more Klan, no more prejudice, no more hatred because I'm not here, I'll gladly go. But it's not gonna happen.'

Sitting in the office of the trailer park where she lives and works, Gail, Henry Hays's younger sister, explained why politics sent her brother to the chair. 'I would still say that the system killed my brother. The political issue meant everything. They wanted the black vote. Our only hope was that there would be someone who was not standing for re-election.'

This small, slightly tubby and very chatty woman in her mid-thirties spoke freely about her brother's death. When I had called a few days before she had declared herself an avid Anglophile. I wondered whether she would feel set up when she discovered I was black. But she was neither fazed (I think Michael Wilson, who helped me set up the interview, may have warned her), nor upset by any of the questions I asked her about her father's behaviour or her brother's crime.

Behind her hung an enormous grid illustrating the layout of the trailer park along with each trailer's inhabitants. Our conversation was continually interrupted as people from the park dropped in either for a chat or to report a problem. One man had just gone to hospital with heart trouble; somebody else had just come out with a colostomy bag; one of the trailers was leaking sewage. Gail's husband called and asked if she knew where his hat was. 'I don't know honey, on your head?' she said, and laughed loudly.

Having her brother die on death row, she said, had changed her: 'The first time I ever went to visit Henry on death row I was scared because I thought I was going into this room full of murderers. But when I got inside there was not a person there who didn't look like a real person. I was expecting them to have horns. They're not animals. Maybe they made a mistake, maybe they should never see the light of day. But they're humans.'

When she discovered that some of the prisoners did not receive any visitors and were not going to get anything for Christmas, she was upset. 'I put a little note around saying if you're not going to get anything for Christmas say your name. There were seventeen names and with the help of churches and civil organizations we got them all presents.'

Not once had black people blamed her for her brother's crime. 'Black people in general have dealt with prison issues and so could understand what was happening. I have never had a black person deal with me in anger.' She still insists that if Henry said he was innocent then she believes him. But it is difficult to reconcile her calm candour with the demeanour one might expect from a person who believes one of their close relatives has been executed due to a miscarriage of justice.

Her brother, she says, was a good-natured, if hopeless, character. 'Henry was a very generous, giving person. It didn't matter if he had one dollar. If you wanted it you could have it. He never got into fights because he was not that type of person. But he could never keep himself together. He could never keep a vehicle. He would always forget that it needed water and oil. If he had a vehicle it would break down.'

She painted a picture of a weak person, completely overwhelmed by his domineering father. 'It all goes back to my father. The Klan was a very violent organization, and my father was a very determined man. I don't resent him. I think he was a disturbed individual. I think he had mental problems and a very violent temper. Hatred covered a very broad area for him. It was not just blacks. It was foreigners and gays, too. Despite his Klan views he did have respect for some black people. In my father's eyes he respected anyone who took care of his family. That's why he didn't respect Henry. Henry couldn't really take care of himself.'

Her mother, who is now dead, was a very quiet person. 'She followed the exact model of what Dad wanted from a wife. He came in and his shoes were removed for him and his bath was run just like he wanted.'

I cannot imagine what it must be like to be raised by a Klansman, but I imagine that to come out of it with any

degree of sanity and respect for humanity is a real achievement. Gail lives with her second husband, and between them
they have seven children ranging in age from four to sixteen.
She considers herself something of a liberal, and compared
with many white Southerners I suppose she is. 'I feel that
there will always be prejudice. We all come from different
backgrounds, and we should respect those backgrounds.'

But the reason she thinks race relations have improved in
the South is because the government has left them to it. 'The
racial problems would never have developed if the federal
government had not gotten involved. If you're told you have
to do something, you immediately don't want to do it.'

The one thing she does have a problem with is black
and white couples having children. 'I don't believe in interracial relationships,' she says determinedly. 'Even though
they do create the most beautiful and clever children I still
don't think it is fair on the children because they don't know
where they belong. It's like if you chose to have a retarded
child. Not if you just had one but if you went out of your
way to have one. I don't feel like it would be a fair thing to
put on a child. I think it's fine if that's what you want to do
but don't do it to your own children.'

After years of negotiating the labyrinthine world of
middle-class racism, upfront prejudices like Gail's are refresh-
ing. The candour with which they are expressed at least gives
you something to engage with. It's not only that Gail says
out loud what more discreet people might think privately;
I'm sure she says what many middle-class Southerners also
say, just never in my presence.

Mobile is a beautiful town, and for two nights I stayed in the
most dingy part of it. When I had arrived, I asked the cab
driver to take me to an inexpensive motel downtown. She

took me to the Budget Inn where I shared my room with bugs in the dim light. The first night there was a terrific thunderstorm – a deluge punctuated by immense bolts and claps from on high. Three doors away, a drunk man was trying to kick my neighbour's door down. His screams, interspersed with heavy kicks against a locked door, were soon followed by sirens and the steady sound of policemen's feet. When I did eventually doze off, it was to the sound of crackling walkie-talkies and the raised voices of inebriated anger. I had booked for two nights, and the next day the hotelier told me there were no refunds. I contemplated forfeiting my night's rent for the sanity and serenity of the nearby Holiday Inn.

I started to clear my room, and as I checked the drawer in the bedside table I found this note, which judging from the date must have been left by the person who stayed there just before me. Written in a childlike scrawl, mixing up capital and small letters, it sat alongside a stub for a Greyhound ticket to Mobile from Biloxi, Mississippi, and an empty packet of long Kool cigarettes.

Dearest David,
I will try and write you while I still have the time. I am sick today. If I go too jail, I may not make it out alive again. I want you to wait for me. I am your wife and there has never been another man but you. But if something happens to me like a hospital or death you will be free to marry again, maybe I am doomed to a jail, hospital and death. I took my poems you wrote me that is all I will have of you. I want something of you in there. The poems will be good. I am sorry I ever started gambling. The money I got from the checks are not worth nothing compared to the cost I have to pay, a fine Christian husband LOVINg KINd AND TRUe. I LOVE YOU SO

MUCH AND WILL MISS YOU TERRIBLe. Thank you for your love and everything you have done for me. you have protected me and loved me. I love you you are a wonderful husband. I only wish I hadn't listened to that devil and gambled. God protect, bless and keep you safe from harm. I pray God will let you bring me home one day soon, David Honey. I LOVE YOU BUT REMEMBeR GOD LOVeS YOU AND CAReS ABOUT YOU. HE WANTS YOU TO PROSPeR AND MAKE IT IN THIS WORLd, THY WORd HAVE I PUT IN MY HEART THAT I MiGHT NOT SIN AgAINST THEE. God IS LOVe. I MiSS YOU. THe OLe MAN gAVe YOU SOME TURKeY. PLeASE TAKe CARe OF YOURSELF.

That night I remained at the Budget Inn after all. At two o'clock in the morning I was woken by the screaming of a woman in the Inn's courtyard. First of all she was shouting at one person in particular. Then she was just shouting. She sounded drunk. 'They let niggers in there,' she screamed into the night. 'Niggers are in there.' A car pulled up, doors slammed shut and then it went quiet.

This, I am anxious to point out, was not Mobile at its best. Walking down Dauphin Street, the main street, on a sunny day, you would think you were in the Mediterranean. The architecture throughout the city bears witness to its Spanish and French colonial heritage. As a coastal town it has more in common with New Orleans and Pensacola, Florida, than it does with the rest of Alabama, and not just aesthetically, but politically too. Which makes it all the more shocking that, of all the places in the Deep South, Donald's lynching should have happened in Mobile.

Joseph Langan, who was Mayor for sixteen years from 1953 to 1969 – a period which spans from before the Montgomery bus boycott to after King's assassination –

believes its position as a port town helped keep Mobile off the civil rights map. 'At first most people in Mobile were of a Spanish or French background. We also had quite a lot of Irish people who came here in the middle of the nineteenth century after the famine. So, unlike in the rest of the South, there were a lot of Catholics and a lot of people coming in from overseas. I think we just had a lot broader perspective than those from rural areas of Alabama.'

With his grey hair slicked back, Langan sat in his attorney's office surrounded by papers. He is a self-made man. He didn't have the chance to go to college but went to help at his uncle's law firm as a boy and became an attorney that way. On the wall there is a picture of Jesus, in the corner an American flag. Langan believes the main reason he managed to keep racial strife off the streets of Mobile during the fifties and sixties is because problems were worked out locally and gradually and, although he probably doesn't even recognize the fact, with a heavy dose of paternalism. He says he met with black leaders every week and even had a cross burnt on his own front lawn.

'During the lunch-counter boycotts, we would start with just a couple of blacks who would go in when other people would be leaving for the end of their lunch hour. Then, when whites got used to it, we would send them in earlier and earlier. On the buses we had it so that whites boarded at the front and blacks boarded at the back. Even if there were only seats available at the front, blacks would have to go to the back to get to the front. We got a black to get on the front and got a policeman to arrest him, and we took it to the court who said the law was unconstitutional. And that was it.

'No local legislation could be passed without me agreeing to it. I cemented a deal to pay black teachers and white teachers equally. The city government wanted something else, and I said I wouldn't agree with that unless they equalized the pay. They needed the money, so they agreed.'

Compared with his contemporaries – Bull Connor in Birmingham, George Wallace in the state capitol in Montgomery and Ross Barnett in Jackson, Mississippi – Langan was undoubtedly liberal. If he had been in Britain during the Thatcher decade he would have been branded a wet, the sort of decent fellow who might pull some strings to save the local coal mine, not realizing that the very fact of pulling strings may solve one immediate problem but perpetuates a far more enduring one.

It is an attitude illustrated in one of Langan's war stories. 'I served in the 93rd Division as a colonel and had a black driver. We were in Arizona and we couldn't find a place where they would let my driver have a dinner with me so I'd get two dinners and we would eat them in the jeep.' It is a touching story, but Langan didn't appear to see that his benevolence only existed because racism existed. But the main point is Langan was progressive when it mattered. Why? Langan is a 'one nation' American, a religious man with a sceptical take on the role of government. 'It is the creed of this country that all people are created equal. That is what we have got to do: respect each other as creatures of God and respect and love and serve each other. And not deal with each other on a racial basis. The flag doesn't represent the constitution, but the declaration of independence. God gave us right and wrong. Government didn't give us anything.'

So why, given that Mobile managed to remain largely untouched by the brutal scenes which were happening all over the rest of the South during the fifties and sixties, did it start making headlines when everywhere else was cleaning up its act?

'You couldn't stop it happening again,' said Michael Wilson, who covered Hays's execution for the *Mobile Register*. It was, he said, an act of violence that was as random as it was brutal. Not the organized terror of the old Southern lynch mobs, but the isolated actions of two twisted individuals. 'If four guys in this room decided they were going to haul someone out like that then they could. But it would be no more likely to happen now than it was in 1981.'

We were sitting in a café called A Spot of Tea and ordering our national beverages – I was sipping tea, Wilson was drinking coffee. This year, said Wilson, had been a big year for murders in Mobile. 'We haven't broken any records yet, but we could. There's been about fifty this year already.'

Many of them were apparently random and without motive although they could have had a racial dimension. 'Recently a white kid, the son of a wealthy doctor, was shot on the sidewalk right there by two black guys,' he said pointing to the street outside. 'They asked him for a cigarette. He walked on and then they shot him.'

I asked him when this was. He couldn't remember and so turned to the waiter and asked him.

'Do you remember when it was that the kid got shot on the sidewalk here recently?' he asked.

'What, the guy three weeks ago?' the waiter replied.

'No, not that one, a while longer – the doctor's son.'

The waiter couldn't remember. It has been a big year for murders.

In the run-up to Hays's execution, Wilson got to know him well. 'By the end of it I probably knew him better than he knew himself. He was like a kid. He struck me as a really impressionable guy. He would just tell you what you wanted to hear. He liked to be liked. In prison he was very popular, even among the black inmates.'

Right up to the end of his life, said Wilson, Henry Hays was in denial. 'He told me there were three stages you go through when you're on death row. The first is denial. The second is an eagerness not to waste any time. You want to do a whole bunch of things and read a bunch of books before you die. The third is when you just say: "I don't care. Just go ahead and take me." Henry was really still in the first stage.'

In the entire time that Wilson went to visit Henry Hays, Hays cried only once, and that wasn't for himself, but for his father, the man whose influence had guided him thus far, whom he still loved and who had died a few years before. 'He cried when he remembered how his confused father, suffering from senility, asked Henry's brother in Ohio why Henry, who'd been on death row for nine years then, didn't come to visit any more,' wrote Wilson in the *Mobile Register*.

Wilson went to see Hays die. 'Three reporters get to see it. The print media from the town is automatically booked in. Then the rest is like a raffle. There are two big windows, and you sit on the other side of one of them. There was his brother Raymond and his lawyer, and then doctors. Behind another window there was Donald's brother with the husband of one of his sisters. They give him a really long time to look around the room and say whatever he had to say. He said I love you to everyone. The warden comes and reads the death warrant. At the side there is a phone which is connected to the governor's office so right up to the last second if the governor wanted to stop it he could just pick up the phone. They pull a shade over the windows and when they pull the shade back up he's got a mask on and you can see him breathe through the mask. You just watch him, and then finally someone flicks a switch. His whole body is real rigid. You could see his throat get really red and that went on for about a hundred seconds. Then the doctors go and look at him and make sure he's dead and then they take him away and that's it.'

Donald's mother, the late Beulah Mae, said that she did not want Henry to die. 'You can't give life, so why take it?' she told the *New York Times* in 1987. 'You kill an innocent person, that person stays with you, day and night.' Donald's brother, Stanley, who watched the execution, told Wilson he would rather have fought him one on one.

Watching it strengthened Wilson's views against capital punishment: 'Before, I thought if it was not wrong then it was at least useless. But then there was always a voice in my head saying, "You'd be all for it if it was your brother." I'm much more against it now. It's such uncivilized behaviour for a country to kill people. The government can have the penultimate power over someone's life but not the ultimate power. And are you killing this guy who committed the lynching fourteen years ago or the guy who's touched so many lives fourteen years since. I don't know how you come away from watching something like that and think it's a good idea.'

Before I heard Wilson's account, I was not so sure. I have always been ambivalent about the death penalty. I remember watching *Schindler's List* and letting out a cheer when the chair is kicked from beneath the Ralph Fiennes character – a Nazi who murders at will and whim – and his fall is caught by the rope which jolts his body upwards and leaves him hanging. I was glad he was dead and could think of no more appropriate punishment for him. And if it was good enough for gassing Nazis then it should be good enough for a lynching Klansman.

It had embarrassed me that Donald's mother could have

wanted Hays's life spared when I, who had never even met Donald, could not, although you cannot change your views on things like capital punishment because you are embarrassed. But by the time I had finished hearing of Henry Hays's miserable life and his even more miserable death, it was obvious that you cannot kill people just to wreak political and social vengeance either. Revenge may be a suitable reaction for human beings, but it is no way for a judicial system to operate. If it is staggering to think that a lynching could take place in 1981, it is no less shocking that a government can retaliate with an execution in 1997.

The bus from Mobile to New Orleans was half empty. It was a pretty drive through the sunset on the coast of the Gulf of Mexico, through the bottom half of Mississippi en route to the bayou. We passed Biloxi, Mississippi, which looked like Las Vegas by the sea – a seemingly endless line of large casinos full of garish colours and bright lights flashing, opposite motels and fast food places. On the bus there was an elderly white woman with brown plastic boots that were undone, an old coat, long, grey greasy hair and a blue industrial-style face mask which she wore over her mouth for the entire journey.

'What is that face mask for?' I asked her.

She pulled it down for little longer than a second.

'Germs,' she said and then put it back on again.

We arrived in New Orleans in the early evening. I had lost the ticket for my bag but managed to convince the young man taking the bags off that it was mine.

'Look at it,' I said, pointing at my tired, battered rucksack with all the support poles at the back bent out of shape. 'Who would want to steal that?'

CHAPTER NINE

Mississippi: Poitier's Last Stand

When the Freedom Riders' Greyhound bus pulled into the terminal in Jackson, a large crowd awaited them. But to Farmer's astonishment, as he led his group towards the sea of white faces, it parted to let him through. They were not an unruly mob of Klan sympathizers but reporters, federal agents and plain-clothes police.

Farmer and his group entered the whites-only waiting room, drank from the whites-only water fountain and then headed for the entrance to the whites-only restaurant. A police captain blocked their way and asked them to move on. When Farmer refused, the demonstrators were arrested and escorted to a police wagon.

John Lewis, who arrived shortly afterwards on the next bus, was apprehended while actually using a urinal in the whites-only toilet.

'Can't you see what I'm doing?' he protested.

'I said move, now,' said the policeman, and Lewis 'zipped up and moved out'.

'It was all very civilized,' wrote James Farmer. 'The nation was watching through newsreel cameras. Bigotry had many faces, and unlike Alabama, where Klan hooliganism had been allowed to run amok, Mississippi was putting its best face forward.'

As the paddy wagon headed for the city jail, with more protesters from all over the country already on their way to keep filling up Mississippi's jails, the Freedom Riders sang 'We Shall Overcome'.

The court proceedings, wrote one protester, were a farce: 'The prosecution got up, accused us of trespassing, took his seat. Our attorney, Jack Young, got up to defend us as human beings. While he was defending us, the judge turned his back [and] looked at the wall. When Young finished, the judge turned around. Bam. Sixty days in the state penitentiary, and there we were, on the road to Parchman maximum security.'

Since I had left Washington DC, my expectations of New Orleans had grown out of all proportion to what the town could possibly have delivered. In Greensboro, one man had talked of his lost weekend there with a degree of hedonistic reverence that the British reserve for their visits to Amsterdam and Glastonbury. In Atlanta, friends had recommended enough jazz clubs to fill two pages in my notebook. From Birmingham on down, layer upon layer of potentially wild times had been predicted in such detail and with such enthusiasm that I expected to go straight from the bus into the arms of a curvy Creole woman who would hand me a joint and a glass of Bacardi and take me straight to a smoky bar where Miles Davis would be blasting out super Cs.

New Orleans – the capital of Cajun country and home of Mardi Gras; a groovy, laid-back party town on the Mississippi River and a safe haven for jazz nuts, where you can take your sensuality with food, music or just have it straight. No wonder the Freedom Riders wanted to finish their protest there – it sounded like paradise.

There really is nowhere in America quite like the French Quarter of New Orleans – a small grid of streets, with delicate architecture, called things like Chartres and Bienville. The place is a magnet for those who like to bump and grind their way through the weekend. For bars, cafés and clubs, it is like a concentrated version of New York. And like New York, it does have attitude, but instead of being in your face, it is mostly in your ears. There is music everywhere. Not all of it is good, and most of it is not live. But walking down the narrow streets of the French Quarter, it is all-pervasive.

Despite the Quarter's small size, my hotelier drew a chequered pattern through about a fifth of the streets on my map and warned me away from them for my own safety – New Orleans has one of the highest crime rates in the country. Then I was on my own in New Orleans on a Saturday night.

It was after nine o'clock, and the blessed El Niño was blowing a biting wind from which there was no hiding. The district's narrow streets were crammed with people with accents from out of town. They queued outside jazz clubs, stamping their feet to keep warm, in groups of six and seven, their glad rags hidden under windcheaters, weekend hair-dos squeezed into bobble hats; couples holding hands through their gloves went from crowded restaurant to packed bar; there were lots of young men shivering in light cotton shirts, well on their way to falling down drunk. It was like eleven forty-five on New Year's Eve: lots of people had heard there was a party, but weren't quite sure where it was. Right there, where Mississippi meets the Gulf of Mexico, it was only the cold that told me I wasn't on the Playa las Americas in Tenerife.

I cruised the streets looking for a club I didn't have to queue for that played music I wanted to hear (soul, rhythm and blues, or, failing that, anything but trad jazz) and after half an hour, defeated by the cold, adjourned to a bar. Over a double Jack Daniels, I chided New Orleans for letting me down.

I was sitting beside a man with a complexion the colour of dishwater and whose teeth were rotten, who was talking to the television which was showing American football: 'Fucking Dallas Cowboys. Don't fucking talk to me about the Cowboys. Bunch of fuckin' pussies,' he said, loud enough for me to hear but not loud enough to create a scene involving the entire bar. His head was ever so slightly too large for his body and, when he turned and started addressing me, I was hit by the smell of stale alcohol. His eyes were of the glazed, staring variety generally associated with maniacs. I couldn't understand most of what he said, because thick accents never do sound too clear when they have been marinating in Scotch all day. It was something about Dallas Cowboys having spent too much money on a bad player, that they cheated their way to the Superbowl several times and that – well, that they were basically 'a bunch of fuckin' pussies'. My job was to nod when he said, 'Know what I'm sayin'?' and laugh when he laughed. When he started talking about his divorce and the money she had taken and the business he had lost, I swigged what was left of my drink and made for the door.

It was nearly midnight, and out on the streets New Orleans was still humming. If I had the energy and the inclination, I could go on all night. After months of travelling through small Southern towns where local people looked on visitors with suspicion, I was now in a place where everybody wanted to be – Somewhere, as opposed to Anywhere.

This was one of the best nights I had spent on my own during the entire trip. The only improvement would have been if I had not spent half of it thinking I was missing out on something.

At the bus station the driver read us our rights and then added a word of caution for those hoping for a long journey north. The road past Jackson was blocked up with snow and getting worse. The bus might not make it all the way to Memphis.

And then we were off, into the night and the marshy

lowlands of the tip of Louisiana and the south of Mississippi. We were in the bayou and, with the help of the reading light, I could see tree stumps poking over shallow waters by the roadside. A short while after Brookhaven, the snow started falling, and by the time we reached Jackson, the ground and air were thick with it.

A white woman at the main entrance to the bus station asked if I would take out her young daughter's earring because her hands were too cold. As I fiddled with the child's lobes, stopping every now and then to blow life into my hands, her mother lit a cigarette, and then followed the flakes from a nearby streetlight to the ground as though hypnotized. She said she'd never seen anything like it.

Mississippi's reputation for racial intolerance and abject poverty is as deeply ingrained a part of its identity as the river that gave the state its name. Renowned as the home of lawless bigotry, cut off from all standards of human decency without any hope of a moral compass, it took even the NAACP, the most conservative of the civil rights organizations, fifty years before it would dare to start organizing there. For the best part of this century, it has been at the wrong end of just about every league table, leading the nation in the number of racially motivated beatings and lynchings but trailing it in the percentage of blacks registered to vote as well as in doctors, accountants, nurses and lawyers per capita. 'The good Lord', said the Governor of Mississippi to the Freedom Riders when they were in the state, 'was the original segregationist. He put the Negro in Africa, separated him from all the other races.'

So entrenched is its redneck image that some black Americans heading along the country's southern shoreline would still rather drive on through the night into Louisiana than stop for a night in the Magnolia State. Before setting off from Washington DC, I had asked a couple of black colleagues at the *Washington Post* if they thought there was anything or anywhere I should worry about on my journey. Mississippi was the one state where nobody would vouch for my safety. Given the progress that has been made in Mississippi over the past twenty years – the election of black officials, the integration of the schools and the virtual extinction of the Klan – they didn't necessarily think anything untoward would happen to me there either. But they wouldn't want to rule it out. 'Just be careful,' they said.

'To be born black and to live in Mississippi was to say that your life wasn't worth much,' said Myrlie Evers, the former head of the NAACP. To be a civil rights worker during the fifties and sixties, your life was worth even less.

On 20 June 1964, the time known as the Freedom Summer, during a drive to register black voters, three activists, two white and one black, went missing. Six weeks later, their bodies were discovered in an earthen dam. They had been shot with .38-calibre bullets, and the black man's skull was fractured.

During the search for them and their killers, which provided the narrative for the film *Mississippi Burning*, the federal agents sent by President Johnson dredged up bodies of other missing black people from the Mississippi River, and found some bodies at the side of the road. But in Mississippi at that time, black people going missing and turning up dead was not even news. It was a fact of life.

The man who ran the civil rights movement in Mississippi during the early sixties, who organized the Freedom Summer and who led the sharecroppers and farmhands in their fight against the most intense and violent racial hatred in the country, was Bob Moses. As a softly spoken and very serious twenty-six-year-old with a graduate degree in philosophy from Harvard, Moses was an unlikely candidate to lead the battle against the country's most racist establishment. During the first few years working there, this self-effacing intellectual found himself shot at, beaten and regularly jailed by the authorities. But his ability to connect with local people and his reluctance to seek the limelight in their name earned him unrivalled respect, which at times bordered on deification, among fellow activists. So concerned was he about the sheer awe in which he was held by his peers that at one stage he seriously contemplated changing his surname in the hope that it would at least strip him of any biblical connotations.

'Moses was aware of the godlike reverence he was accorded by others,' writes John Lewis in his autobiography, *Walking with the Wind*. 'At one meeting, he complained out loud, "Nobody would ever call *me* a motherfucker." He said it with such a lament, with sadness. He wished someone *would* call him a name like that.'

The day I met him, he was due to be presented with an award at the Jackson City Hall by the city's first black Mayor, not for his services to the civil rights movement, but for his contribution to the teaching of algebra. Moses's big idea is maths literacy, which is the key, he believes, to the participation of black urban youth in a modern economy. The Algebra Project aims to teach algebra to inner-city children and transform the way in which maths is taught. The Project, which involves as many parents and teachers as it can, tries to facilitate children's understanding of maths by using accessible tools – including anything from school trips to African drums – and a problem-solving method in which teachers do not spoon-feed children with answers but try to take them to the question they need to ask to find the answer they want. The Project, which is based in Jackson, also operates in Oakland, San Francisco, Los Angeles, Chicago, Milwaukee and Boston, and it is still growing.

When I called the day before and asked for an interview, Bob Moses told me he would be at the City Hall, but when I arrived, nobody was sure whether he would turn up or not; nor did they seem particularly surprised at the possibility of his absence. A group of ageing gospel singers had received their award, and now the chamber was filled with the sound of restless fidgeting and the rustling of a stalled municipal agenda. One of the parents from the Algebra Project suggested they should pick up the award on his behalf, but the council members wanted to wait just a little longer and agreed to move on to the other business in the hope that he would turn up later. They praised the Mayor for the effective manner in which the snow had been cleared the day before. It was the largest snowfall since 1929. A meteorological shock to the city's system that had closed schools, kept many people away from work and cut off many of the outlying rural areas. And just when their congratulations were exhausted, Moses sailed in on a tide of relief and some eyebrow-raising. A small man with a paunch and a goatee, he listened to his warm introduction without any reaction. 'After years dedicating his life to the civil rights struggle in Mississippi, Mr Moses has now returned to invest his talents in the state's most prized resource: children,' said a council member. 'If we are going to keep up with people all over the world, we cannot afford to be behind in mathematics. We are so very proud that you have come back and not run away from our people.'

Moses then ambled up to the microphone, muttered something about geometry, calculus and pre-calculus and then walked off, making way for the teenagers from the Algebra Project to address the council about what they had learnt from the scheme.

This, at least in part, is Moses's political modus operandi. He is not interested in awards, honours or publicity. Self-aggrandizement would probably bring him out in a rash. When Franklin McCain said, 'What we need is small enclaves of dedicated people, not someone who can rally a hundred thousand people and give a good speech,' he was talking about the likes of Bob Moses. For unlike so many of those who made headlines during the civil rights era, Moses is less concerned with securing his place in the radical history hall of fame than cementing himself in the community that he is still trying to serve, building on the work he undertook during the sixties. He is focused, resolute, gifted, self-effacing and, to an extent, a disciple of Machiavelli. He will turn up at the City Hall to receive the award so that the children can speak and maybe gain some confidence. He will allow a boring businessman to pontificate about his views on maths teaching so that he can get his business card, because he comes from a town where the Algebra Project is not yet operating and – who knows? – maybe one day might be useful.

He has a grand plan, which is to advance not himself but the movement, and in his professional life at least, everything seems to be subordinated to that goal or to be irrelevant. All of which makes him a fascinating man to read about, and an irritating and frustrating man to try to interview.

When I introduced myself to him in the corridor of the Jackson City Hall, his eyes lit up. 'I had no idea that you were black,' he said, and his mind whirred on how best to capitalize on the situation: how could he introduce me to the children and let them ask me questions, give them the opportunity to speak to a young black professional male from England? He had no idea what I would say, but felt pretty sure it could do no harm.

He asked someone if he could borrow a room in the city

chambers, procured a councilwoman's office and sat me at the head of the table in front of about twelve of his teenagers, who were between the ages of about fourteen and sixteen, as well as some of their parents. They were as polite, confident, articulate and smart a group of teenagers as you are likely to meet anywhere, much of which was down to Moses; they had just addressed a city council chamber – they were not going to have any problems speaking to a British journalist. I answered lots of questions about England and spoke some French and Russian; a couple of months ago I would have considered it boastful, but now I felt I might be opening a window on what they might make of their future. Then suddenly, halfway through answering a question about Lady Diana, Moses, the man I had come to interview, put on his coat and made for the door. He told the youngsters he would see them all the next day at the Superintendent's office and informed me that one of the parents would show me around the Project tomorrow.

The next morning, one of the parents who worked with the Algebra Project came to pick me up at my hotel and drove me around. We went to a school which was one hundred per cent black – 'we had one white student who graduated last year,' the principal said – and where ninety-seven per cent of the children were on free and reduced lunch. We ate some soul food in what looked like a shack and went to visit my guide's wife at her office.

Her colleagues kept calling other black colleagues into her office to hear my accent. When they were all in the room, she asked me to speak some Russian again, just as I had done the previous day. Momentarily caught between bashful and bullish, I baulked.

'What do you want me to say?' I asked

The women in the room were amazed. 'Damn, did you

hear that?' said one. 'How the hell you get to speak languages like that?'

It took me a couple of seconds to realize that they thought I had been speaking Russian.

'That was English,' I said, and then said it again, enunciating carefully: 'What–do–you–want–me–to–say?'

By the time I got to Lanier High, where the Project is based, it was past two o'clock, and I had not yet spoken to Moses. When I entered his class room, I found him wandering around in a pair of yellow kitchen gloves cleaning out bins. He nodded hello to me and carried on.

It suddenly became clear that he had no intention of giving me an interview. It was not that he was too busy to talk to me; he just didn't want to. And I was irritated. I understood that he had no interest in self-promotion. But if he had said no when I first asked him for the interview, I would have done something else with my time. As it was, he had said yes, and not only kept me waiting but had forced me to follow the agenda he had set. He wanted me to learn about the Algebra Project, which was fine. It was interesting. But I wanted to talk to him. And he was messing me around.

'I need to speak to you now,' I said. He muttered something about exams and bells and a limited amount of time, and then walked out with another bin. I followed him out and stood in the doorway, watching, while he lined the bin with a plastic bag. I couldn't make him speak to me, but could possibly make him feel bad if he didn't. He came back in, peeled off his gloves and observed that there were a few minutes to go before the bell.

With no time for courtesies I asked him what the link was between his civil rights activism in the sixties and the Algebra Project.

'The link is that it's organizing with a target population.

The target used to be the sharecroppers and domestic labourers, and we organized around the right to vote. The work now is with young people in urban areas, people who were not picked up by the gains of the movement – they are sort of the sharecroppers of the nineties. In the fifties and sixties the adult population was marginalized by plantation economics; their sons and daughters are similarly marginalized today with regards to the economy.'

It sounded at first like an odd battleground in the struggle for equality. But Moses's priorities definitely chimed with those in the wider black community. Throughout my journey, when I had asked people what they thought the main issues were today, they had talked about their children's education and the need to compete in a modern economy. White flight from cities was leaving urban areas with depleted resources to fund state education. The result has been a huge number of poorly educated black youths who are growing up ill-equipped to compete in the job market. But where does algebra fit into this?

'In this country, math is used as one of the subjects by which you separate those who will have a function in society from those who will not. They sift students to decide who will move to the next level and into the larger economy, and the way they do that is through algebra. There is nothing to say it has to be algebra. In France, it is geometry. There is nothing in the math that says it has to be used that way. But algebra has been the subject in this country that we use to gain command of abstract representations of quantum data. That is the data that are used in computers and other technologies.'

If he is concentrating on those blacks who have not reaped the gains of the civil rights movement, who does he think benefited?

'A small percentage of blacks who were present as the

black middle class and lower middle class in the sixties and whose sons and daughters were invited to attend elite colleges, and to work for companies which were looking for a certain percentage of black students who could move on to the corporate world. It was this small proportion who picked up the gains. But while they had money, they didn't have real wealth, and they weren't able to pass these gains on to their children. So their sons and daughters are in a difficult position. They have grown up accustomed to a certain level of affluence, but their parents are not able to guarantee it because it's not clear that their own position will prevail.'

Then the bell went. There were many more questions I wanted to ask, but there was no time. He stood up and left.

At the office of the Mississippi NAACP, the State Secretary, Wendell Paris, was on the phone.

'He fired you? Who else has he fired? Are they black, too? And he is white? You have to make sure that your equal rights are being violated ... Oh, well that is certainly using fear and intimidation. Is anyone who works at the store white? Have they been fired? ... There are four things that the Equal Employment Opportunities Commission will move against: age, religion, race or sex. Which one are you going to file under? ... No, no, no, you can't go on age, because you're under fifty. Make sure you put race discrimination on this. This is a white person doing this to you.'

Paris hung up and shook his head. I wanted to take a drive up the Delta, but I needed to know if there was anywhere I should avoid, and thought the NAACP would be the place to find out. One of Paris's predecessors, Medgar Evers, was shot dead on his doorstep in Jackson in 1963. If anyone could tell me how much of Mississippi's reputation was still justified, Paris could.

Paris said that the degree to which things had progressed varied from town to town. 'Unless you had folks changing things in the community years ago, then often nothing has changed there. You can have one town that has changed, but you go fifteen miles up the road, and nothing has changed. In Belzoni, the catfish capital of the world, there are still places where blacks aren't allowed to eat.'

When I told him I was thinking of going up to Leflore, Tallahatchie and Quitman counties, he sucked his teeth and shook his head again. 'I wouldn't advise you to stop around there, or ride around at night. Try and take the major highways.'

I asked him what he thought might happen. He said he didn't know, but a young man was run over by a car up that way recently, which then reversed over his legs several times.

'I wouldn't say that would happen to you. But you just never know what people in those places are going to do.'

This, I now knew, was the standard black Southern response to questions about my personal safety. Whites would generally treat any anxiety about the prospect of a racial assault as a personal insult and shrug it off with assurances that everything was different now. Blacks always started by admitting that they had no idea what might happen but would advise me to beware all the same. They would then back up their counsel with a gory tale of a recent maiming, or paint a scenario in which I would end up the hapless and injured victim. It was a gulf in perception highlighted in the aftermath of the lynching in Jasper, Texas, in 1998. White people were shocked; black people, even as they mourned their dead, clearly felt that an atrocity like this had been only a matter of time. One of the consequences of racial violence, which is often overlooked, is that it not only physically injures and even kills individuals, but also stops entire communities from living normally because they are suffocated by fear.

Reading between Paris's pauses, sighs and hesitations, what he appeared to be saying was: 'We know there are some scary people around here, but we don't know who they are, and they are generally not the type to show themselves in daylight. Just because things look normal doesn't mean they are.'

The next evening, once night had fallen, I drove up the Delta, stopped by the Tallahatchie River and stood for as long as I dared. There was no bravado in this. I did not deliberately ask Paris what not to do so that I could then just go ahead and do it. But I was motivated by that perverse element of human nature that finds some primordial satisfaction in being terrified. I knew what had happened there, and I wanted to taste the fear.

There was a full moon floating in the Tallahatchie. In nearby Money – a tiny place for which there are no road signs, only directions – the shops that once made up the town centre are now derelict, their roofs collapsed, their fronts faded and small trees and shrubs sprouting from their charred innards. During fifteen minutes, not one car passed. The only noise was the occasional flap of the Stars and Stripes hanging outside the makeshift post office. Standing on the banks of the Tallahatchie, I thought of Emmett Till, all the stupid things I did when I was fourteen and the fact that the only thing scarier than the sights and sounds of rural Mississippi at night is its history.

Emmett Till did a stupid thing when he was fourteen. On an August night in 1955, on a dare from his friend, the black teenager, who was on holiday from Chicago, said, 'Bye, baby,' to a white woman in Money's grocery store, and maybe even whistled at her. Three days later, his body was fished out of the Tallahatchie with a bullet in his skull, an eye gouged out and his forehead crushed on one side. His body was so mangled that his uncle could identify it only by his initialled ring. When the body was sent home to his mother in Chicago, she demanded an open-casket funeral so the world could see what the Southern racists had done to her son.

Two men were acquitted of his murder by an all-white jury, but later confessed to the killing, for a price, to a magazine. They said they wanted only to scare him, but when he refused to beg for mercy, they 'had to' kill him.

Of all the stories of Southern racist atrocities, Till's has had the greatest effect on me, not only because it was such a bloody and cowardly murder, but also because, from the pictures I had seen of Till, and from what I had read about him, he looked and behaved much as I did at that age. He was a little chubby adolescent with a mischievous smile who liked to show off and did not know when a joke had gone too far. 'He was known as a prankster, a risk-taker and a smart dresser who nevertheless did well in school,' wrote Stephen Whitfield in *A Death in the Delta*. In every aspect but his dress sense, he could have been me.

Standing alone on the banks of the Tallahatchie, I was shivering with cold and getting my wish. I was tasting fear and it made me want to retch. I felt alone in a dark place, a long way from anywhere, not just physically, but politically, morally and culturally. I was afraid for the first time on my trip: afraid of all the small, ugly personal histories that might be hidden by the night, the river and the long grass; haunted by the bodies that went missing, the indignities that went unavenged and the lies that stood uncorrected.

For as long as I stood on the banks of the Tallahatchie,

the world was stripped of all moderating influences. Right there, right then, it felt as though, if a group of white youths drove past and saw me, nothing would matter but my race. There would not be one joke I could tell them, one certificate I could show them, one anecdote I could share or one drink I could buy them that would make them see anything but the fact that I am black and no saying what that simple fact might mean to them.

I got back into the car and drove away quicker than I should have. Fear, Mississippi-style, is a very ugly dish.

Driving north from Money, I stopped that night in the small town of Senatobia and pulled up at the Comfort Inn, just off I55, at around nine o'clock. Senatobia, according to the 1990 census, has 4,770 inhabitants and sits in a very quiet, sleepy part of the world. There were no more than three or four cars in the car park but the young white woman at the desk said there were no rooms. This was the first time since the beginning of my journey that I had been turned away from a motel – even in Greensboro during homecoming weekend and the barbecue festival I had found a room. And this was the smallest place I had stopped on my travels.

'None at all?' I asked.

'No. We're all booked up and not taking any more reservations for tonight,' she said.

This was annoying; I didn't want desperately to stay in Senatobia, but I was sure this woman was lying and I couldn't work out what to do about it. I walked back to my car and put my Sidney Poitier hat on.

It was the first time something like this had happened to me since I was fifteen, and I was stunned. I knew quite definitely that people could do things like this, but I hadn't quite expected that I could encounter such bigotry without either having the foresight to avoid it, or without outsmarting it.

In the summer of 1984, I was in the Dordogne on a French exchange. My penfriend, Richard, came into our room with a tent under his arm and tears in his eyes, explaining that there was a 'big problem'. His father said he couldn't bear having a black person in the house, and I would have to go. 'Tell me your thinks,' said Richard; 'I think we'd better go,' I replied, and we walked silently in the sunshine to the local campsite where I pitched my tent and, since I had not counted on having to pay for food and lodging, waited for my mother to send me some money. At the time, I was simply amazed that someone would go quite that far. It added a whole new dimension to the despiser clan I had grown up with in Stevenage. I wasn't embarrassed, apart from for Richard, and I didn't feel insulted. I just felt numb. I was fifteen, and this man didn't want me in his house. What could I do about that? Nothing.

In the subsequent years that I had to deal with this level of discrimination – which, as it happened, was often in France – I would react in a similar way, helpless in the face of a hopeless case. 'This person is a bigot. What can I do about that? Nothing.' And nothing is what I did.

As I grew older and started earning more money – it is easier to be stroppy when you have a regular income – I became bolder. I also decided that it was the responsibility of people with either cash or clout to complain so that the perpetrators did not simply assume that since black people are generally poor and powerless they would never fight back.

Back in my car in Senatobia, Poitier fedora firmly on my head, I decided the only reasonable thing to do with a situation that belonged in the sixties was to try to expose it with a sixties technique. I went to the petrol station over the road and called the Comfort Inn to ask if they had any rooms.

From here, I imagined, the tale would go one of two ways, either of which would serve me well. If the receptionist said no, then I would know she had been telling the truth, and it would prove that one of Mississippi's main problems was not that it had not changed but that the rest of the world did not trust that it had. If she said yes, then I would have a classic Southern moment, a personal illustration of how little things had really progressed, which I might cap by returning to the motel, demanding the room and watching her fluster.

As I dialled the number, I didn't think of option three.

'I would like to make a reservation,' I said.

'Didn't you come by here a minute ago?'

She recognized my accent. Englishmen probably do not pass through Senatobia that often. My ruse was heading towards a brick wall at breakneck speed. I slammed on the gas.

'Yes, I did,' I replied. 'But I didn't believe you.'

I replaced the handset. It never happened like that in the movies.

At the food counter at the Jackson bus station, I was fuelling up for a long journey with a plate of potato salad, fried chicken and green beans. The bus was scheduled to leave Jackson at seven in the evening. I would have to change in Memphis around midnight for a bus that would go straight to DC, arriving at around nine the following night. I planned to bail out a few hours earlier in Roanoke, Virginia, where my girlfriend would pick me up and drive me back.

The woman ahead of me in the cafeteria queue was

desperate to get back to St Louis, Missouri. She had spent the previous four days in jail after the police had stopped a car she was in and found drugs on her travelling companion. With no money for bail, she had to wait for her boyfriend to wire some from St Louis. When the cashier offered her a routinely cheery, 'Come visit us again,' she replied, 'I hope not. I don't care if I never see this place again.'

This was a no-nonsense travel day, the last Friday evening before Christmas. The buses were packed, the station which had been practically empty the week before was buzzing. The prospect of being turned away from a full bus afforded nobody the security of waiting quietly.

When I had finished my meal, I got the tags for my bag, milled around with everyone else and then joined the crush when the bus was announced. This proved pointless because Greyhound had put on an extra bus to Memphis; once we were on board, confusion kept our bus right where it was for about forty-five minutes.

There were no spare seats. I sat next to a balding man called Craig with false teeth who delivered mobile homes all over the country. Once he had made a delivery, he would get a bus back to Chicago, where he lived with his second wife and her grandson, the son of her daughter who was abandoned by her boyfriend and unable to take care of her child.

Craig was a seasoned bus traveller. On the road, he carried a pillow, a book – Stephen King – and a small briefcase with some toiletries in it. He just came from a delivery in Biloxi. He doesn't rush for buses because he knows there is no point. 'There's not one time when I think if I'd have gone running it woulda made any difference at all,' he said. When I tell him my final destination is DC, he winced.

'I've been there a couple of times, but I wouldn't want to

live there,' he said. 'Too many diplomats. They could just run up and shoot you and walk off, and there ain't nothing you can do about it because they've got that diplomatic immunity.'

I told him that while that was probably technically true, I had never heard of it actually happening.

'But it *could* happen,' he said, and would not let the matter rest until he had forced me to agree.

Soon after, he rested his pillow on the window and went to sleep. Had it not been for the man who kept belching a few seats behind us, and the small boy in front of me who kept reclining his chair, pulling it up and then reclining it again, until I stuck my knee out to let him know there was a limit to my patience, it would have been a fairly uneventful journey.

When we arrived in Memphis, I went to pick up my bags and was shooed away by the man whose job it was to pick up my bags. I told him that I would prefer to see them on to the next bus myself; he waved me away and told me that it would be fine. I was too tired to argue.

Inside the bus station, the staff wore foam reindeer antlers which bobbed up and down as they mopped the floor and served burgers. The two longest queues reflected the country's two most significant post-war migrations. The line for Chicago, one of the magnet cities during the surge to the North during the great migration, was mostly made up of black people, whom I assumed were either from the South going to visit family or from the North returning home from visiting family. The line to Texas was mostly Hispanic: immigrants, new citizens and some seasonal labourers going home, I guessed, to either Texas or Mexico. Many of them were leaning their heads on cardboard boxes filled with microwaves and television sets.

Midnight in Memphis, and I was wilting. Every so often,

a rush of excitement would pass through the queue, making everyone think the bus was about to arrive; we would get up, get in line, wait for ten minutes and then realize it was a false alarm. Then a weird thing happened; I spotted the woman with the plastic boots and the blue face mask, the woman I had seen a week previously on a bus between Mobile and New Orleans. The United States is a big place. Unless she had a twin sister with the same dress sense and phobia about germs, this was a big coincidence. I nodded hello, but she didn't recognize me.

Just after one in the morning, the call came for people for all stations to New York to step forward. As we walked through the gate, a man whom I would very much like to meet again sometime rushed us on to a bus saying NASHVILLE.

'Is this going to DC?' I asked him.

'Yes,' he said. 'After Nashville, it's going to DC.'

I got on the bus, fell asleep and woke up in Nashville. 'How long have we got here?' I asked the driver.

'This is it,' he said. 'The bus stops here.'

'What about the bus to DC? The man at Memphis said you were taking us all the way.'

'The bus stops here,' he said, then he picked up his hat and walked off.

At the ticketing desk in Nashville, there was already a long line of people who had just got off the bus I was on. There was a woman with three small children who had been travelling from Tulsa, Oklahoma, since the previous morning and should already have been in DC; a man going from southern Arkansas to Boston; and a Korean student on his way to North Carolina. All of us, with about twenty others, had been put on the wrong bus.

The staff at Nashville were unsympathetic. 'Well, I'm afraid you have missed your bus. You should be here half an hour before the bus is due to leave. It left about twenty minutes ago,' said a man.

'We missed it because you put us on the wrong bus,' I shouted from the back of the queue.

'One person at a time, sir,' he said, and started to patronize the woman from Oklahoma who had already started crying. Her smallest daughter, who had silver bells tied to the laces of her white shoes, joined in. It was four o'clock in the morning. The next bus was in three hours' time.

I went to the customer service office to complain. The woman to whom I complained, whose name was Mona, said it had nothing to do with her. 'I didn't tell you to get on the wrong bus,' she said.

'But you do work for Greyhound, don't you? That suit you wear does mean that you all work for the same company, doesn't it? Well, somebody who wears the same suit as you told me to get on the wrong bus, and now I'm stuck here for three hours,' I said.

'What do you want me to do about it?' said the ever obliging Mona.

'Well, you could apologize,' I said.

'What for? I haven't done anything wrong,' said Mona as she left the room.

I left with her on a hunch, the hunch being that the only reason she left the room was to get away from me. And I was right. Mona had nowhere to go. So I followed her as she wandered aimlessly around for a few minutes, telling her (not shouting, just telling) that if I was as bad at my job as she was at hers, I would give up and join the circus; that the firm she worked for was a bad joke; and that I was going to write to her manager and tell him or her just how bad she was at her job. After five minutes of watching Mona pretend that I did not exist – she went back into her office at least twice, and I was right behind her both times – I got bored, sat down and listened to the bells on the little girl's feet.

When the bus arrived, dawn was breaking. By the time we got to Knoxville, a camaraderie had built up among the passengers. To my left, across the aisle, was a nineteen-year-old woman who was heavily pregnant; the father was a forty-two-year-old man she had married the year before. She was younger than some of her stepchildren.

Sitting next to me was a man called Smokey, a wiry-framed character of medium height with a wispy goatee that had a life of its own, and a large head of hair that was all combed back. He looked like Sean Penn in *Dead Man Walking* but acted like a character from a Coen brothers movie. Smokey was about twenty-six and grew up in Ohio. He had been doing some work down South and was now coming back to be with his girlfriend, who he hoped would soon be his wife. 'I'm going to give her that ring on Christmas day and see what she says,' he said.

The woman in front of us asked Smokey how he got his name.

'Well, my dad was a hash-head, and while my ma was giving birth, he went into the hospital bathroom to roll up a joint. He'd just taken his first puff, when the nurse came in and told him I was a boy. He took a deep breath, blew out a whole lot of smoke and said, "We'll call him Smokey."'

Smokey liked to talk, mostly about fighting: the fights his ex-wife and current girlfriend had over him, the fights with his older brother, and about the number of times he had been in jail for fighting, in particular the time his neighbours had called the police on him and his brother.

'My brother got back in the house, but I gave the police the finger, and they took me in. Got fined fifty bucks to get my ass whupped by my own brother in my own front yard,' he said, laughing uproariously, apparently unaware that he came out of the story looking neither particularly smart nor particularly tough.

Once he and his brother were on the same side. 'There were these three guys walked past my house with one girl and a dog and they started making like they wanted to start something. So me and my brother kicked their asses. *And the girl. And the dog,*' said Smokey triumphantly. When I asked him how on earth he managed to beat up a dog he turned to the woman across the aisle and started talking about child-birth. Smokey had two children. That was probably the most scary fact about him.

At one stop, a cross-dresser propositioned one of the passengers at the front of the bus. For a while, the entire bus was engaged in one conversation: everyone was quiet as the passenger told his story, and laughed when he had finished. And then Smokey chimed in: 'You should have told him you're a pitcher, not a catcher,' and the bus dissolved into a swamp of hilarity and homophobia.

On the eastern tip of Tennessee, I heard an English voice. It belonged to a young man of about twenty from Folkestone, who was fed up of getting plastered in his home town and had recently moved to the States to stay with his American father and stepmother and get plastered there. He had not been getting on with his stepmother, and was bored in the suburbs of Virginia Beach, so his father had sent him down to Kentucky to spend some time with one of his uncles where, he boasted, he had drunk everybody under the table. 'It was mental,' he said. 'I feel rough now, I can tell you. Everyone was giving it large last night. Jesus. Wallop, wallop, wallop.' He poked his thumb up from a clenched fist and lifted it to his mouth and away again to the beat of each 'wallop', which symbolized him drinking a lot, fast. Not one of the Americans who was standing around smoking as he told the story could understand a word he was saying but found him very entertaining. It was when he started trying to explain what hair of the dog meant – 'Cos you see, it's like if a dog bit you and then you would be having a hair from that dog ... you know, like if I had a beer now it would be like taking a hair' – that everyone started to walk away.

Shortly after we reached Virginia, the police came on with sniffer dogs and searched everybody's luggage. It was then that I realized I had not seen my rucksack since Jackson. I checked in my pocket; I still had the precious stub.

When we arrived in Roanoke, I made the futile gesture of waiting for my luggage to be unloaded, and then went and told the man at the ticket desk it was not there.

'Where did you lose it?' asked the man.

'I didn't lose it; *you* lost it. But the last time I saw it, it was in Jackson, Mississippi.'

He told me to come back the next day.

The next day, another Greyhound employee was at the desk, and I had to tell the story all over again. Two sailors were also waiting. 'Lose your bag?' they asked, with big smiles. I handed the woman behind the desk my ticket, and she disappeared into the back. She came back with my bag. I had a quick look through and found a shoe was missing. I told her. She asked if I was sure it had been in there in the first place. I told her that it is a rule of mine never to travel with one shoe. She asked me to empty out my rucksack. I told her the shoe had been right at the top. She said unless I emptied my rucksack, she could not sign the form saying that the shoe had been lost.

'You lose my bag, you lose my shoe, and now you want me to unpack my whole rucksack?'

'I didn't lose your shoe, sir,' she said.

If anyone at Greyhound ever revises the company's core standards, they might want to put in collective responsibility.

I proceeded to pull out my underwear, newspaper and T-shirts and throw them over her desk while muttering the words 'fucking', 'Greyhound' and 'crap' in various combinations loudly enough for her to hear. I then filled out a form with my address and phone number, and she told me I would get a reply within ten days. Three months later, I received a letter from Greyhound. 'Based upon our investigation of this incident, we do not find any evidence that your property was tampered with while in the care and custody of Greyhound Lines. Accordingly, we will be unable to honor your claim.'

CHAPTER TEN

History's Shadow

In the White House East Room, there were songs and tears. A month after I had returned from the South, James Farmer, the former leader of CORE, the architect of the Freedom Ride, who is now blind, diabetic and a double amputee, was finally being honoured.

'He has never sought the limelight, and until today, I frankly think he's never got the credit he deserves. His long-overdue recognition has come to pass,' said President Clinton as he awarded the Presidential Medal of Freedom, the highest civilian award in the United States, to Farmer. After the White House ceremony, Farmer attended a reception in his honour at the Hay Adams Hotel in Washington DC, where crowds of applauding supporters and admirers were waiting for him.

Lying in his bed in his rural home in Spotsylvania County, Virginia, the seventy-seven-year-old civil rights veteran said it was the best day of his life. 'It was just like the old days. But this time I felt like I was finally being vindicated. That the years of invisibility were over, and that my work was now being recognized by the President of the United States of America.'

He said it reminded him of the day he returned to New York after he had been released from jail in Jackson following the end of the Freedom Ride. 'When I walked into the airport and there were two hundred or more people there

268

singing, "James Farmer is our leader" and "We Shall Not Be Moved".'

I had arrived a little early, and he was just finishing lunch. Lying in bed, with a bar hanging just over his head: a torso in a vest with two large, muscular arms and what is left of his body covered with a tartan sheet, he was struggling with a yoghurt. He had a full, warm face, a low, booming, gravelly voice, a good sense of humour and a raucous laugh. On a table by the bed there was his medicine, all laid out in rows, and next to that a prosthetic leg with a sock and a shoe on it. Hanging on the wall was a street sign reading JAMES FARMER STREET, from his home town of Holly Springs, Mississippi. Outside were a small lake and acres of woods.

I asked him why he thought his contribution to the civil rights struggle was never fully recognized. He grabbed the bar and pulled himself up.

'One reason is that I was in the shadow of Martin Luther King, and that was quite a big shadow. It was King who made the "I have a dream" speech. And King was assassinated, and that always enlarges a person's image. The other reason was because I had a white wife, which would not be such a big deal now, but at the time it definitely was. A civil rights leader with a white wife.' He laughed.

In terms of national publicity, the Freedom Rides were Farmer's finest hour. A few years after the campaign, he went on the speakers' circuit, and some time after that he made an unsuccessful bid for a Congressional seat in Brooklyn, New York. Like Shuttlesworth and, to an extent, McCain, he was concerned that his place in history would be either diminished in importance or erased altogether.

In fact, were it not for the honesty with which Farmer refers to his desire to be honoured, it could come across as sour grapes. But almost forty years after the Freedom Rides, there will soon be two generations who have never seen Farmer's name on the front pages of newspapers. If he does not battle for his place in the history of the civil rights movement, then who will?

'At that time, I was one of what used to be called the big four. There was Roy Wilkins [the NAACP lobbyist at Congress], Martin Luther King, James Farmer and Whitney Young [the leader of the National Urban League]. It should really have been the big six, because there was John Lewis [national Chairman of SNCC] and Dorothy Height [the President of the National Council of Negro Women], but age bias and sexism were even more rampant then than they are now.'

With the possible exception of John Lewis, who is now a congressman, the only person that most Americans – blacks and whites – would be able to identify from this six today is King. Farmer admits he has had trouble coming to terms with that. 'I resented it at the time. There was an element of envy. I think that was inevitable, but I lived with it. I do not detract at all from Martin Luther King, because he was a great man.'

One other factor that confuses his legacy is that he spent some time working in the Nixon administration in a top post at the Health, Education and Welfare Department. He did have serious concerns about taking the job at the time, which he expressed to Robert Finch, Nixon's secretary-designate to the department: 'Ninety-five per cent of the blacks in this country are Democrats, and Nixon is very unpopular. For me to work in that administration might be political suicide. I would be painting a bull's-eye on my chest, my back and both sides.' But his reasons for accepting had a political logic. 'For a long time, it has been my conviction that blacks achieve maximum political leverage by not being "in the bag" for either party,' he told Finch.

When he left the job eighteen months later, saying privately that the administration lacked 'moral leadership', but offering no public criticism of Nixon, he was assaulted from the left and the right. Much of his life now takes place on this bed. He gets out on Mondays and Tuesdays to teach civil rights to packed classes at the Mary Washington College in Fredericksburg and then has someone read term papers to him so that he can mark them. 'I lie down, think, sometimes I roll outside and I travel, too,' he said. I asked him where he had been. He mentioned Barbados, and I told him that my parents were from there.

'So, are you black?' he asked, sounding slightly astonished.

And only then did it occur to me that Farmer assumed, from my accent, that I was white. I had told him I was black when I first came in and was explaining the book, but he must have not heard. Now he was intrigued. He wanted to know 'how black'.

'Just a little bit lighter than you,' I said, and then explained about my parents' immigration. We talked for a while about black people in Britain. He said that since he had been legless, he had not been as active as he would have liked. I told him that 'being legless' in Britain meant being drunk. His laugh filled the room, and he assured me he was sober.

Then we went back to history. I asked him how he chose the people to go on the Freedom Ride. His answer shocked me. 'We had to screen them very carefully because we knew that if they found anything to throw at us, they would throw it. We checked for Communists, homosexuals, drug addicts. They had to be twenty-one or over, and have the approval of their parents. I personally interviewed people, and then would talk to their friends.'

Like the Montgomery bus boycott, which had dropped

Claudette Colvin, the Freedom Rides were not a purely moral crusade. They had excluded black people they thought might embarrass them. Politically and tactically, given the mores of the time and the degree of prejudice ranged against them, they may have been right to act in this way. But one wonders who else was left out.

What was the best political decision Farmer ever made? 'Rejoining the Freedom Ride in Montgomery,' he said immediately. He recalled the moment he decided to board the bus in Montgomery after he bid farewell to a white female volunteer already on the bus. 'I said, "Have a safe trip," and her eyes were as big as saucers with fear. She said, "Aren't you coming with us, Jim?" I was hoping they weren't going to ask me. I went through a litany of reasons. We had just buried my father. Two deaths would have been too much for the family. Somebody had to stay free to meet with the President and raise money. I said, "Don't worry. I'll be with you in spirit." She said, "Jim, please." Now, there had been some ambivalence about how I would approach it. So I had packed my suitcase and put it in the trunk of the CORE rental car. I was hoping that I would get the courage to go. Her pleading gave me the courage, and I thank her for it.'

Any regrets? 'The worst decision I ever made was staying in jail during the March on Washington.' Farmer was in Plaquemine, Louisiana, leading a march against police brutality when he was arrested with more than two hundred other marchers. Bail was set at $500. He refused to bail himself out, because those he had marched with were not in a position to do the same. On the day of the demonstration when King made his 'I have a dream' speech, he wept in his cell.

'I should have bailed myself out. I missed an opportunity to speak in front of a worldwide audience – TV, radio, print media. Such an opportunity had never come before and would never come again. That was the thing that made Martin Luther King a saint. It was a great speech. Great orientation.'

Instead, he listened to it on the radio. When King wound up one of the great oratorical performances of the century with the words, 'Free at last, free at last, thank God Almighty, free at last,' Farmer turned to the radio and jokingly retorted:

'OK, Martin, give me the key. Give me the key.'

Homecoming

Trips to the United States make me bold and sassy. Returning to the UK is always tricky. Until the confidence of the New World has been drained from my system, I talk louder, walk faster and generally act like a Technicolor cartoon character that has bounced on to a black and white screen. Having spent six months roaming around the South, I had been confirmed, assured and supported: Black Southerners might have been confused by my British accent, but they were keen to embrace my blackness. They talked about it and engaged with it. They gave me access to another dimension. All that, I felt, would be confiscated at Customs: *Ladies and gentlemen, we are about to land at Heathrow. Please stow away your tray tables, put your seats in the upright position, ensure your seatbelt is securely fastened and that your racial identity is put away carefully in a safe place as otherwise it may well pop out and cause you injury.*

Coming home is always the same. Once I am through the hoops, I am fine. Past the barriers and far away, there are friends to whom I will not have to explain myself: people who don't think I'm speaking Russian when I'm actually speaking English; people who are not stunned by the very fact of me and who live in a country where nationalism is still viewed with scepticism and segregation is not de rigueur. But first I would have to go through the hoops – the ones where the faceless man in the forgettable attire matches my melanin to the crest on my passport and his colleague piles through my dirty washing.

It is a long way from the arrival gate to passport control at Heathrow, past the advertisements and along a seemingly endless number of moving walkways. But I didn't rush. Because even if I sprinted from a seat in first class, I would never be first to the baggage carousel. I just wanted to get through the next fifteen minutes with some integrity, but as I got closer to my target I felt the spring in my step uncoiling.

The human traffic split in two: EU and Others. Once, in Rome, a guard with a gun whistled at me from the other side of the room and ordered me out of the EU line. When I refused to move, he strutted over, snatched my passport, held it as though I had just handed him a turd, grunted and then gave it back to me. But if there must be humiliation, then let it be this. Then at least any self-respecting human being could walk past and be revolted. In London, they address you as 'sir' and ask you insulting questions with such a polite demeanour that everyone walking past thinks they are just doing their job.

I opened my passport at the page with my picture on it and handed it over to the passport controller. He looked up at me, down at the page and then up at me again before passing it carefully under an ultraviolet light. Around me, other passengers strode past. He passed it back under the light, throwing me another glance. No question this time. No 'Is this your only passport, sir?' or 'Could you tell me your place of birth, sir?' None of the ruses so predictable and pathetic that I am tempted to put on a West African accent just to make all our lives that little bit more interesting. Just the ultraviolet treatment and the sound of your white fellow passengers moving on.

I picked up my bags and headed for customs, where a small man pointed my trolley to a layby in the green channel

and started with the usual questions: Where have you come
from? How long were you there? Did you buy any duty
free? Where is your ticket? Where is your passport? He was
intrigued by the number of stamps in it.

'Do you work, sir?'

'Sorry?'

'Do you work?'

'Yes.'

'What as?'

'A journalist.'

'Do you have any work ID, sir?'

I went for my pocket and paused.

'What has it got to do with you whether I work or not?'

'It's a routine question, sir. Do you have any work ID?'

I reached in my wallet, pulled out my National Union of
Journalists membership card and looked away, feigning indifference. The only other person to have been stopped was a
black man of about my age. He looked at me and raised his
eyebrows. And that look was enough to spark a change in
me, from weary and resigned to bold and sassy.

'Is it your policy, then, just to stop young black men?'

'I'm sure as a journalist, sir, you like to see all sides of
the story.'

'The only story I see here is lots of white people walking
through and two young black men being stopped.'

'If you were here for more than five minutes, I'm sure
you'd see that we stop all sorts of people, sir.'

He handed me back my card and tapped my bags in a
way that suggested he had finished. I started repacking what
he had taken out.

'If I've only been here five minutes and this is what you
do, I'd hate to see how many of us you stop in a day.'

I was irritating him. And I was glad.

'Do you think we're prejudiced, sir, is that your problem?'

'No, I think it's *your* problem.'

I loaded my bags back on to the trolley.

'So, sir, are you going to put this in your paper?' he asked, with a sneer.

'I might,' I said.

'Good,' he said to my retreating back, with a laugh designed to make everyone around think we were having a joke. 'Put it in your paper. I look forward to reading it.'

In the papers that day there was not one story about race. I was back home, to a bigotry I understand.

Bibliography

Applebome, Peter, *Dixie Rising: How The South is Shaping American Values, Politics and Culture*, Harcourt Brace, San Diego, 1997

Bass, Jack and Nelson, Jack, *The Orangeburg Massacre*, Mercer University Press, 1984

Branch, Taylor, *Parting the Waters: America in the King Years 1954–1963*, Simon & Schuster, New York, 1988

Carson, Clayborn (ed.), *The Eyes on the Prize Civil Rights Reader: Documents, Speeches and First-hand Accounts From the Black Freedom Struggle 1954–1990*, Viking, New York, 1991

Farmer, James, *Lay Bare the Heart: An Autobiography of the Civil Rights Movement*, Arbor House, New York 1985

Fryer, Peter, *Staying Power: The History of Black People in Britain*, Pluto Press Ltd, London, 1984

Hampton, Henry and Frayer, Steve, *Voices of Freedom: An Oral History of the Civil Rights Movement for the 1950s through the 1980s*, Bantam Books, New York, 1990

Kilpatrick, James, *The Southern Case for School Segregation*, Crown-Collier, New York, 1962

Kluger, Richard, *Simple Justice: The History of Brown v Board of Education and Black America's Struggle for Equality*, Vintage, New York, 1975

Lewis, John, *Walking with the Wind: A Memoir of the Movement*, Simon & Schuster, New York, 1998

McPherson, James M., *Battle Cry of Freedom: The Civil War Era*, Oxford University Press, Oxford, 1988

Moskos, Charles M. and Butler, John Sibley, *All That We Can Be: Black Leadership and Racial Integration the Army Way*, Basic Books, New York, 1996

Payne, Charles M., *I've Got That Light of Freedom: The Organizing Tradition and the Mississippi Freedom Struggle*, University of California Press, Berkley, 1995

Peck, James, *Freedom Rider*, Simon & Schuster, New York, 1962

Raines, Howell, *My Soul is Rested: Movement Days in the Deep South Remembered*, Penguin, New York, 1983

Reed, John Shelton and Reed, Dale Volberg, *1001 Things Everyone Should Know About the South*, Doubleday, New York, 1997

Robinson, Jo Ann Gibson, *The Montgomery Bus Boycott and the Women Who Started It: the Memoir of Jo Ann Gibson Robinson*, University of Tennessee Press, Knoxville, 1987

Savage, Kirk, *Standing Soldiers, Kneeling Slaves: Race, War and Monument in Nineteenth-century America*, Princeton University Press, Princeton, 1997

Tolnay, Stewart E. and Beck, E. M., *A Festival of Violence: An Analysis of Southern Lynchings, 1882–1930*, University of Illinois Press, 1995

Walker, Alice, *You Can't Keep a Good Woman Down*, Harcourt Brace, New York, 1981

Whitfield, Stephen J., *A Death in Delta: The Story of Emmett Till*, John Hopkins University Press, Baltimore, 1988

Williams, Juan, *Eyes on the Prize: America's Civil Rights Years 1954–1965*, Viking, New York, 1987

Wilson, Michael, *Mobile Register*, 1–4 June 1997

Wittstock, Melinda, 'For Those Watching Black and White', *Guardian*, London, 2 March 1998